The Paradoxes of Integration

The Paradoxes of Integration

Race, Neighborhood, and Civic Life in Multiethnic America

J. ERIC OLIVER

THE UNIVERSITY OF CHICAGO PRESS   CHICAGO AND LONDON

J. ERIC OLIVER is professor of political science at the University of Chicago. He is the author of two previous books, *Democracy in Suburbia* and *Fat Politics: The Real Story behind America's Obesity Epidemic.*

Equations for figure 3.1 can be found in an online appendix at the publisher's Web site: http://www.press.uchicago.edu/books/oliver.

The University of Chicago Press, Chicago 60637
The University of Chicago Press, Ltd., London
© 2010 by The University of Chicago
All rights reserved. Published 2010
Printed in the United States of America

19 18 17 16 15 14 13 12 11 10   1 2 3 4 5

ISBN-13: 978-0-226-62662-8 (cloth)
ISBN-13: 978-0-226-62663-5 (paper)

ISBN-10: 0-226-62662-8 (cloth)
ISBN-10: 0-226-62663-6 (paper)

Library of Congress Cataloging-in-Publication data has been applied for.

♾ The paper used in this publication meets the minimum requirements of the American National Standard for Information Sciences—Permanence of Paper for Printed Library Materials, ANSI Z39.48-1992.

Contents

Acknowledgments

As with any academic endeavor, this book is the product of much collaboration. My work in this area started with two early colleagues, Tali Mendelberg and Janelle Wong. In 1999, while at Princeton University, Tali and I started talking about race and social environments. At the time I was writing about how suburban social contexts influence civic participation, and she suggested it might be interesting to examine their impact on racial attitudes. This piqued my interest, and, working together, we published a paper examining how economic and racial contexts shaped whites' racial attitudes. A year later, while at Yale University, Janelle and I began to wonder if these same effects might be evident among minority populations as well. As an undergraduate at UCLA, Janelle had worked as a researcher on the Multi-City Study of Urban Inequality (MCSUI) and told me the data might be a great source for testing some hypotheses about interminority attitudes. Working together, we later published a paper using the Los Angeles portion of the MCSUI study. I am greatly indebted to both Tali and Janelle for helping me first engage this difficult topic and work through many core issues in this analysis.

An equally large debt is owed to the principle investigators of the various data sources that this book draws on. Although I helped consult on the construction of the Citizenship, Information, and Democracy survey instrument, all of the other surveys this book uses were actually designed for other purposes. Getting funding, designing, testing, and implementing these surveys is a Herculean labor, and I am extremely grateful not only for the efforts of my colleagues but also for their generosity in making the data and geocodes available to me. I am particularly indebted to Larry Bobo, Marc Howard, Vince Hutchings, and Robert Putnam. It is a great privilege to piggyback on the expertise and efforts of others, and I hope this book is a further credit to their enterprise.

Over the past years, I have also enjoyed a number of comments, suggestions, and support from other sources. In the 2002–2003 academic year, I was a resident at the Russell Sage Foundation, where an early draft of this book was first written. There I received great feedback from the other resident scholars, particularly Frank Bean. I am indebted to the foundation for the financial support on my leave of absence and for allowing me to take the manuscript to the University of Chicago Press. Here at the University of Chicago, the book took greater shape after comments from my colleagues John Brehm, Cathy Cohen, and Michael Dawson. I also had the great pleasure of having Shang Ha as a graduate research assistant and later collaborator. Shang was instrumental in helping design some questions we submitted to the Citizenship, Information, and Democracy survey and contributed much of the statistical analysis that is in chapter 6. I also enjoyed helpful feedback from seminars at Harvard, Dartmouth, Northwestern, and the University of California, Berkeley.

This book would not have emerged without the unflagging patience and support of John Tryneski at the University of Chicago Press, who tolerated innumerable delays as I waited for yet another data source. His comments and those of the anonymous reviewers, as well as the editorial assistance of Sharon Brinkman and Rodney Powell, all have greatly improved this book. Finally, I owe a large debt to my wife, Thea, for her comments, feedback, support, and understanding as this project lingered along.

Introduction: Place and the Future of American Race Relations

To catch a glimpse at the future of American race relations, a good place to look is Chicago, Illinois. Like many American cities, Chicago is mixed between similarly sized white and African American populations and fast-growing Latino and Asian American populations. And, like many cities, Chicago's different racial and ethnic groups tend to live in sharply defined neighborhoods. Despite the fact that more than two-thirds of Chicagoans are not white, few minorities live in many of Chicago's northern neighborhoods like Lincoln Park or the Gold Coast. Meanwhile, many of Chicago's southern neighborhoods are entirely black, and large parts of the western city are completely Latino. Although these racial boundaries are not formally codified, the norms that define these places are clearly evident. An African American on North Halstead Street or a white person on South State Street is quite likely to draw suspicious glances and feel some unease. If Chicago is emblematic of America's racial future, then that future would seem to hold high levels of racial diversity, segregation, and mistrust.

But for an alternative vision, one can also walk around the intersection of Clark and Devon on Chicago's far north side. Within blocks one might hear English, Spanish, Hindi, Chinese, and Polish, with all sorts of ethnic and regional dialects in between. Music from passing cars and open windows straddles the cultural spectrum, jumping from hip-hop to classical to Tejano. Surrounding restaurants and kitchens emit smells ranging from curry to kielbasa. Yet in the midst of all this ethnic difference, there is a palpable sense of social ease. People make eye contact and share friendly hellos, and, although it is part of such a large and sprawling city, the area has a feeling of neighborliness. In a city notorious for its hypersegregation and chronic racial tensions, the Rogers Park neighborhood in Chicago stands out not only for its heterogeneity but for its relative social cohesion.

Like Chicago, the United States is in the midst of a massive racial transformation. New waves of immigration from Asia and Latin America are rapidly turning America from a country monochromatically divided between blacks and whites into a multiethnic society composed of at least four sizeable ethnic groups. African Americans have already been surpassed by Latinos in population size, and by midcentury whites will no longer be an outright majority of the American population. Latinos and Asian Americans, already emerging as distinctive ethnic groups in American society, are expected to continue to grow in number. America has become a truly multiracial nation.[1]

But while America's racial destiny may be clear, the future of its race relations is not. Race continues to be an important social issue, separating Americans in their views of themselves and their neighbors. Sharp racial and ethnic differences persist in employment, health, education, and almost every other indicator of social and economic status. In many cities, social relations between the races remain potentially explosive. Most glaringly, America's racial groups are highly segregated by neighborhood and municipal boundaries. Across neighborhoods, cities, and suburbs, America's ethnic and racial groups continue to live more apart than together.

Of all aspects of American race relations, few are more telling than these patterns of segregation. If America were a technically integrated society, then the racial composition of its neighborhoods and cities would reflect the proportion of its four major groups. In other words, most neighborhoods would be about 70 percent white, 13 percent black, 13 percent Latino, and 4 percent Asian American.[2] The actual patterns of residential segregation in the United States, however, reveal a far different arrangement. Figure 0.1 depicts an "average" racial composition of each neighborhood for all four major racial groups. The average American of any racial group lives in a neighborhood with a disproportionately high number of his or her own race. For example, the "average" white American lives in a neighborhood that is at least 82 percent white, while the "average" African American lives in a neighborhood that is at least 50 percent black. Both of these figures are far higher than what the average neighborhood should look like based on the national figures.

In fact, these statistics actually understate the extent of racial segregation in the United States. According to data from the 2000 U.S. Census at

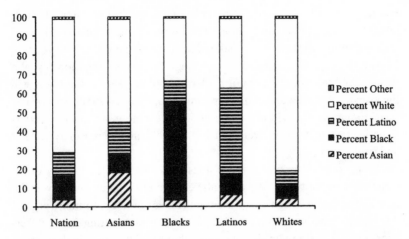

FIGURE 0.1 Average American neighborhood racial composition by racial group, 2000 (2000 U.S. Census).

least four out of every ten Americans would need to change residences to achieve some proportionate level of neighborhood integration relative to the racial makeup of their region. For example, nearly six out of ten blacks would need to move into white areas to alleviate the high levels of racial isolation of African Americans; in addition, roughly one in two Latinos would need to move to be proportionally integrated.[3] Although Asian Americans are more integrated in white communities, they still remain quite isolated from blacks and Latinos. To put these numbers in perspective, sociologist Douglas Massey notes that even at the peak of immigration in the United States in the early 1900s, the most sharply defined ethnic enclaves within America's cities rarely had segregation levels so high and that these tended to be quickly dissipated with time; yet, unlike a century ago, our current levels of segregation, particularly among blacks, Latinos, and whites, are changing very slowly, if at all (Massey 2001; Logan 2001).

Such high levels of segregation are troubling because they seem to contradict so much of the progress in race relations over the past several decades. According to surveys of public opinion, racism and racial animosity in the United States appear to be fading away (Kinder and Sanders 1996). Unlike a generation ago, most Americans today strongly embrace norms of racial equality, and it is difficult to find substantial numbers of people who publicly express hostility or bigotry toward other racial or

ethnic groups. And, in 2008, Americans took the historic step of elect-
ing the first nonwhite president. Yet, given all these gestures toward
racial equality, what are we to make of the extreme geographic separation
of America's racial groups? Does the high level of segregation reveal a
latent racial hostility that is not evident in polite society? And how will
the growth of Latino and Asian American populations affect Americans'
racial experiences? Will racial distinctions become more pronounced as
America becomes more diverse, or will they become increasingly blurred
and irrelevant?

Within public discourse, these questions elicit a wide variety of responses. Some note that the dramatic change in racial attitudes over the
past forty years is a significant accomplishment in itself. In many arenas,
Americans have made substantial progress in eliminating racial differences, and, despite their glacial rate of change, historically high segregation levels are beginning to recede (Patterson 1997). Others argue that
the slow integration of America's racial groups will promote greater understanding and that race is declining in significance as an indicator of
social status (Sowell 1994; Wilson 1980.). An even more optimistic view
sees the construct of race becoming undone as black/white divisions are
blurred by new ethnic groups and more Americans embrace principles
of racial equality (D'souza 1996; Thernstrom and Thernstrom 1999). In
contrast, many commentators view racism and segregation as "a permanent and indestructible component of American society" (Bell 1992).
Although slightly less segregated than they were thirty years ago, whites
and blacks still live largely in two separate worlds. Other commentators fear
that growing numbers of Latinos will balkanize the United States between
English- and Spanish-speaking populations (Huntington 2004; Buchanan
2006). Still others observe that America's intractable levels of geographic
segregation reveal how its sense of community extends only as far as a
racial boundary (Massey and Denton 1993). From this perspective, the
racial diversification of the United States will only exacerbate existing racial
tensions, leaving multiethnic communities especially prone to strife.

Social science offers limited and seemingly contradictory answers to
these questions as well. Although scholars have been examining patterns
of racial segregation and racial attitudes for decades, many of their findings seem at odds: some find that racial diversity promotes antagonism,
others find that diversity reduces it. Furthermore, there is very little
research on the racial attitudes of minorities, particularly toward each
other, and almost nothing is known about the ways that social environments shape the racial attitudes among Asian Americans, blacks, and

Latinos. In fact, it is not even clear whether whites' racial attitudes are categorically different in multiracial versus biracial environments. Quite simply, social scientists have not offered a clear vision of what impact America's growing diversity or its high levels of segregation will have on the future of its race relations.

This book looks to shed some light on America's racial future by examining segregation, racial attitudes, and neighborhood life in an increasingly multiethnic America. In chapter 1, I theorize on why people's environments are so important for their racial views and draw some hypotheses about how such contexts might affect their patterns of interracial contact, particularly in a multiethnic nation like the United States. The remaining chapters then put these hypotheses to empirical tests. Analyzing specially constructed data compiled from the census and four national surveys, I compare the racial attitudes of four major racial groups in the United States (chapter 2) and examine how these attitudes vary across different types of racial environments (chapters 3–5).[4] But while the approach of this book is primarily a quantitative analysis of survey and census data, it is more than just an aggregation of statistical facts. In examining patterns of racial attitudes, segregation, and social and civic involvement, the book touches on several larger issues of race and community in a rapidly diversifying America.

My central argument is that America's patterns of spatial and social integration present some fundamental paradoxes for the future of its race relations. The first is the paradox of diversity: living among more people of other races, no matter what one's own race is, corresponds with both higher and lower levels of racial animosity. The key to unraveling this paradox is in the different ways of defining what it means to live "among" others. At the metropolitan level living among people of other races corresponds with greater racial intolerance, particularly for America's white majority. The findings replicate a large body of evidence that shows higher feelings of racial competition and resentment in metropolitan areas with larger minority populations. The same processes also occur among minorities, that is, blacks who live in metropolitan areas with more Latinos exhibit more hostility toward Latinos and vice versa. When looking at the macrolevel, diversity seems to breed greater feelings of racial competition, conflict, and resentment.

But at a different level of geography, an opposite trend occurs: at the neighborhood level, living among people of different races corresponds with less racial resentment. No matter what the race of the individual, the trend is almost always the same—people who live in racially integrated neighborhoods are generally more tolerant, while people in segregated neighborhoods exhibit more racial resentment. In other words, whites, blacks, Latinos, and Asian Americans residing in integrated neighborhoods tend to be more positive toward other races; those who are sequestered in neighborhoods of only their own racial group tend to be more racially hostile.

The middle portion of the book explores the sources of the diversity paradox. The higher level of racial antagonism at the regional level has a commonsense answer: ethnic diversity breeds greater competition for resources and status, which then translates into greater intergroup animosity. In that racial antagonism arises partly from competition between groups, racial animosity will often arise as a function of diversity, particularly when that diversity is within a geographic arena where resources such as jobs, housing, and public services are interchanged. From this perspective, one might conclude that the regions with the highest growth rates of Latinos and Asian Americans are likely to experience the greatest levels of racial tension in the decades to come.

The higher level of racial tolerance in integrated neighborhoods, however, is more difficult to explain. The most obvious source appears to be geographic self-selection—people in segregated neighborhoods may be more racially hostile because racially biased people are more likely to choose such neighborhoods to begin with. Indeed, this type of self-selection is often identified as a cause for the hypersegregation seen in most metropolitan areas—throughout American history, whites have used a variety of methods, both state sanctioned and not, to keep themselves apart from minorities.[5] Chapter 4 examines the self-selection explanation and finds some surprising results. Although geographic self-selection undoubtedly accounts for some of the differences in racial attitudes between integrated and segregated neighborhoods, it is not the sole reason, or even most important reason, for this trend. Most of the geographic differences in people's racial attitudes are not attributable to wanting neighbors of their own race, particularly among minority groups, who often express a preference for integrated neighborhoods. Geographic self-selection by preexisting racial attitudes is primarily a white phenomenon and, in spite of this fact, has limited explanatory power even in accounting for the overall neighborhood patterns in whites' racial attitudes.

Another possible explanation for the high levels of tolerance in integrated neighborhoods is the greater interracial contact that putatively occurs within more diverse neighborhoods. Because people in integrated neighborhoods are more likely to be familiar and friendly with people of other races, the thinking goes, they are less likely to harbor racist sentiments. According to social capital theorists, one of the primary mechanisms by which integrated neighborhoods bridge racial and ethnic differences is through voluntary civic organizations: people who join voluntary organizations not only gain the benefits of greater trust, happiness, and well-being, they make themselves available for having the types of positive interracial contact that promotes greater understanding (Putnam 2000; Varshney 2002). Chapter 5 shows that, indeed, people who live in integrated neighborhoods have more interracial social ties, participate in more interracial civic associations and, most importantly, work in more integrated jobs. Moreover, people who have meaningful interracial contact are also less likely to harbor negative attitudes about other groups, and this effect is particularly strong for whites.

From these findings, one might leap to the conclusion that integration has the practical benefit of reducing racial tension and hostility. But this conclusion suffers from a big problem—the causal pathway linking neighborhood integration, interracial contact, and greater racial harmony is not clear cut. Although the evidence shows correlations among these phenomena, the data available do not allow us to draw any causal inferences about the relationship between integration and racial attitudes. And this is more than simply a methodological problem. According to social psychologists and social capital theorists, interracial proximity is not sufficient for reducing racial hostility; rather, if people are to overcome their racial animosities toward other groups, they must do so through contact in very specific circumstances (that is, all parties must be of equal status and work together toward a shared goal). In short, people in integrated neighborhoods need to have structured interactions with other races, whether it is in a work setting or within a local civic organization, to overcome their racial animosities.

This, however, brings up another paradox of integration in America: the paradox of community. As demonstrated in chapter 6, residential integration may foster greater racial understanding, but it also diminishes people's involvement in their communities. For minorities, living in a more integrated neighborhood means being less socially connected in general and more alienated from one's neighbors in particular. This is partly because integration into a white community generates reciprocally negative feelings from whites—whites who live in more integrated (that is, less white) neighborhoods often exhibit fewer social ties with and less trust of their neighbors—because, for most Americans, same-race neighborhoods provide a feeling of community not available in a larger, diverse society.

From these findings, it appears that residential integration is not a simple panacea for America's racial ills. What might be good for improving race relations (that is, integration) may not necessarily improve community ties among groups. Conversely, segregation may instill a greater sense of community with one's own racial group but ultimately undermine social connections to a larger and more diverse population. In other words, integration may contribute to some bridging across different groups, but it comes at the cost of bonding with one's immediate community and being more active in the public realm.

In the book's conclusion, I explore the implications of these findings in light of America's changing demography and debates over multicultural-ism. The increasing racial diversity of the United States is likely to cre-ate racial hostility and competition—adding sizeable Latino and Asian populations is only likely to increase perceptions of racial competition and the potential for racial strife among different groups. Unfortunately, there appear to be no simple solutions to this dilemma. While we may hope that integrating America's neighborhoods, civic associations, and other areas of social life will promote racial tolerance, we must be cognizant of the costs that such integration imposes—costs that are most heavily borne by dark-skinned minorities. For many groups, incorporation into American society often comes at the expense of an indigenous cultural identity and creates enormous conflicts in self-perception. Although one may argue whether this is desirable or not, processes that sustain social cohesion are usually in direct tension with processes that maintain cultural differences. It is also important to be cognizant of the mechanisms by which cultural assimilation takes place. Many scholars argue that Asian Americans and Latinos can only transcend racial barriers by "becoming white" and set-ting themselves in opposition to African Americans. These issues are the ultimate paradox presented by an integrated, multiracial America: will the real transformation in American racial attitudes require the elimina-tion of the ethnic, cultural, and social markers that many groups hold as a fundamental part of their identity? And if so, will it do so at the expense of darker skinned peoples? The final chapter of the book tries to offer some answers to these questions and a prognosis on America's racial future.

On Studying Race and Racial Attitudes in America

Given the potency of race in American society, the study of racial attitudes and race relations is fraught with peril. The scholarly literature is replete with contentious and acrimonious debates on virtually every dimension of this topic. Readers often take issue with even the simplest of claims. In fact, one cannot even begin to discuss the idea of race without encountering a debate: because most "racial" differences in human behavior have virtually no biological basis, some question whether using racial categories serves to reify and sustain already pernicious and artificial social divisions; others note, however, that racial categorizations still have important and material implications for those who live under them and cannot simply be dismissed (Berry and Henderson 2002; Patterson 1997). This type of debate is evident in everything from theories of racial attitudes to the construction of racial measures. Because so much in the study of race can be subject to disagreement, it is imperative to be very clear about one's approach from the outset.

Although race may be a social construct, this book seeks to show how this racial construct operates in American society, particularly in the relationship between segregation, social life, and public attitudes. That point noted, this book is not a comprehensive study of racial attitudes in America. It does not purport to explain all the reasons why people hold negative views of other races or the many ways in which the construction of race gets regenerated in American society. There are many other works that tackle such tasks quite well, and there are likely to be more in the future.[6] Rather, this book has a far more specific agenda. It seeks to examine the interrelationship between racial attitudes and racial environments and to do this in a very singular way, using data constructed from individual surveys and the census. In the end, it has something unique to say about why people of many different races have negative views about other groups and how the practice of racial differentiation is sustained, but it is just another perspective on a rich and complicated topic.

In short, this book is primarily an empirical inquiry into the relationship between segregation patterns and racial attitudes in multiethnic America. It relies primarily upon data from the 1990 and 2000 U.S. censuses and several public opinion data sources including the 1992–1994 Multi-City Study of Urban Inequality (MCSUI), the 2000 Social Capital Community Benchmark Study (SCCBS), the 2004 Citizen, Information and Democracy Study (CID), and the 2004 National Politics Study (NPS). A full description of these data sets is given in appendix A. Taken together, these studies, coupled with the census measures, are probably the best available data for gauging the effects of social environments on racial attitudes. They provide a full range of measures of individual racial attitudes and civic involvement, and they contain both a large national sample as well as large samples of communities with higher percentages of Asian Americans and Latinos.

Of course, this type of survey-based research has some weaknesses. The biggest drawback to this type of research is that it cannot fully describe the process by which social environments influence racial attitudes. For instance, one of the claims this book tests is that meaningful interracial contact fosters greater racial tolerance. Although the data reveal less racial hostility among people with integrated social ties, they cannot specify how exactly this process occurs. The claim is simply based on relationships in a broad data sample at a particular point in time. To truly understand how racial dynamics operate in multiethnic contexts, one also needs to pursue ethnographic research that studies such venues in greater depth or to conduct experiments that show changes in racial attitudes as the consequence of such participation. The survey research utilized in this book may describe the contours of the forest, but it cannot account for the variety within the trees.

The other limitation of a survey approach is the inherent constraints of survey instruments. Survey data are only as good as their questions, samples, and interview procedures. Although the data in this study were gathered by professional survey organizations and represent the state of the art with regards to sampling methodologies and question formation, they are still limited because of the propensity for response biases and nonresponses among the people interviewed. Most Americans acknowledge the social norms surrounding racial tolerance and equality and may alter their responses in order to conform to such standards, even if their own racial attitudes are far different.

Furthermore, one may even question the viability of surveys for capturing something as nuanced and complicated as contemporary racial attitudes. People's views about other racial or ethnic groups involve a host of different psychological, social, and political processes. People may exhibit extreme prejudice toward someone of a different race in some instances and not in others; their racial attitudes may be exacerbated or attenuated depending on other phenotypic cues; and many people may have deep ambivalence about other groups. Cross-sectional survey data can only capture the tendencies of racial attitudes in a single and crude snapshot.

Bearing these caveats in mind, survey data can still be useful for describing the broad contours of racial attitudes in America. There is a long and highly informative body of survey research that has explored racial dynamics over the past several decades. This work has provided us with a good picture of the changes and variances in racial attitudes across the American public. Moreover, given the limited generalizations that can be derived from laboratory experiments or ethnographies, surveys remain the most powerful instruments for social scientists interested in examining questions of race in America. Although the survey findings in this book are more of a first than a last word on racial attitudes, they do provide a remarkable picture of the different ways Americans views themselves and people of other races depending on where they live.

CHAPTER ONE

Why Place Is So Important for Race

The 2008 election of Barack Obama to the presidency of the United States was a historic occasion. Less than fifty years after the end of Jim Crow, an African American man had been elected to America's highest and most powerful office with nearly 53 percent of the popular vote. For many, this event seemed to usher in a new era of race relations as a broad coalition of whites, Latinos, and African Americans came together. Some claimed that Barack Obama was a "postracial" candidate whose victory signaled the ability of all Americans, but whites in particular, to look beyond their racial biases and embrace a new, multiethnic future.

But the electoral map comparing the vote margins between 2004 and 2008 shows a somewhat different pattern. Of particular note was the broad swath of counties running from Oklahoma and East Texas through Arkansas to Kentucky and West Virginia where the Republican vote margins actually increased from 2004. On its face, the Republican increase in votes in these places was very surprising. After all, 2008 was a terrible year for Republicans: their incumbent president had the lowest approval ratings in modern history, they lost numerous seats in the House and Senate, the economy was plummeting, an unpopular war continued in Iraq, and the McCain-Palin campaign was beset by gaffes and missteps. Given these conditions, one would hardly expect to see increases in the Republican vote share, particularly in those counties where, four years earlier, the Republican vote margin was already quite high. Nevertheless, in over six hundred counties, the McCain margin of victory over Obama was actually higher than Bush's margin of victory over John Kerry.

Why, in an election year so dominated by Democrats, did these counties go from merely "red" to "scarlet"? To answer this question, it is important to identify what is distinctive about "scarlet" counties. This may not reveal the motivations of any individual voter, but it can give some

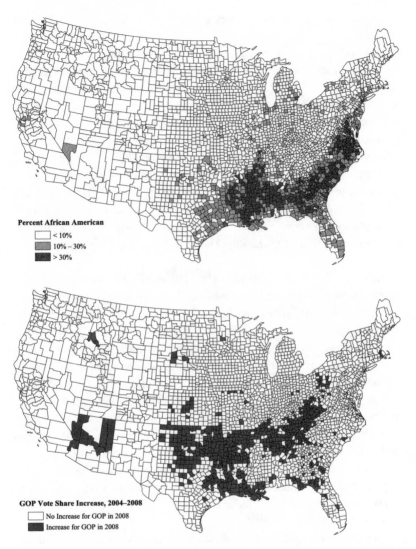

Percent African American
- < 10%
- 10% – 30%
- > 30%

GOP Vote Share Increase, 2004–2008
- No Increase for GOP in 2008
- Increase for GOP in 2008

hints about why the scarlet counties zigged while the rest of the country zagged. Based on census data, scarlet counties were less wealthy and educated, more rural and southern, and had higher unemployment rates than the national average. For example, in scarlet counties, only 13 percent of adults hold a college degree, on average, compared with 17 percent for the "azure" counties (the places where Democratic margins increased). Seventy-three percent of the scarlet counties are rural, compared with 59 percent of azure counties. Interestingly, the scarlet counties were not older or more white: their populations average about 85 percent white and

15 percent over age sixty-five, rates nearly identical to the national county averages.

But perhaps the most important factor in explaining these voting patterns is the racial composition of nearby counties. As illustrated in Map 1, nearly all of the counties that went scarlet were proximate to counties or states with large black populations. In fact, 72 percent of the scarlet counties are in states that are over 10 percent black, compared with only 49 percent of the azure counties. Regression analyses of county-level election data reveal that the best predictor of county-level shifts (that is, the color patterns depicted in the map) is the racial percentage of a county relative to its state's black population size. In other words, the counties in which Republican margins grew the largest tended to be predominantly white places in otherwise racially mixed states. Clearly race was a factor in people's vote choice, but the importance of this factor depended a lot on the racial environment.

As the voting patterns in 2008 reveal, if we want to understand what people think about other races, we need to look at where they live. Our social environments are essential for shaping our racial attitudes because they make our racial identities salient. Where people of different groups have no contact or exposure to each other or share no common geography or other resource pools, then it is highly unlikely they will have meaningful attitudes toward one another or even recognize themselves in racial terms. Few Americans, for example, have opinions about Tamils from Sri Lanka or Creoles in Guyana, even though in their home countries such ethnic identities are the source of great social tension. Nor did isolated tribes in the Amazon or the Arctic typically think of themselves in racial terms until they had contact with Europeans. It is only within a shared, diverse context, be it a nation, a neighborhood, or a classroom, that racial identities become important. So fundamentally, the study of race itself must be a study of social environments.

After decades of research, social scientists largely agree that racial attitudes are profoundly influenced by people's social surroundings. From the pioneering studies of John Dollard and V. O. Key to the most contemporary research using multilevel survey data and hierarchical linear models, scholars have repeatedly demonstrated that much of what people think of other races, or the strength of their own racial identity, depends upon the types of people they live around (Dollard 1989 [1957]; Key 1949). But while the influence of social environments on racial attitudes is unquestioned, the direction of their effect is not. Sharp divergences exist in the psychological, sociological, and political science literature about whether or how intergroup proximity affects the construction and regeneration of racial identities.

On one side, there is a substantial amount of evidence that racial diversity fosters negative racial sentiments. Part of this tension arises from a seemingly innate tendency of humans not just to categorize people according to in-groups and out-groups but to also discriminate against people who seem different (Brown 1986; Tajfel and Turner 1979). Part of this tension arises because conflicts over resources and status escalate when minority groups grow in size (Blumer 1958; Blalock 1967; Bobo 1983). For example, white Americans tend to be more racially hostile in counties or metropolitan areas with higher percentages of blacks because the larger minority population is a putatively greater threat to white racial privilege (Fossett and Kiecolt 1989; Giles and Buckner 1993; Glaser 1994; Key 1949; Quillian 1996; Taylor 1998). On the other side, another body of research suggests that racial diversity alleviates racial antagonism. Utilizing the theory that interracial contact can promote racial understanding, several studies have documented how integrated work and neighborhood settings nurture greater racial understanding (Allport 1954; Carsay 1995; Deutsch and Collins 1951; Welch et al. 2001). Then there are those who question whether diversity has any impact at all in contemporary settings (Sears et al. 2000). From past studies, it seems that racial diversity simultaneously increases, decreases, and has no effect on race relations.

Adding to this confusion are a host of different (and sometimes competing) theories on what causes racial prejudice. In the past fifty years, researchers have offered dozens of explanations of why certain racial and ethnic groups sustain negative judgments toward nonmembers. For example, racial attitudes have been linked to evolutionary imperatives, basic cognitive processes, socially learned cultural norms, moral principles, psychodynamic processes, and economic and social competition, just to name a few (Sidanius and Pratto 2001; Tajfel and Turner 1979; Sears et al. 2000; Kinder and Sanders 1996; Bettleheim and Janowitz 1964; Bobo 1999). Many of these differences also arise from different hypotheses about how social environments shape racial attitudes—some studies see environments largely in terms of social structures and resource pools, while others emphasize interpersonal dynamics (Bobo and Hutchings 1996; Welch et al. 2001). And some of these differences can be linked to the different ways that social environments are conceptualized. A social environment can be as intimate as one's family and as broad as one's country, and each type may have a different effect depending on its size and scope.

The impact of racial contexts becomes even more perplexing when multiracial environments are considered. The addition of two sizeable new racial groups to the American ethnic panoply not only makes thinking about racial environments more complex, it challenges many of the traditional notions about the sources of prejudice. For example, are the same theories that explain white prejudice toward blacks equally valid in explaining their attitudes toward Latinos and Asians? This question has no immediate answer because virtually all of the research on American racial environments has focused on whites' racial attitudes regarding blacks. While these studies offer important insights into the dynamics of race relations, their applicability for explaining how other racial groups respond to racial contexts or how whites view other minority groups has not been established. There is considerably less research on how blacks, Latinos, and Asians view other groups, much less how they respond to their racial contexts.[1] Moreover, there has been little research on whether whites respond to increasing populations of Latinos or Asians in the same way they do to larger black populations (Taylor 1998; Hood and Morris 1997). We do not know whether whites or blacks respond to nearby Latinos or Asians from concerns of race or nativism or both. As most theories that explain how social contexts shape racial attitudes pertain to white racial antagonism toward African Americans, their usefulness for predicting how racial attitudes operate in multiethnic contexts is unknown.

Finally, the relationship between racial attitudes and social environments is even more difficult to conceptualize when one considers that racial environments themselves, particularly at the microlevel, are the consequence of racial attitudes. The high levels of American segregation are partly the consequence of a long history of racial intolerance within the United States. The legacy of white racism is largely responsible for the segregation that exists in most metropolitan areas. Thus even if one is to find a clear pattern of racial attitudes that vary across different social environments, it is not necessarily clear that the social environments are to blame. For example, people with strong biases against other races may seek to live in places composed primarily of their own race and may discourage people of other races moving in as well. Racial animosity may be higher in segregated communities primarily because the segregated communities themselves arise because of the preexisting racial animosities of their residents.

This chapter reviews what past research has discovered about the relationship between social environments and racial attitudes and speculates on how these diverse theories and findings might apply to multiethnic set-

tings in the United States. In an effort to distill this broad and complicated topic down to a manageable size, the chapter starts by examining
how racial attitudes operate in a biracial context, primarily by reviewing
studies of how the racial views of dominant groups (namely, whites in the
United States) vary across social environments. When these theories are
applied to minority groups, the implications are largely the same: the environmental dynamics that shape whites' racial attitudes toward blacks
will also operate in relationship to interminority attitudes, although some
exceptions will also apply.

The Environmental Determinants of Whites' Racial Attitudes

Perhaps the most commonly held view among contemporary race scholars
is that white racial resentment arises from the competition between groups
for status, privileges, and resources. In what is often called the "threat" or
"real conflict" hypothesis, racial attitudes are believed to derive from the
perceived conflict between racial groups over economic and political position. Prejudice emerges as different races within one society jockey for
social power or when a dominant group feels its position of preeminence
is threatened. Among American whites in particular, it is believed that the
anxiety over social position and resources translates into increased hostility toward blacks (Bobo 1983, 1999). As sociologist Herbert Blumer sum-
marized over fifty years ago, "The sense of group position is . . . a sense of
where racial groups belong. The source of race prejudice lies in a felt challenge to this sense of group position. It functions, however short-sidedly
[*sic*], to preserve the integrity and the position of the dominant group"
(Blumer 1958, 5). As whites feel economically or politically vulnerable,
they will increasingly guard their privileged racial status by denigrating
minorities. American racial hostility primarily comes, in this view, from
white status insecurity.

These feelings of white racial insecurity can be affected by the environment in many ways, such as through cultural histories or economic
conditions.[2] Yet, perhaps more than any other component, the single most
important environmental factor shaping whites' racial attitudes is the size
of nearby minority groups. According to many scholars, whites' feelings of
racial threat are believed to increase as a linear function of minority group
size: as the percent of minorities in a region increases, they putatively become a greater threat to white racial privilege. Numerous studies over
the past several decades have demonstrated that whites' negative racial

attitudes increase with higher percentages of blacks in the county, state, and metropolitan area (see Fossett and Kiecolt 1989; Giles and Evans 1985; Giles and Hertz 1994; Huckfeldt and Kohfeld 1989; Pettigrew 1959; Wright 1977). For example, in her examination of national data spanning twenty years, sociologist Marylee Taylor finds consistent patterns of prejudice and opposition to policies encouraging racial equality among whites as the black percentage of their metropolitan area increases (Taylor 1998). Similarly, sociologist Lincoln Quillian, looking at white racial attitudes in both Europe and the United States, concludes that "prejudice is a function of the relative size of the subordinate group to the dominate group" (Quillian 1995, 1996). Higher black populations have been found to increase the likelihood of racial violence, opposition to school desegregation, and support for racially conservative party politics and policy preferences (Green, Strolovitch, and Wong 1998; Olzak 1994; Giles and Buckner 1993; Glaser 1994). Across all of these studies, researchers have concluded that whites feel more threatened and are therefore more racially antagonistic in environments with larger black populations.[3]

Thus the prevailing view within social science is that white racial resentment will be highest in areas with the greatest percentage of African Americans. According to the threat hypothesis, larger numbers of subordinate group members breed the greatest levels of status insecurity. This insecurity is translated into a heightened sense of racial competition and is manifest in greater racial animosity, stereotypes, and violence as well as through political mechanisms such as support for racially conservative political efforts. Other research suggests that these levels of resentment should also be highest in areas that have experienced the greatest recent changes in racial populations or where racial boundaries are still fluid.[4]

The Benefits of Interracial Contact and Interracial Civic Ties

An alternative view to the "threat" explanation is what is commonly known as the contact hypothesis. Unlike the earlier explanation, the contact hypothesis sees racial prejudices as originating not in the competition between groups for material resources but from attitudes learned early in life that are not derived from direct experience. According to some psychologists, white racial prejudice is based on irrational, psychological processes that largely arise in childhood—negative stereotypes and feelings of racial resentment fundamentally are socially learned attitudes (Allport 1954; Sears 1983). Although these sentiments can be firmly rooted and quite strong, they can be undone by later life experiences and social contact, particularly if this contact is under conditions of equal status, shared goals, intergroup cooperation, and the support of dominant institutions and customs (Pettigrew 1998). Psychologist Gordon Allport believed that as whites interact with blacks in contexts of social equality, the racial preconceptions that are learned early in life and reinforced by a formally prescribed racial hierarchy can be corrected. Buoyed by other norms of equality and social justice, whites will realize that their negative stereotypes about African Americans are inaccurate. Early research from the 1950s generally found that when all four conditions were met, white racial antagonism toward blacks diminished with increased social contact (Allport 1954; Wilner, Walkley, and Cook 1955). In other words, as whites interact with blacks on a one-on-one basis, particularly in settings in which they share goals and work in equal status, their negative stereotypes about African Americans diminish or disappear.

Many scholars, however, have questioned the validity of the contact hypothesis. Part of the problem arises from self-selection—whites who are less racially hostile are more likely to enter into situations in which they will have interracial contacts that meet the conditions Allport required (Jackman and Crane 1985). Part of the problem arises from whether the process of interracial contact actually changes racial attitudes—it is still unclear whether simply interacting in shared, equitable situations will generate better understanding (Brewer and Miller 1988). Finally, advocates of the threat hypothesis might suggest that the very nature of the American racial hierarchy precludes the conditions under which contact might have its beneficial effects. Although the cultural and institutional norms about race relations over the past forty years have conferred equal status to the races, some question whether it is possible to have a situation of shared goals and intergroup cooperation (Hamilton, Carpenter, and Bishop 1984). According to the threat hypothesis, it is precisely the presence of out-group members that threatens white racial preeminence and alleviates the potential benefits of interracial contact.

But while the contact hypothesis continues to have its critics, many recent studies purport to find strong correlations between racial contact and positive out-group sentiments (Bledsoe et al. 1995; Sigelman and Welch 1993; Stein, Post, and Rinden 2000; Welch and Sigelman 2000; Pettigrew and Tropp 2000). The strongest case has come from a recent long-term study of Detroit by political scientist Susan Welch and her colleagues (Welch et al. 2001). Looking at survey and census data over two decades, they find that residential integration promotes interracial contact and reduces interracial hostility. Whites who live in neighborhoods with larger numbers of blacks were less likely to oppose interracial marriage and were more likely to have black friends, factors that also related to less racial hostility. From their findings, they derive the optimistic conclusion that neighborhood integration could gradually improve interracial relations. Yet, as compelling as these findings are, many still question whether the casual contact that occurs between neighbors can promote racial understanding, and many argue that simple proximity between races without conditions of equal status and goal sharing can actually exacerbate racial tension. Neighborhood integration has the potential for providing positive contact between races, but it is important to specify where, exactly, the interracial contact is taking place. In other words, whites in integrated places may be more likely to have blacks as friends, but these friendships rarely come out of thin air; rather, interracial friendships usually only emerge from structured social situations.[5]

The most likely situation in which people in integrated places can befriend people of other races is through voluntary associations, such as a neighborhood group or church or other civic organizations, and workplaces. During the past decade, social scientists have begun to pay increased attention to the important benefits of people's voluntary groups and organizations. Participation in voluntary civic organizations can increase one's health, wealth, and mental well-being by solidifying social connections between people and building "social capital" in communities (Putnam 2000). Others have argued that civic organizations may also alleviate racial hostility. Research on ethnic violence in India has shown that the existence of integrated civic and business associations was one of the most important factors in predicting whether or not a city would have ethnic riots (Varshnay 2002). Since many civic associations, particularly the ones that build social capital, draw their members from the immediate vicinity, it makes sense that voluntary organizations in integrated neighborhoods could provide an ideal venue for bridging the differences between racial and ethnic groups.

Another situation in which people in integrated places may have positive racial contact is at work. Since most Americans work within a few miles of their homes, people in integrated communities are also more likely to have integrated work lives. In fact, the American workplace may be the most integrated sector in American society. Law professor Cynthia Estlund argues that America's workplaces have become one of the most important sites for providing the benefits of social capital, particularly in regards to promoting interracial understanding (Estlund 2003). Of course, not all jobs necessarily provide beneficial experiences of racial contact: one can easily imagine racial animosities being heightened by competition for promotions, pay raises, or even a better office. Nevertheless, for many jobs, people must come together with coworkers in teams to accomplish shared tasks with joint rewards.

In this regard, integrated voluntary organizations and workplaces may be the missing link that bridges the gulf between various groups living together in integrated settings. From the perspective of the contact hypothesis, this makes sense. Civic associations and many work situations are the ideal space for promoting positive intergroup contact under the conditions that Allport specified: their members are of equal status, associations have members that work together for shared goals, they provide a venue for frequent contact, and they allow for new superordinate identities to be formed that can coexist and even transcend racial identities. For instance, white members of a fraternal civic organization, such as the Rotary Club or Elks Lodge, may identify with black or Latino members as fellow Rotarians or Elks, thereby supplanting perceptions of racial difference. These types of superordinate identities often help to increase the positive feelings of participants toward other races and reduce bias in general toward out-groups (Gaertner and Dovidio 2000). If racial antagonism derives originally from social learning, then presumably, such ideas and attitudes can be unlearned. Integrated work sites and shared, voluntary organizations where new identities crosscut racial and ethnic boundaries can be an important mechanism for restructuring people's racial biases.

But while the notion of an integrated associational life may seem quite alluring, it must also be viewed with some caution. One problem is that American stocks of social capital— the resources and support that people gain from their social connections—appear to be declining at a dramatic rate. In Robert Putnam's famous terms, Americans are no longer joining bowling leagues but are now "bowling alone," that is, they are becoming less active in voluntary civic associations and are spending more discretionary time in isolated pursuits such as watching television (Putnam 2000). With only a minority of Americans active in such organizations, the opportunities for such contact are limited. Furthermore, we know very little about whether people in integrated settings are any more or less likely to be civically active than people in segregated places. People in integrated neighborhoods are typically less trusting in general and seem to be more socially alienated (Marshall and Stolle 2003). It very well may be that integration, so important for providing opportunities for contact, diminishes the likelihood that people will take advantage of these opportunities.

Resolving the Contradiction between Threat and Contact

In reviewing these two dominant areas of research, there appears to be a contradiction in the hypotheses on how social environments shape racial attitudes. The power-threat hypothesis suggests that proximity to blacks promotes white status insecurity and hostility; the contact hypothesis suggests that interracial friendships and participation in interracial associations can promote mutual understanding. What accounts for the difference between the threat and contact hypotheses? Does living among more African Americans make whites more racially resentful? Or does it decrease racial hostility by allowing for greater interpersonal exchange?

Although at first glance such theories may seem contradictory, both theories actually might be complementary. One reason is related to the unit of geography. Most evidence supporting the power-threat hypothesis has come from large geographic units, typically the county or the metropolitan area. The negative effects of proximate minority populations on white racial attitudes seem to exist only relative to larger geographic areas—no quantitative research across a large number of settings has found negative attitudes among whites to be higher in integrated neighborhoods.[6] Conversely, most evidence supporting the contact hypothesis comes from smaller contexts such as housing developments, neighborhoods, or classrooms. Just as the dynamic of racial threat primarily operates in terms of larger macrosettings, the impact of proximate minority populations for fostering contact exists primarily relative to microsettings.

This, however, brings up an essential point regarding race and place: which types of contexts are most important for racial attitudes? After all, racial contexts can be as small as a household or as large as a nation-state. When thinking about the appropriate level of context to consider, one must identify which one is relevant to the hypotheses at hand. For example, some researchers use states as units of geographic analysis. States are important arbiters of public services and political power, thus we might want to consider states as a meaningful category of geographic difference. However, the problem with using states as units of analysis is their internal heterogeneity. Many large states, such as New York, California, and Texas, have regions that are diverse and other areas that are quite homogeneous. Racial issues may flare up during some political campaigns or around state policies regarding affirmative action or immigrant service provisions, but in big states, it is unlikely that race will have the same impact across the board.

As noted above, the major way that social environments affect racial attitudes is through determining the parameters of social conflict and the opportunities for social contact. The units of geography most influential in this regard are the metropolitan area and the neighborhood. The metropolitan area is a primary arena for racial competition. It determines the labor market, housing market, and provision of many public services such as schools. Neighborhoods, by contrast, are much bigger predictors of people's social and civic experiences. The people we see on a day-to-day basis and whom we join in groups and community projects are likely to be drawn from the immediate vicinity.

Of course, it is also important to consider not just the right level of geography but several levels of geography at the same time. Obviously, if there are few minorities in a county or metropolitan area, then the potential for whites to have positive interracial social contact will be reduced. As the percent of minorities in the metropolis increases, the potential for racial competition increases but so too does the importance of neighborhood racial composition. If whites in racially mixed metropolitan areas spend all of their time in predominantly white suburbs, jobs, or social activities, they may have few opportunities for interracial contact yet still feel competitive pressure from nearby minority populations. The contention that the proximate, yet unseen, minority population creates will not be undone by positive contact for whites in segregated neighborhoods. In short, race relations can be influenced by several levels of geography at once, often in opposite ways. A racially mixed metropolis may influence racial attitudes in a much different way than a racially integrated neighborhood.

Another factor to consider when thinking about the relationship between racial contexts and attitudes is self-selection. If high levels of segregation are sustained by white racial animosity, then presumably geographic differences in racial attitudes will occur not because the environment causes people to have certain beliefs but because people are spatially sorting themselves according to their racial preferences. Racially tolerant people, because they are more racially tolerant, are more likely to live in heterogeneous settings; racially intolerant whites will seek to live in all-white areas. In fact, this is the biggest weakness with many studies on the positive benefits of racial contact—whites who seem to be more racially tolerant because of their interracial friends and social contacts may simply be more tolerant to begin with (thus explaining why they have more interracial friends in the first place).[7] Any attempt to disentangle the relationship between racial environments and racial attitudes must somehow come to grips with this self-selection issue.

Finally, it is also important to consider the interaction between different geographic units. Choosing to live in an all-white neighborhood does not necessarily signal a strong racial preference if one also lives in a predominantly white region. In New England and parts of the American West, where minority populations are quite small, many people live in all-white communities because there are only all-white neighborhoods in their region. Conversely, in metropolitan areas heavily populated by minorities, such as Atlanta, Detroit, or Los Angeles, choosing an all-white neighborhood is more likely to signify a strong racial bias, particularly since whites in these regions allegedly are also more likely to feel racially threatened. Neighborhood differences in racial attitudes should be greatest in those macroareas with larger black populations.

Whites in Multiethnic Contexts

The hypotheses above were derived largely from research on whites in relationship to African Americans; what remains undetermined, however, is whether these same patterns also hold true in multiethnic contexts. Both the conflict and contact hypotheses were formulated largely about two racial groups in a sharply defined historical relationship, and their suitability for explaining white attitudes toward Asian Americans and Latinos is unclear. For example, the threat that Latinos or Asian Americans may present to whites is not self-evident. If whites view all ethnic out-groups as similarly alien or threatening, then presumably they will respond to increasing populations of other minority groups with the same degree of animosity.[8] In his research on both Europe and the United States, Quillian (1995, 1996) offers the general rule that racial threat is related to the numerical size of the subordinate group relative to the dominant group. The long history of white racial dominance and the subjugation of Latinos and Asian Americans suggest that whites would be equally threatened by other racial or ethnic groups. Indeed, the relatively high economic power of Asian Americans may make them more of a threat than other racial groups.

Yet there are many factors that differentiate whites' attitudes between different minority groups. Many scholars have identified an "exceptionalism" of white attitudes toward African Americans because of the long history of slavery and their particular place in American history. Conversely, the economic successes of Asian Americans can generate a "model minority" stereotype that may make them seem more virtuous or less threatening than Latinos or blacks (Kim 1997). The racial status of Latinos is difficult to assess because the category Latino includes a broad range of racial groups, with Latinos themselves very divided over their own racial identities. The large immigrant proportions of both Asian American and Latino populations raise the question of whether whites' attitudes toward these groups arise from racial or nationalist sentiments or both. Thus between the recent growth of the Latino and Asian populations and the absence of research on whites' attitudes toward these groups, the impact of multiracial environments on whites' racial views of all minority groups remains undetermined.

Summing up Research on Whites' Racial Attitudes

Although two bodies of research on the environmental determinants of white attitudes toward blacks seem to be contradictory, they actually can be seen as complementary. The question still remains, however, as to how well these accounts explain white attitudes toward other minority groups. Given this caveat, the existing research on social contexts and white racial attitudes can be synthesized in the following set of predictions:

- The greater the number of blacks in the larger macrocontext (that is, county, state, or metropolitan area), the more racially threatened whites will be and the greater their racial hostility.
- The greater the number of blacks in the smaller microcontext (that is, neighborhood, workplace, civic association), the greater the possibility for interracial contact, and, if contact occurs, the more likely whites will be racially tolerant and accepting.
- Neighborhood differences in racial attitudes will be greatest in more racially diverse metropolitan areas and less severe in predominantly white metropolitan areas.
- To whatever extent whites view Latinos or Asians as similarly alien or categorically different as blacks, these same contextual dynamics should occur, although distinctions should be made between whites' racial attitudes and their attitudes toward immigrants.
- The differences in racial attitudes across microsettings may also come from racial contact or self-selection but may also be strongly influenced by participation in racially mixed civic associations and work sites.

- However, participation in multiracial organizations may be affected by integration—whites in integrated neighborhoods may be less likely to participate in
  community affairs than people in segregated places.

Environmental Influences on African Americans'
Racial Attitudes

Although there have been some general studies on blacks' racial attitudes, there is very little research about how social environments shape
those views (Schuman et al. 1997; Bobo and Hutchings 1996; Bobo and
Massagli 2001). Most research on how segregation shapes racial attitudes
has focused almost exclusively on whites, and the research on blacks has
concentrated mostly on in-group cohesion (Lau 1989; Welch et al. 2001).
While it seems likely that social context will be just as important for shaping blacks' attitudes as it is for shaping whites' attitudes, it is not self-
evident that they will operate in the same manner. After all, because
African Americans constitute only 13 percent of the population, being
black in America means inevitably living amidst people of other races.
Yet, residentially speaking, most blacks are also highly isolated from other
racial groups. To understand how social contexts shape blacks' racial
attitudes, particularly those toward other minorities, hypotheses must be
extrapolated from other research.

The most logical place to develop such hypotheses would seem to be
existing research on social environments and whites' attitudes. It seems
plausible that blacks' racial attitudes should be affected by racial environments in many of the same ways as whites' racial attitudes. In other words,
blacks should be more racially hostile toward nonblacks in metropolitan
areas with larger nonblack populations and should be less racially averse
in integrated neighborhoods. Such a conclusion, however, assumes that
blacks' racial attitudes are roughly the same as those of whites.

But is this a fair assumption to make? The answer depends on which
racial attitudes are considered. With respect to feelings about whites,
blacks' racial attitudes are not likely to be the same. As a demographic
minority and a historically disenfranchised racial group, blacks' experience with race in American society is far different from that of whites:
African Americans have been denigrated in American culture to an extent far beyond what occurred with any of its white ethnic populations,
and blacks, as a more economically and politically marginalized group, do

not have the same racial prerogatives to defend. Whites are also less accepting of integrated neighborhoods and are less willing to acknowledge
discrimination in American society than blacks (Schuman et al. 1997). In
terms of black-white relations, blacks' racial attitudes are more liberal
than those of whites. But while blacks may be more tolerant of whites,
they are not necessarily more accepting of Latinos and Asian Americans.
Other research has demonstrated that blacks hold more negative stereotypes of Asians and Latinos than whites do (Bobo and Johnson 2000).
So it is unclear whether existing theories about how social environments
shape racial attitudes that were developed for white populations need
modification when applied to African Americans. To understand this further, it is important to examine more closely the major theories on the
environmental determinants of racial attitudes with an eye to how they
may relate particularly to African Americans.

Racial Competition

As noted above, the most popular explanation of social contexts and racial
attitudes is the real conflict or group threat model. The threat hypothesis views racial attitudes as originating from the competition between
racial groups for material, political, and economic resources. Although
proponents of this model understand that these racialized conflicts will be
historically and contextually situated, they nevertheless argue that racial
attitudes arise primarily from a reasoned assessment of group interests
and are equally applicable across groups. Most notable has been sociologist Lawrence Bobo's refinements of Herbert Blumer's theories on racial
attitudes, where racial attitudes originate not just in competition between
groups for power and resources but from an understanding of racial status
position: "Feelings of competition and hostility emerge from historically
and collectively developed judgments about the positions in the social order that in-group members should rightfully occupy relative to members
of an out-group" (Bobo and Hutchings 1996, 955).

According to Bobo, this feeling of racial status competition explains
not just the resentment whites may have toward minorities but also the
racial attitudes of blacks toward other groups. Blacks may resent Latinos
or Asians if they feel these groups are threatening or denying them their
rightful social status. The increased presence of Latinos and Asians in
many metropolitan areas may be seen as a competitive force against black
interests, particularly if these groups form political coalitions that exclude

African Americans. If Bobo is correct about how feelings of racial competition for status and position shape racial views, then blacks' racial attitudes toward Asian Americans and Latinos should be influenced by social environments in the same way as whites' attitudes toward all minorities: the greater the number of Asians or Latinos in an area, the greater threat blacks will feel and the higher their level of racial resentment will be. If blacks' attitudes are similar to those of whites in this regard, these environmental effects should occur relative to metropolitan area or counties. In short, as the percentage of Asians or Latinos in a region increases, there should be greater levels of black racial antagonism toward these groups.

Yet, at the same time, theories about racial status and threat seem ill suited for explaining environmental variations in blacks' racial attitudes toward whites. Since blacks historically have occupied a subordinate position to whites in American society, it is unclear how blacks' social and political status could be hampered or diminished by the increasing numbers of whites within a region. If anything, one might expect that blacks who live in predominantly white areas will experience less racial discrimination and feel less threatened by white populations since those white populations putatively are less racially hostile. Furthermore, Blumer's theories about racial status position are meant to explain the attitudes of dominant groups. Although the racial status theory might work in explaining the attitudes of blacks toward other minorities, it does not seem applicable for blacks' attitudes toward whites because whites are still the overwhelming majority of the population in most metropolitan areas and whites continue to hold a preeminent position in American society. Therefore, to explain the environmental determinants of blacks' attitudes toward whites, another factor needs consideration: feelings of group identification and solidarity.

Racial Solidarity

Human beings are cognitive categorizers: a natural human tendency is to organize all the information processed through the senses into distinct mental schemas. According to social psychologists, this categorizing tendency has important social implications because when thinking about other people, humans immediately categorize them as either in-group or out-group members. More importantly, even under conditions of the most minimal information, humans are likely to favor members of in-groups over those of out-groups. In a famous series of experiments, psychologist Henri Tajfel demonstrated that when randomly assigned to make-believe groups, human subjects repeatedly favored other in-group members (Tajfel and Turner 1979). Where social groups in a society are hierarchically ordered, like races in the United States, membership and identification with a low-status group has negative consequences for both material and psychological well-being (Hogg and Abrams 1990). As with any organization, those who find themselves in low-status groups are under pressure to disavow their group membership and emphasize their personal characteristics or to disguise themselves as members of another group or to voice a challenge against the group hierarchy, what could be called exit, pass, and voice, respectively.[9]

Social environments are particularly important for shaping feelings of group solidarity or isolation because they determine the possible response to a negatively ascribed group identity. In particular, people who belong to groups with negative social connotations are more likely to affirm their group membership and voice a challenge to the group hierarchy if there are more fellow group members around. For example, a New York Yankees fan visiting Boston is more likely to wear a Yankees baseball cap if there are other Yankees fans around than if not (Brown 1986). Similarly, African Americans should be more likely to challenge racial hierarchies and avow a stronger sense of racial solidarity in areas with higher proportions of blacks. And this is precisely what some research suggests: blacks who live in predominantly black neighborhoods express greater feelings of racial solidarity and greater solidarity among members of black churches, which in turn contributes to higher levels of political activity (Bledsoe et al. 1995; Allen, Dawson, and Brown 1989; Shingles 1981).

If living in predominantly black neighborhoods gives African Americans a stronger sense of racial identity, they may be more likely to feel a sense of "linked fate" with other blacks. (Dawson 1994). What effect, in turn, this has on their attitudes toward whites is unclear. Psychologists have found that feelings of in-group solidarity only correspond with out-group denigration under conditions of group competition (Branscombe and Wann 1994). What is not clear is whether blacks who feel a stronger sense of racial solidarity are also more racially resentful toward whites or racially competitive with other minority groups. Theories of social identity would suggest that African Americans who live in regions or neighborhoods with higher populations of blacks will have a stronger sense of group identification and possibly be more judgmental of whites, particularly if they feel unjustly denigrated. Blacks with a stronger sense of racial identity may also have a stronger sense of distance from out-groups, particularly whites, which may then be manifest in a higher level of racial animosity.

Interracial Contact

Although Allport's hypotheses about socially learned prejudice and the benefits of social contact were oriented primarily around whites' attitudes toward blacks and Jews, they should, in theory, be universally applicable for other groups. Several studies have found that blacks who have greater opportunities for interracial contact with other groups, particularly under favorable conditions such as in neighborhoods or among friendship groups, are more likely to have positive racial attitudes toward those groups (Schuman and Hatchett 1974; Welch et al. 2001). For example, among African Americans, early childhood contact with whites was important for determining later patterns of interracial friendship, which are then important for shaping their adult racial attitudes (Ellison and Powers 1994).

The contact theory of racial attitudes has important implications for understanding the relationship between social environments and blacks' racial attitudes. Obviously, the extent to which blacks can have social contacts with whites and particularly Asians and Latinos will depend on their exposure to these groups in work and neighborhood settings. Their exposure to Asians and Latinos will also depend upon the size of these groups in the region as well—blacks in Atlanta are far less likely to come into contact with Asians or Latinos, irrespective of the level of segregation in their own neighborhood, than blacks in Los Angeles. But as with whites, blacks who live in more integrated neighborhoods should belong to more multiracial civic organizations, should be more likely to have friends of other races, and, as a result, should harbor less animosity toward other racial groups.

The most important aspect of contact theory to consider with respect to African Americans is where the contact is occurring. Because of the long history of racism toward blacks in the United States, many other groups may continue to exhibit negative behaviors when coming into contact with African Americans. Casual contact between blacks and other races may not promote racial understanding but be an experience of bigotry and hostility. As Ellison and Powers explain, "black Americans often have no choice but to come into contact with whites. Much of this contact takes place under hierarchical conditions . . . and the sorry legacy of racial animosity in the United States almost surely adds a dimension of suspicion" (Ellison and Powers 1994, 396). The more important types of social contacts for lowering racial animosity, therefore, will have to occur in settings of equal status and sharing.

Other Considerations

Issues of self-selection also are important to consider when thinking about the relationship between social environments and blacks' racial attitudes. As with their white counterparts, blacks with a strong aversion to other races may seek to locate in all-black areas. Although this is less likely to explain regional differences in racial attitudes, it might account for higher levels of black racial solidarity and out-group aversion in all-black neighborhoods. But while self-selection may be an important explanation for geographic differences in whites' racial attitudes, spatial self-selection among blacks is unlikely to follow the same patterns. First, blacks still experience high levels of discrimination in urban housing markets and may find many neighborhoods effectively closed off to them. As blacks have a much more limited geographic mobility, they have fewer opportunities to sort themselves spatially according to their racial preferences. Second, unlike whites, blacks typically prefer racially mixed neighborhoods; several studies have shown that while whites typically prefer all-white neighborhoods, blacks prefer neighborhoods that are only 50 percent black and relatively few prefer all-black neighborhoods (Farley et al. 1993; Charles 2001).

This also brings up another important and overlooked factor: the difference in the significance of black population sizes compared with whites. Blacks are only 13 percent of America's population, whereas non-Latino whites are around 70 percent. The difference in size means that the racial composition of a neighborhood will have far different implications depending on which group is considered. A neighborhood that is 50 percent black is not an evenly integrated neighborhood—relative to the size of the African American population, it is a disproportionately black neighborhood. On the hand, a neighborhood that is 50 percent white is a relatively underpopulated neighborhood relative to the size of the white population. Consequently, the same types of constant effects should not occur for both blacks and whites as the neighborhood percent of their own race increases. The cultural differences between a neighborhood that is 50 percent black and 80 percent black are far less than those between neighborhoods that are 50 and 80 percent white. When examining how racial environments shape blacks' racial attitudes, particularly in comparison with whites, it is important to consider the relative distribution of racial populations.

Summation

Previous research suggests that many of the same environmental factors that shape whites' racial attitudes also hold for blacks, but the distinct position of African Americans as a relatively small minority in American society and a racial group with a history of profound racial discrimination also means there are some unique processes that will influence their attitudes. With these considerations, the dominant theories on racial attitudes generate the following hypotheses:

- The greater the number of Asians or Latinos in a region, the higher the level of perceived threat and antiminority resentment there will be among African Americans.
- Because most metropolitan areas are largely white, there should be fewer differences in blacks' attitudes toward whites according to the size of the white regional population.
- Blacks who live in either neighborhoods or metropolitan areas with more blacks should exhibit greater feelings of racial solidarity, which, in turn, may shape their racial attitudes.
- Blacks who live in neighborhoods with people of other races should be more likely to have contact with out-groups, belong to racially mixed civic organizations, work in more integrated settings, and be less racially resentful.
- Greater levels of discrimination in housing for blacks will mean that self-selection effects should be less pronounced among blacks than whites and that neighborhood effects will be different in scale.

Environmental Influences on Latinos' and Asian Americans' Racial Attitudes

Unlike with whites or African Americans, very little is known about the racial attitudes of Latinos and Asian Americans. Partly this arises from the recent growth of these populations. Prior to the 1970s, Latinos and Asian Americans were very small minorities within the United States. Although their numbers have increased substantially in the past three decades, their relatively small numbers have still made them difficult to study with most survey data. Most national surveys on racial attitudes, for example, draw representative samples of the population and end up having too few cases of Asians and Latinos to make independent analyses of these groups. Research that has focused on these groups has tended to come from specific states or metropolitan areas where Latinos and Asians are in high numbers (Lee 2000; Portes and Bach 1985; Saito 1998). Although these studies provide interesting portraits of Latinos and Asians in particular settings, it is unclear whether the findings of this research can be generalized for the population of the entire country.

Latinos and Asian Americans also present a unique challenge to researchers on racial attitudes because of their great internal diversity. Some scholars even have questioned whether it makes sense to group people according to the title of "Latino" or "Asian American" because of the tremendous variation in nationality, race, and immigrant status within these groups (Portes and Truelove 1987). While some Latinos and Asian Americans come from families who have lived in the United States for decades, the large majority of Asian and Latinos are either first- or second-generation immigrants. Many of these immigrant groups continue to have strong ties to their country of origin and retain an identity more strongly defined by nations than by panethnic association (Jones-Correa and Leal 1996). It is not clear whether groups that define themselves so strongly by nationality have a strong sense of racial differentiation with the rest of the population. Furthermore, Latinos themselves are not racially homogenous and are divided in their own racial self-identification between white and black and some other category that is distinct from either (Frey, Abresch, and Yeasting 2001).

Consequently, it is difficult to know how the racial attitudes of Latinos or Asian Americans will be shaped by their social surroundings. Much of this may vary with a level of incorporation into white society. For Latinos who identify themselves as white, live in integrated settings, and speak mostly English, their racial attitudes toward other minorities, particularly blacks, may be no different than the white majority. For others, particularly those who are not fully incorporated into American society or who do not identify as white, their racial attitudes may follow the same dynamics as African Americans. As with blacks, Latinos and Asian Americans also experienced systematic discrimination throughout American history and, as a racial minority, may still face biases from the majority white population. What remains in question, however, is whether the same hypotheses about context and racial environment that were generated for whites or African Americans will also hold. On the one hand, if Asians and Latinos are incorporated into white society, they may see their racial identities in relative opposition to African Americans; consequently, their racial attitudes may vary less with the percent of their own group in the neighborhood and more with the percent of whites in their area. On the other hand, if Latinos or Asians see themselves as a minority group similarly in opposition to a white-dominated racial hierarchy, they may react as blacks do, that is, those who live in same-race neighborhoods should have more negative views of other groups, particularly in metropolitan contexts of greater racial diversity.

In short, given the internal diversity of the Asian and Latino populations, other factors must also be considered when examining their racial attitudes. Most important will be their length of residence and country of origin. Newly arrived immigrants may not have a strong sense of racial identity in the United States, but they may have a strong sense of national identity that comes in opposition to other groups. Furthermore, many immigrants may import the cultural stereotypes or biases from their home country or even see themselves in opposition to other Latinos or Asians based on strong national or ethnic differences. New immigrants may also see themselves as greater competitors with other minority groups, particularly among the unauthorized, who often come with few job skills or little education. Finally, the linguistic differences of many immigrants may preclude their ability to interact with other racial groups and build various types of interpersonal connections. The national origin and linguistic isolation of many Latinos and Asian Americans mean that differences by nationality, English language usage, or level of incorporation may far outstrip the effects of social environments.

Thus, in addition to the patterns described above, Latinos and Asian Americans offer other complexities to the relationship between racial attitudes and social environment. New immigrants who are more likely to live in ethnic enclaves may have fewer opportunities for social interaction with other racial groups. Strong national differences may exist in the attitudes of Latinos and Asians, which may be further heightened in particular social settings. Linguistic barriers may affect economic opportunities, residential choice, and patterns of social interaction, which all in turn may shape racial attitudes. As these are all issues that social scientists have yet to fully investigate, the impact of racial environments on the racial attitudes of Asian Americans and Latinos is still largely unknown.

Nevertheless, we can still summarize a few predictions based on past research. These would include the following:

- Because most American metropolitan areas are largely white, there should be fewer differences in Latinos' or Asian Americans' attitudes toward whites according to the size of the white regional population.
- However, the greater the number of other minorities in a region, particularly African Americans, the higher the level of perceived threat and antiminority resentment there will toward that group.
- Asian Americans or Latinos who live in places with more of their own ethnic group, particularly their own nationality, should exhibit greater feelings of ethnic solidarity which, in turn, may shape their views about other groups.
- Asian Americans and Latinos with limited English language abilities will have fewer opportunities for positive contact with other groups and may harbor more negative views, particularly if they live in ethnic enclaves.
- The social and civic integration of Asian Americans and Latinos depends largely on their level of incorporation—citizens with English skills should be less adversely affected by living in white areas.
- Asians and Latinos who are more incorporated into mainstream American society may be affected not by the percentage of their own racial group but by the percentage of whites in their neighborhood.

Conclusion

Given past research, we have some pretty clear expectations about how people's racial environments will shape their perceptions of other groups, even in an increasingly multiethnic America. Nevertheless, for these theories to be truly applicable for all racial groups, several important considerations must be noted. First, the specific locations of social contact must be identified. If the positive effects of racial contact are predicated upon races interacting under conditions of equality, goal sharing, intergroup cooperation, and the support of dominant institutions, then we need to find out where such patterns of contact are occurring and how participation in such settings varies with the racial composition of people's surroundings. If most Americans are not meeting people of other races in workplaces, civic associations, or under other conditions of equality, they may have few opportunities to improve their racial views.

This also means considering the reality of integration in the United States. For most Americans, integration will entail minority migration into predominantly white areas. Such a pattern is likely to hold different consequences for each racial group. Whites in integrated neighborhoods may have less contact with their neighbors, be less involved in community affairs, and feel more estranged from their communities. Among minorities, it is likely that the greater the level of social or economic incorporation of a minority group into white society, the less alienating this cohabitation will be. In other words, for Asian American and Latino citizens with English language skills and for African Americans with resources and education, migration into white areas is less likely to be met with resistance or be a source of social dislocation. However, for minorities without such resources, integration may be a further jarring and alienating experience. In examining the social consequences of integration, it is essential that its difficulties be acknowledged.

Second, racial environments may have an additional effect on minorities' racial attitudes by instilling a sense of group solidarity. Residing in what is still a largely white society, African Americans, Latinos, and Asian Americans may have a stronger sense of their own racial identity if larger numbers of their own racial group are present. Research from social identification theory suggests that when minorities are a smaller fraction of the population, they may downplay their own racial identification and may express less racial resentment toward other groups (Hogg and Abrams 1990). Conversely, when their fraction of the population grows, minorities may exhibit a stronger sense of group identity and have stronger racial views about other groups. In short, racial environments shape minority attitudes not simply by determining the nature of racial competition or the opportunities for intergroup contact but by altering the minority's own sense of racial solidarity.

Finally, the level of social and economic incorporation of Latinos and Asian Americans needs to be considered. It is not self-evident that Latinos or Asians, particularly among new arrivals to the United States, have a strong panethnic identity, and new immigrants may see themselves more as Mexican or Chinese than as Latino or Asian American. They may also see themselves as similar to whites in being differentiated from blacks; that is, Latinos or Asians may, along with whites, group themselves as "not black" rather than as a minority group. This racial self-identification may vary by nationality and English language usage and may have a strong impact on their attitudes toward other groups in American society. To test these hypotheses, we now turn to some data.

CHAPTER TWO

Racial Attitudes among Whites, Blacks, Latinos, and Asian Americans

Cablinasian. For most Americans, this term is unrecognizable, but for one very famous person, it is an effort to carve out a new and more authentic racial identity. After Tiger Woods won the 1997 Masters Golf Tournament, many commentators and political activists celebrated the victory of the first "African American" in this historic event. Yet Tiger Woods balked at this characterization. He said that it bothered him to be labeled as African American given that his father was of mixed ancestry of Native American, Caucasian, and African decent and his mother was of Thai and Chinese descent. Rather than seeing himself as African American or Asian American, he coined the term "Cablinasian" (for Caucasian-black-Indian-Asian) as a self-description. This created a minor controversy among some black commentators who saw Woods as "selling out" and trying to "pass" for something he was not. For Woods, it was simply an attempt to better acknowledge his diverse background.

In many ways, the controversy over Tiger Woods's identity epitomizes the increasing complexity of race in the United States. As America becomes more racially diverse, its residents' racial attitudes are growing more complicated. Racial and ethnic identity in the United States has always been a fluid and contested phenomenon, but the increasing number of Latinos and Asian Americans and the greater integration of American society mean that Americans' racial perceptions are subject to a wider set of influences than ever before. Consider the fact that over seven million Americans identified themselves as having multiple racial identities in the last census. By this count, nearly 3 percent of the population do not see themselves as fitting neatly within any single racial category. This racial jumble is further exacerbated among Latinos, who are divided in their own racial self-categorization as being either "white," "black," or some unnamed "other" racial category. On top of this, it is also unclear whether most Latinos or Asian Americans see themselves primarily in terms of Latino or Asian or a single panethnic identity or whether they identify more particularly with their country of origin (for example, Mexican American or Korean American). Finally, America has just elected a president with a Caucasian mother and an African father, a man who is often described as "transcending" race in a very self-conscious way.

Such complexities within American racial identities make it hard to anticipate how its growing racial diversity will influence its race relations. As we found in the previous chapter, one of the key factors in predicting the future of race in the United States is the impact of racial geography on perceptions of group competition and opportunities for positive interracial contact. Whom people live around should be a good indicator of how they feel about different groups and which groups they might get to know. Yet when we take into account the blurring lines of race in America, the impact of geography also becomes less clear. After all, most of our knowledge about how racial environments influence racial attitudes is based on studies of whites in biracial contexts; very little research has examined how whites might respond to other minority groups or how blacks, Latinos, or Asian Americans might be affected by their surroundings. Before we can begin to examine racial environments in a multiethnic America, we first need to address three unresolved questions regarding racial identity in contemporary America.

First, do whites have consistent attitudes toward all minority groups, or do they view blacks, Latinos, and Asians in systematically different ways? Decades of research have yielded a trove of studies on white Americans' patterns of racial hostility toward blacks. Although few whites publicly express the outward bigotry and racism of decades past, many whites continue to behave in racially biased ways or express racial hostility in more subtle ways, what some researchers call "symbolic racism." Many questions remain, however, about whether or not the same factors that underlie whites' attitudes toward blacks also drive their attitudes toward Latinos and Asian Americans. It is not self-evident that whites perceive similar levels of threat from Latino and Asian populations as they do from nearby black populations or that whites couch their resentment of Latinos and Asian Americans in symbolic terms.[1] Indeed, we do not know if whites' negative perceptions of Latinos and Asian Americans arise from xenophobia or ethnocentrism.

Second, are minorities' racial attitudes categorically different than those of whites? Because of their historically subordinate place in America's racial hierarchy and relatively smaller population proportions, minorities will surely not think about whites in the same way that whites think about them. It is unlikely, for example, that African Americans would utilize the same symbolic terms that whites use to express their racial resentment toward other groups. But we do not know whether minorities have distinctive types of racial attitudes, either toward whites or each other. Many of the same group dynamics that drive racial and ethnic perceptions among whites, such as feelings of group competition and threat, are also likely to influence minorities' racial attitudes, but, given the history of racial discrimination, minorities' perceptions of their own racial identity are likely to be different from those of both whites and other ethnic groups. For example, Latinos and Asian Americans may be threatening to blacks in a way they are not to America's white population or to each other. To understand how minorities might react to their increasingly diverse social surroundings, we must first identify whether they think about themselves and other groups in unique ways.

Third, how are Latinos' and Asian Americans' racial attitudes affected by the diversity of their populations? It is not self-evident that most people who fall under the heading of "Latino" or "Asian American" necessarily view themselves or others according to these group-based terms. A recent immigrant may see herself first as a Korean, then as an immigrant, then as a Christian, and then maybe as an Asian American. Her views of whites, blacks, or Latinos may, in turn, be shaped by these various categories—as an immigrant, she may see she has more in common with Latinos, yet as a Korean, she may see herself differently than Chinese or Filipino Americans. We know very little about the feelings of panethnic solidarity among the diverse sets of people who trace their ancestry to Latin America or Asia or whether systematic differences occur in how these people view other racial groups. As with whites and blacks, before we determine what shapes Latinos' or Asian Americans' racial attitudes, we must first understand whether the peoples who fall under these categories have a coherent sense of racial identity or racial views toward other groups.

In sum, to anticipate the impact of America's growing racial diversity, we need to first ascertain whether each group's racial attitudes are categorically similar or different and whether it even makes sense to generalize about the racial attitudes of some, such as Asians and Latinos. Luckily, this is an empirical question that can be answered partly with survey data. By comparing the differences in racial attitudes among the four major racial categories (non-Latino white, non-Latino black, Latino, and Asian American), we can explore some baseline conditions of racial identity and perception. While there are some important differences in the racial attitudes measured by the survey instruments (minorities have higher levels of racial solidarity; Asian Americans' and Latinos' attitudes are internally divided by levels of incorporation and country of origin), there are also strikingly similar patterns. Racial animosity, perceptions of intergroup competition, and negative stereotyping of other groups are evident among all races In terms of out-group perceptions, whites, blacks, Latinos, and Asian Americans are probably more alike than different, although each of these groups differ in their own racial self-conceptions.

Whites' Racial Attitudes

When thinking about whites' racial attitudes, it is essential to consider their distinct and privileged position within American society. Despite its increasing ethnic and racial diversity, the United States remains a nation dominated by its white population. Americans of European origin continue to be the overwhelming majority (roughly 70 percent) of U.S. residents. Whites still hold the vast majority of elected offices, corporate executive slots, and other positions of economic, social, and political leadership (Anderson 2001). Whites also enjoy higher incomes, education levels, employment rates, and better social status, on average, than either blacks or Latinos and many Asian nationalities (Oliver and Shapiro 1987). In fact, by almost any imaginable indicator—culturally, socially, or economically—America continues to be a predominately white nation.

Much of this racial predominance traces back to the long history of white racial discrimination and exclusion. From slavery to Jim Crow, from the nineteenth-century disenfranchisement of Chinese Americans to more contemporary immigration restrictions, whites in America historically excluded people from other races and nationalities from the full benefits of citizenship, often to their own advantage. Although tremendous progress has been made in eliminating white racial hostility and the legal barriers to nonwhites since the Civil Rights Movement of the 1950s and 1960s, race is still a defining part of American society, and whiteness, in particular, still confers social status.

Yet, as America's racial composition rapidly changes, the legacy of this racial domination remains unclear. As we saw earlier, previous research would suggest that the increasing racial diversity of the United States is pushing whites' racial attitudes in seemingly opposite directions. On the one hand, the shrinking size of the white population relative to other minority groups is likely to generate more feelings of white status insecurity. As the white majority contracts and other racial groups gain in social status and position, the white monopoly of racial privilege is rapidly eroding. It seems likely that this loss of preeminence should lead to a greater hostility toward other races or ethnic groups; evidence of racial backlash is already evident in the politics of immigration reform and "English only" movements. On the other hand, the increased exposure of whites to Latinos and Asians also creates opportunities for interpersonal friendships and the building of social bonds, factors that can alleviate racial tension. As the United States becomes slowly more integrated, as Americans of European ancestry encounter more peoples from Asia and Latin America, and as the American white hegemony fades, the traditional mechanisms of bias and bigotry may come undone.

But such prognostications are largely speculative because our knowledge of whites' racial perceptions is based almost exclusively on the relationship between whites and African Americans, a relationship that is still in flux. For example, over the past fifty years, whites have demonstrated a major change in their support for the principles of equality between races. Where previous survey data from the 1950s and 1960s revealed that large majorities of whites openly embraced negative characterizations of blacks and opposed interracial marriage and desegregation, very few whites today openly espouse any of these opinions (Schuman et al. 1997). On paper, the overwhelming majority of white Americans seem to fully embrace the ideal of racial equality. Not all observers, however, believe that whites are willing to accept other groups as brothers and sisters. Some scholars argue that the "old-fashioned" racism of the 1950s has been replaced with a new "symbolic racism," in which antiblack affect is fused with a sense that blacks violate Protestant norms of work and self-reliance (Sears 1993; Kinder and Sanders 1996). Whites, knowing it is unacceptable to publicly voice racist sentiments, couch their bigotry in coded terms: blacks are not called lazy or inferior, but they are seen as unwilling to work, be self-sufficient, and take responsibility for their own welfare. Persistent differences in black levels of unemployment, poverty, and social welfare are explained, not by structural problems of white racism, but by blacks' inability to conform to Anglo-Protestant cultural norms of individual responsibility.

Yet it is unclear how this type of racial resentment translates across the board in terms of a general ethnocentrism. After all, the impact of social environments on racial attitudes is believed to operate through relatively

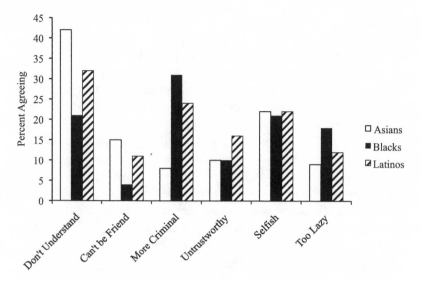

FIGURE 2.1. Percent of whites agreeing with negative characterizations of other races (2005 CID).

crude mechanisms: competition for resources or group contact. If whites view Latinos and Asians as similarly threatening as blacks, then presumably the impact of geography will be the same regardless of the group in question. But for this to be the case, we would expect to find relatively high and uniform levels of white racial bias—whites should view all minority groups with equally high levels of negative stereotyping or, if whites know enough to suppress their racial bigotry in public, they should express alternative forms of discrimination or distance toward all groups.

In order to sort through these various processes, we can first examine differences in whites' attitudes using some measures of crude stereotypes. Figure 2.1 depicts the percentage of whites in the 2005 Citizen, Information, and Democracy (CID) survey who agree with each of six particular traits that describe Asians, Latinos, or African Americans. These traits are as follows: that [OUTGROUP] is *hard to understand*, that they *couldn't imagine being friends with* that group, or that people in the out-group are more *criminal, untrustworthy, selfish*, or *lazy*.[2]

In terms of these six characteristics, it is clear that whites do not view all minority groups in the same terms but employ different stereotypes for each. For example, whites are twice as likely to report not being able to understand Asian Americans than not being able to understand blacks:

over 40 percent of whites agreed that they find Asians difficult to understand; in contrast, only 30 percent of whites agreed that they find Latinos
and 21 percent agreed that they find blacks difficult to understand. Similarly, whites reported it harder to imagine having friendships with either
Asians or Latinos compared with blacks—less than 5 percent of whites
said they could not imagine being friends with someone who is black, but
over 10 percent said they felt that way about Latinos and 15 percent said
they felt that way about Asians. Yet whites seemed to also view Latinos
and African Americans in more deviant terms. Over 30 percent of whites
agreed that blacks were more criminal, and 18 percent saw them as lazy
(24 percent thought Latinos were more criminal and 12 percent thought
Latinos were lazy). Less than 10 percent of whites thought either of these
traits applied to Asians. Whites also viewed Latinos as less trustworthy
than blacks or Asians. Interestingly, the only trait that was consistently
applied across all racial out-groups was selfishness; roughly 21 percent of
whites saw all three other races as being selfish.

Two trends are immediately apparent from these findings. First, whites
do not employ consistent stereotypes about all other minority groups.
Outside of seeing all other groups as selfish, whites view African Americans as more socially accessible but also in more negative terms regarding
issues of order and drive (findings that were also evident in the National
Politics Survey [NPS] data as we will see); Asians and Latinos may be less
familiar to whites, but Asians, at least, are not viewed negatively in terms
of character. Second, negative stereotypes of other groups are not widely
admitted among whites. Less than a quarter of whites would publicly agree
with a statement calling other races untrustworthy, selfish, or lazy.

It is difficult to know whether these seemingly low levels of racial stereotyping reflect the full extent of whites' racial predispositions because
many whites feel that it is unacceptable to publicly articulate whatever
racist sentiments they may hold. But even using more subtle measures of
symbolic racism (that is, measures of why whites think that other groups
do less well in American society), similar patterns emerge. Respondents
in the Multi-City Study of Urban Inequality (MCSUI) data set were
asked how much they agreed with various reasons for why either blacks
or Latinos have worse jobs, income, and housing than whites.[3] Two of
these reasons were arguably symbolic, that blacks/Latinos do not have
the "ability" or the "willpower" to rise up. Roughly 18 percent of whites
sampled agreed that black and Latino poverty was related to ability, although whites split on views about motivation: 44 percent of whites agreed

that Latinos lack motivation, compared with 52 percent who thought that blacks lack motivation. Interestingly, both of the measures are highly correlated with the negative stereotype measures.[4] In other words, whites who agree with statements of symbolic racism are also more likely to endorse negative stereotypes of such groups. Although whites score slightly higher on measures of symbolic racism than on measures of negative stereotypes, less than 20 percent of whites still attribute racial differences in social status to any innate differences between races.

Nor do many whites see themselves in greater competition with blacks than with other minority groups. Respondents in the NPS survey were asked two questions about whether more jobs or political influence for other racial groups would result in fewer jobs or political influence for whites.[5] Overall, whites expressed low feelings of zero-sum competition with other races. In no case did more than 22 percent of whites agree strongly with either of the zero-sum competition measures on either jobs or politics. Nor were there any statistically significant differences in the percent of whites based on the target group in question. For instance, 21 percent of whites agreed that blacks posed threats of zero-sum competition, nearly the same percentage that felt that way about Latinos. Although there may be regional difference in these attitudes, in this broad national survey there was remarkable similarity in feelings across groups.[6]

These findings have mixed implications for the relationship between of racial environments on whites' racial attitudes. On the one hand, if whites hold fewer negative stereotypes of Latinos and Asian Americans, then living among more of these groups may not trigger greater racial animosity. In fact, this is what some other research suggests. Sociologist Marylee Taylor finds that whites' negative attitudes toward Latinos or Asian Americans, unlike their attitudes toward blacks, do not increase as the population of these groups increases in metropolitan areas, although admittedly the percent of Latinos and Asians in these areas was quite small (Taylor 1998). On the other hand, whites do not feel significantly less zero-sum racial competition with blacks than they do with Asians and Latinos. They also report feeling closer to blacks than to Asians or Latinos, sentiments driven partly by the foreign language and cultural practices of many of these groups. Thus if feelings of racial competition or alienation are what underlie white racial attitudes, then whites may react to proximate Latino or Asian populations with greater resentment or hostility, depending on whether they have any social contact. In short, racial geography may end up corresponding to whites' attitudes in similar ways for all three minority groups, but the underlying mechanism behind these patterns may vary with the particular group in question.

Racial Attitudes among Nonwhites

If race is still a force in the United States, it is especially so for its minority populations. The legacy of slavery, exclusion, disenfranchisement, and state-sanctioned racial segregation has not been easily undone in America. Recent improvements in the social, economic, and political condition of most minorities have been notable, but considerable gaps still exist between America's white (and increasingly Asian) population on one side and its black and Latino populations on the other along nearly every measure of health and economic well-being including education, income, mortality, employment, and poverty. Yet despite these differences, social scientists have not determined whether the particular social position of minorities translates into categorically different types of racial attitudes, particularly in comparison with whites. Asians, blacks, and Latinos may still be marginalized to varying degrees within American society, but the impact of this marginalization on their racial attitudes remains unclear.

Part of our ignorance comes from a lack of data. Because of their smaller population sizes, it is difficult to get sufficient numbers of minorities in most national surveys to conduct a systematic comparison of their racial attitudes. Most national surveys simply do not sample a large enough number of minorities to allow for meaningful statistical comparisons across all groups. Here the NPS data are a true exception. The NPS is the first study to provide a comprehensive, national sample of minorities in a survey of racial attitudes. These data are truly unique and provide a firsthand glimpse of interracial attitudes using the same survey instruments. As listed in table 2.1, they also provide some intriguing findings.

One of the simplest measures of racial attitudes is about closeness among racial groups. NPS respondents were asked a battery of questions of how close they felt to all four major racial groups in their "ideas, interests, and feelings about things," and respondents could choose "very close, fairly close, not too close, or not close at all." The first set of findings in table 2.1 lists the percent of each racial group reporting feeling "very close" or "fairly close" to each group. The one consistent pattern is that all respondents are most likely to feel closest to their own racial group: over 90 percent of blacks, Latinos, and whites feel close to their own group; only

TABLE 2.1 **Comparative perspectives on racial closeness, competition, solidarity, perceived discrimination, and immigration-related issues among racial groups**

	Asians (percent)	Blacks (percent)	Latinos (percent)	Whites (percent)
Feel close with Asians	85	43	41	57
Feel close with blacks	47	91	56	72
Feel close with Latinos	41	69	91	62
Feel close with whites	76	61	71	93
Zero-sum competition with Asians	—	48	41	18
Zero-sum competition with blacks	43	—	42	21
Zero-sum competition with Latinos	38	48	—	22
Zero-sum competition with whites	67	69	62	—
Feelings of racial linked fate	17	33	19	15
Feel blacks have gotten less than they deserve	44	71	45	38
Agree that if minorities are poor they have only themselves to blame	59	60	73	61
Agree immigrants take jobs away from natives	24	52	23	30
Agree immigration levels should be decreased	10	33	15	35
Believe ethnic groups should blend in to larger society	38	52	56	51
Agree being born in the United States is important to be "true" American	36	80	74	51
N	447	720	716	873

Source: 2004 NPS.

85 percent of Asians reported feeling close to Asians. Beyond this similarity, however, feelings of closeness vary in asymmetric patterns across the different racial groups: Asians and Latinos are much more likely to report feeling close to whites than to blacks or each other; more blacks feel close to Latinos and whites than they do to Asians; whites, meanwhile, are most likely to feel close to blacks, then to Latinos, and then to Asians.

From the closeness measure, it would seem that the most alienated racial group in the United States is Asian American. Not only do they report some of the lowest levels of closeness with other minority groups, they consistently garner the lowest ratings of closeness from others. Partly, this may be a function of their relatively small population size and geographic concentration in just a few states. Partly, this may relate to the non-Western cultural origins of many Asian immigrants, which could seem more remote to whites and blacks than the Catholic-Hispanic traditions of most Latinos. Regardless of its origin, in terms of general affect, Asians appear to be the most socially marginalized minority group.

The other notable differences are the asymmetries in feelings of closeness among blacks, Latinos, and whites. A greater percentage of whites feel closer to blacks than vice versa, as do blacks to Latinos and do Latinos to whites. The pattern resembles a love triangle with each member having stronger feelings toward another but no two sharing the same object of adoration. Now granted this measure of closeness is somewhat fuzzy—it is impossible to know whether "closeness" refers to a sense of group affect, obligation, sympathy, salience, or some combination of these factors (Wong 1998). Either way, the seemingly positive news from these data is that large majorities of blacks and Latinos do feel close to both whites and to each other.

A slightly different picture emerges when racial attitudes are gauged relative to feelings of zero-sum competition. NPS respondents were asked how much they agreed with a series of statements about whether "more good jobs" for another racial group meant fewer good jobs "for someone like themselves" and whether "the more influence" another racial group had in politics meant less influence for someone like themselves. The percentage of respondents who agreed with either one or both of these statements is reported. As with the measures of closeness, there are considerable asymmetries in perceptions of zero-sum racial competition, although these are largely between whites and nonwhites. Across the board, only about a fifth of the whites in the NPS sample thought that good jobs or political power for any of the other racial groups would come at their expense; over 60 percent of all three minority groups, however, believed that increased jobs or power for whites would come at theirs. In addition, all three minority groups are much more likely to perceive zero-sum racial competition be it with whites or with each other. Yet, beyond these differences, perceptions of zero-sum competition among minorities show remarkably similar patterns. For all three minority groups, the percent of each group that sees itself in zero-sum competition with the other minority groups is in the ten-point range between 38 and 48 percent. Minorities are not only three times more likely to see themselves in competition with whites, they are also twice as likely as whites to see themselves in competition with other minorities.

While minorities may have similar views about racial competition, they do not share the same view of their own racial identity. African

Americans, in particular, have much stronger attitudes about racial solidarity and discrimination. As discussed in chapter 1, political scientist Michael Dawson has noted that African Americans have a pronounced sense of "linked fate," that is, a perception that their own individual life chances are inexorably bound with what happens to blacks as a whole.[7] This pattern is also evident in the NPS data. Although a sense of linked fate is shared by a small portion of all four racial groups, none sense it as strongly as African Americans: 33 percent of blacks in the NPS study had a very strong sense of linked fate, compared with only 19 percent of Latinos and 17 percent of Asians. In addition, African Americans are far more likely to perceive racial injustice toward their group than other minorities: 71 percent of blacks agree with the statement that "blacks have gotten less than they deserve," a view endorsed by only 45 percent of Latinos or Asians. Interestingly, however, large majorities of Asians, blacks, and Latinos agree that minorities are largely responsible for their own poverty. The NPS asked this poverty-attribution question to all groups, even though it is commonly used to gauge white racial resentment, yet Asians and blacks are no less likely than whites to endorse this view. Attributing minority poverty to individual responsibility appears to be a sentiment widely held across all racial groups.

The other significant differences in interminority racial views occur, not surprisingly, along issues of immigration. NPS respondents were asked several questions about multiculturalism and the threats of immigration. Two of these yielded interesting differences among minorities. First, African Americans are far more likely to feel threatened by immigration than other groups. When asked how much they agree with the statement, "Immigrants take jobs away from people who were born in America," 52 percent of blacks agreed compared with only 24 percent of Asians, 23 percent of Latinos, and 30 percent of whites. Roughly 33 percent of blacks in the NPS survey also thought that immigration levels should be decreased, compared with only 10 percent of Asians and 15 percent of Latinos. Second, Asian respondents are far less supportive of cultural assimilation than other minorities. Only 38 percent of Asian respondents agreed with the statement that it is better for different ethnic groups to "change so they can better blend into the larger society," compared with 52 percent of blacks and 56 percent of Latinos. Similarly, Asians are much less nativist in their conceptions of what it means to be "truly American."[8] Only 36 percent thought that being born in America was important for being "truly American," compared with 80 percent of blacks and 74 percent of Latinos.

As with the data on whites, these findings would seem to present very mixed implications for the relationship between racial contexts and minorities' racial attitudes. On the one hand, racial diversity is supposed to correspond with greater racial animosity as racial groups compete for economic and political privilege. But here, the greatest expression of racial competition arises not among minorities toward each other but from minorities toward America's white majority. Clearly, living among a substantial white majority corresponds with an asymmetric perception of zero-sum racial competition for its minority groups. This perception of competition is not nearly as high as it is between minority groups. Although there has been much ink spilled over the putative tensions among Asians, Latinos, and African Americans, these animosities are not evident in a national survey, and interminority competition pales in comparison with the level of competition minorities feel toward whites.

On the other hand, there is significant variation in the nature and quality of racial attitudes among Asians, blacks, and Latinos, variation that could contribute to greater interminority racial hostility. African Americans are much less likely to report feeling close to Asians, feel much more racial solidarity with other blacks, and feel much greater competition from immigrants than from other minorities. Asian Americans also feel less close to blacks and Latinos and are much more likely to support sustaining their own cultural differences rather than wanting all minorities to assimilate into a single culture. Latinos are less likely to feel close to either Asians or blacks than to whites and, in terms of economic self-sufficiency, have the most conservative racial views of any group in America.

Consequently, from these findings one might expect that minorities will respond to increasing portions of other minorities in a manner that is similar to whites. For example, if increasing Latino or Asian populations generate more feelings of racial threat, then blacks who live in more racially diverse areas should be more racially hostile. However, the environmental influences on minorities' views toward whites might also depend on other factors. Living in a predominantly white society, it seems unlikely that minorities' racial attitudes will be sensitive to white population sizes, particularly with regard to larger geographic units such as metropolitan areas. Rather, minority attitudes may be more affected by the size of their own populations, particularly among African Americans who have a strong sense of racial solidarity. Other research has shown that feelings of group solidarity tend to be higher among African Americans as the percent of blacks in their area increase (Welch et al. 2001). This racial solidarity may fuel a greater sense of linked fate with other blacks and a greater perception of racial competition with other minority groups, both of which may translate into higher levels of racial resentment both toward whites and other groups. When thinking about the distinctive aspects of minority racial attitudes, the salience and strength of their own group identity will need to be taken into account. Which leads us to our third question—how unified are Asian Americans and Latinos as a racial group?

The Diversity of Asian Americans and Latinos

One of the most significant changes in American society during the past thirty years has been the rapid growth of its Latino and Asian populations. In 1970, Asian Americans and Latinos were a relatively small minority in the United States, comprising less than 5 percent of the population and geographically concentrated in a few states. But after a tremendous immigration following both immigration liberalization in the 1960s and a massive wave of unauthorized immigration, the population of both groups surged. Latinos are now over 13 percent of America's population and today outnumber African Americans as America's largest minority group.[9] The Asian American population has grown from less than 1 percent of Americans to over 4 percent. If these rates of growth continue, by mid-century, Asian Americans will be nearly the same proportion of the population (11 percent) as African Americans are today (Frey, Abresch, and Yeasting 2001).

With such rapid growth, the position of Asian Americans and Latinos in America's racial hierarchy remains in flux. Consider Asian Americans. In one light, they seem like other minorities in that they too face many racial hurdles in a predominantly white society. Like African Americans and Latinos, Asian Americans historically have experienced significant amounts of discrimination ranging from the Chinese Exclusion Act in 1882 (which effectively halted immigration from China) to the internment of Japanese American citizens during World War II. And while the state-sanctioned racism of decades ago may no longer be present, many Asian American writers continue to note the prejudices and stereotypes that still exist and that keep Asian Americans as "permanent aliens" in American culture (see, for example, Espiritu and Omi 2000; Kim 2000). But, in spite of these facts, Asian Americans have been very successful at overcoming racial barriers to economic advancement and incorporation into a predominantly white society. In education, employment, homeownership, and economic status, Asian Americans have rates of achievement that are above even America's white population. For example, over 40 percent of adult Asian Americans have a college degree, compared with only 28 percent of non-Hispanic whites.[10] However, while Asian Americans are also more likely than whites to have earned a college degree, they are also more likely to have less than a ninth grade education, a by-product of having so many immigrants and refugees from Southeast Asia in this population.

A similar indeterminacy also exists for Latinos. Because of their racial complexity, Latinos often straddle the divide between America's black and white populations. Some Latinos are following the path of other immigrant groups before them, adopting English language skills, achieving a higher education, and "incorporating" into the mainstream of American life. Many Latinos are attaining positions of social and economic prominence, participating in American civic associations, and moving into predominantly white neighborhoods. The larger proportion of Latinos, however, is not incorporating so rapidly and seems trapped in the lower rungs of American society. A majority of Latinos, particularly among unauthorized immigrants, experience a persistent divide with America's white population in their income, poverty, employment, infant mortality, and homeownership (Bean and Stevens 2003). According to some scholars, Latinos are following a path of "segmented assimilation," where the linear trajectory of social and economic incorporation has been stalled for a large number of second- and third-generation immigrants (Portes and Rumbaut 2001).

This intraethnic polarization highlights one important, if often overlooked, feature of the Latino and Asian American population: their tremendous internal diversity. Consider just the range of nationalities in these populations. Chinese Americans, the largest Asian ethnic group, are only 25 percent of Asian Americans; Filipinos are 18 percent; Asian Indians, the fastest growing Asian American population during the past twenty years, are 16 percent; Koreans and Vietnamese are each roughly 10 percent; and Japanese are 9 percent. The remaining 12 percent are from many other countries in Asia such as Cambodia, Laos, Bangladesh, Pakistan, and Indonesia. Not only do these countries offer a tremendous variety of languages, religions, and cultures, China and India also have significant ethnic and cultural differences within their own populations. Although America's Latino population is predominantly Mexican in origin (58 percent), significant portions also claim a heritage from Puerto Rico

(11 percent), Cuba (4 percent), and the Dominican Republic (4 percent), as well as from all other Latin American countries.

This begs the question of whether it even makes sense to expect any uniformity or consistency in the racial attitudes of peoples who fall under these overly broad ethnic and national categories. Although Asian Americans and Latinos are commonly lumped together as distinct racial or ethnic groups (this book being no exception), this singular classification entails a tremendous linguistic, cultural, and national variety. In fact, the very notion of "Asian" or "Latino" as an ethnicity is largely a political construct generated by activists, policy advocates, and the federal government. Such constructs are fundamentally problematic. For example, the designation of "Latino" or "Hispanic" refers primarily to cultural and social traits, such as Spanish language usage, a national origin from a Latin American country, and Latin Catholicism; using a single term to describe all the peoples whose ancestors or themselves were born in Latin America basically asserts a uniformity in the identity relative to a colonial past. This is akin to thinking that Canadians, Australians, Kenyans, and Indians are all essentially the same because they were once part of the British Empire (Portes and Truelove 1987). Similarly, it is hard to see what Asian Indians, Chinese, and Indonesian peoples all share that is somehow categorically different than the rest of the planet.

Given the national heterogeneity of the Latino and Asian American populations, any generalizations about their attitudes or allegiances as a single ethnic or racial group must be made with extreme caution. For many members of these groups, their primary ethnic identity is with their home country—they are much more likely to see themselves as Mexican or Korean than as Latino or Asian American (Espiritu 1992; Jones-Correa and Leal 1996). It is unlikely that they would all share a common identity that supersedes their own indigenous linguistic and cultural traditions. For instance, it is hard to imagine that a Filipino Catholic would feel more ethnically aligned to a Pakistani Muslim than a fellow Catholic from Mexico or that a new Korean immigrant who speaks little English would feel a strong commonality with a fifth-generation Japanese American. It is unclear whether some of the nationalities have fundamentally different conceptions of race or racial opposition to other groups.

This brings up an important facet in regards to Latino and Asian identity: their levels of incorporation into American culture. One of the strongest determinants of whether a Mexican American feels Latino or a Korean American feels Asian is probably their length of residence in the United States. Because the Asian and Latino population explosion has been fueled largely by immigration, there are divisions among these groups by their members' length of residence and level of incorporation into American society. Consider the case of Latinos. While a small portion of adult Latinos are from families that have lived in the United States for over three generations, nearly 40 percent are foreign-born, and nearly half of these immigrated within the past twenty years (Therrien and Rameriz 2000). These levels of incorporation also vary by nationality. Most Japanese Americans have been in the United States for generations, and most are fluent with English and have a strong sense of American identity; conversely, many Mexicans, Chinese, and Koreans are new arrivals with strong nationalist identities and whose English skills and understanding of American culture are still nascent.

These differences in levels of incorporation could have profound implications for their own sense of ethnic identity. Researchers have found that feelings of Asian panethnic identification typically come in the second or third generation of residence in the United States and may vary considerably by nationality (Espiritu 1992). It is precisely through greater American socialization and civic participation that a Chinese, Korean, or Vietnamese becomes self-identified as an Asian American; many Asian and Latino immigrants simply have not had time to move beyond their own nationalistic identities (Lien 2001). In other words, living in America helps transform the diverse group of peoples from Latin America into Latinos or Chinese, Korean, and Japanese Americans into Asians.

Immigrant incorporation may not only affect Asians' and Latinos' perceptions of having a coherent panethnic identity but may affect their attitudes about other groups in society as well. Newly arrived immigrants may come with preconceived notions of other racial groups or be unfamiliar with American commitments to racial equality; conversely, some Latinos, such as Cubans, may come from multiracial societies in which racial hierarchies are less delineated and they may become more racially conscious as their time in the United States grows. New immigrant groups, seeking to find jobs and resources, may see other minorities as competitors and express greater hostility as a result. Latino noncitizens or new immigrants, with less education, may express less sophistication in their racial attitudes or less understanding of other groups. Finally, the high number of younger Latinos means that a significant portion of the Latino population has been raised in the United States with full exposure to American racial conflicts. These second-generation immigrants may feel less connected to their countries of origin and have an identity and view of others that fall in between dominant racial groups.

Finally, given the question of racial attitudes, it is important to recognize that Latinos are also highly differentiated in their racial self-categorization, which, in turn, varies significantly by nationality. As a whole, about 48 percent of Latinos consider themselves white, 2 percent identify as black, and 42 percent identify with neither racial group and consider themselves a distinct, if unnamed, other.[11] These percentages vary considerably across countries of origin: for example, 82 percent of Cuban-origin Latinos consider themselves white, compared with under 25 percent of Panamanian or Dominican Latinos, of whom over 20 percent identify as black; Mexicans divide almost equally between those who identify as white and those who identify as other (Frey, Abresch, and Yeasting 2001). Obviously, such differences in racial self-conception should translate into differential attitudes about other groups; for example, it seems reasonable to assume that Latinos who identify as black should be less antagonistic toward blacks.

Thus before we can examine the relationship between segregation and racial attitudes among Asian Americans and Latinos, it is essential to first determine whether these ethnic labels make any sense as organizing principles for the racial views of the peoples who fall into them. As with the other aspects of Asian Americans and Latinos, the differences in their racial views or ethnic self-perceptions have not been systematically studied. Although researchers have examined the racial sentiments of particular immigrant groups, there are no studies that examine the wide range of racial attitudes among Asians and Latinos by virtue of nationality, incorporation, or racial self-identification. Therefore, it is important to conduct a firsthand analysis of the data available to see if there are any systematic differences by these divisions.

In comparing nationalities, the NPS and MCSUI data show few consistent differences in racial attitudes. Figure 2.2 depicts the average scores, by country of origin, on a variety of measures of Latinos' attitudes both about other racial groups and about their own in-group ethnic identification.[12] These include measures of closeness to other races, average scores on a four-point negative stereotype scale, a zero-sum competition scale, the average score on the linked fate scale, a measure of feeling of ethnic belonging, and the average score on the preference for Latino neighbors scale.[13] In terms of closeness to other groups, Mexicans are slightly less likely than Cubans or Puerto Ricans to report feeling close to blacks, and a greater percentage of Cubans report feeling close to whites, but these differences are not large in magnitude. Similarly, Latinos' average negative stereotype scores of other groups tend to stay within a narrow range: average scores on anti-Asian and antiwhite stereotype scales stay within a one-tenth range on a four-point scale. There is greater variability in Latinos' attitudes toward blacks, however, with Mexicans and Salvadorans reporting much higher negative stereotype scores, on average, than other groups, particularly Puerto Ricans.[14] Mexicans also report higher feelings of zero-sum competition with Asians and blacks, but like with the stereotypes, this may be attributed to regional differences.

In terms of ethnic identification, the pattern is the same. In the Social Capital Community Benchmark Study (SCCBS) data, Mexicans, Puerto Ricans, and other non-Cuban Latinos had roughly similar percentages of feeling a sense of belonging from their ethnicity, with roughly 75–79 percent reporting a sense of ethnic belonging, although a higher percentage of Cubans (85 percent) reported this feeling. For feelings of linked fate with other Latinos, Salvadorans reported the highest rate at 51 percent; Mexicans (42 percent), Puerto Ricans (37 percent), and other Latinos (42 percent) have slightly lower levels of linked fate; Latinos who identified themselves as Mexican American reported, not surprisingly, the lowest rate of ethnic solidarity, with only 30 percent reporting a feeling of linked fate. Finally, on the five-point "preference for Latino neighbors scale," most groups score between 2.5 and 2.8 on average, with only Mexicans being out of this range. On average, Mexicans report the highest average preference for Latino neighbors.

Although we must hesitate when drawing inferences from these data, from the limited information available there are a few clear patterns in Latinos' racial attitudes by nationality. Mexicans in Los Angeles have greater resentment toward blacks than toward other groups; Cubans report the greatest sense of ethnic belonging; and self-identified Mexican Americans report the lowest levels of feeling linked to other Latinos, and lower levels of racial stereotyping of other groups, compared with self-identified Mexicans. But beyond these instances, what is most remarkable about the findings reported in figure 2.2 is the absence of any consistent patterns by nationality. Across all national groups, Latinos' views of other groups and of themselves as an ethnic group are roughly similar. Despite the tremendous variation in the national origin of Latinos and its importance in their self-conception, there are no clear, systematic differences in racial attitudes toward other groups in the data available here. This is not to imply that nationality is irrelevant to Latinos' sense of ethnicity or their place in American society; rather, it simply means that according to the data that are available, these national differences do not shape racial attitudes in any consistent way.

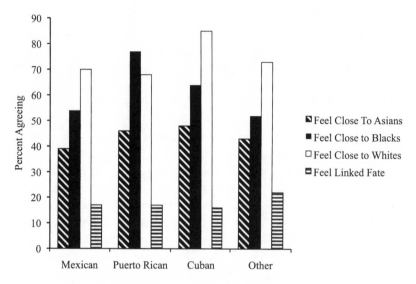

FIGURE 2.2A Latino racial attitudes by nationality (2004 NPS).

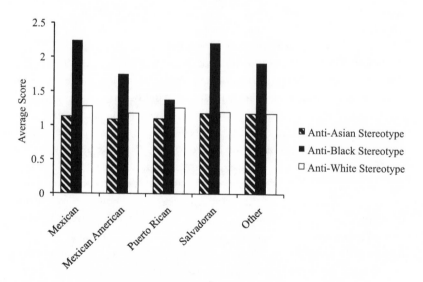

FIGURE 2.2B Latino racial attitudes by nationality, continued (1992–1994 MCSUI).

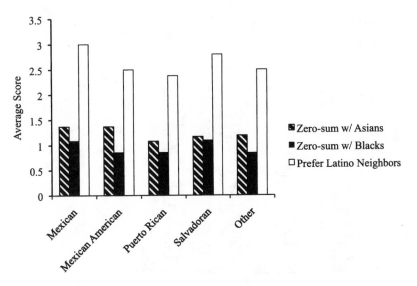

FIGURE 2.2C Latino racial attitudes by nationality, continued (1992–1994 MCSUI).

Among Asian Americans, a similar lack of difference among nationalities is also evident. Part of this may be attributable to the data. The combination of both a relatively small population size and tremendous heterogeneity makes testing attitudinal differences by nationality quite difficult in the Asian American subsample. The NPS does have a large subsample of Japanese, Chinese, and Korean Americans to make robust comparisons, but the SCCBS and CID data do not differentiate Asian nationalities, and the MCSUI data only focus on Los Angeles. With those caveats in mind, the NPS data show only a few clear differences by nationality. Figure 2.3 depicts the average rates of response to feelings of closeness to racial groups, feelings of zero-sum competition with other groups, and linked fate with Asians as a whole. Self-identified Chinese respondents were less likely to report feeling close to other groups compared with other Asian nationalities: only 35 percent of Chinese respondents reported feeling close to blacks or Latinos, a rate roughly half of the rest of the Asian sample. Chinese respondents also were no more likely to feel zero-sum competition with these other groups. Japanese Americans reported more closeness to whites, lower rates of linked fate, and lower levels of zero-sum competition with other groups than other Asian nationalities reported. Yet these differences are rather small and, given the small sample sizes, it is hard to differentiate these patterns from other effects such as their level of incorporation.

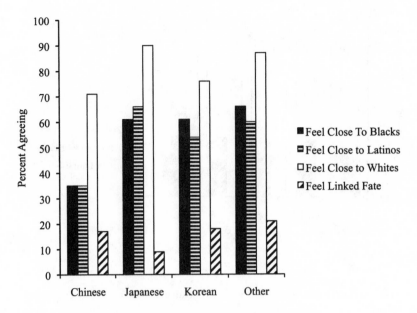

FIGURE 2.3A Asian American racial attitudes by nationality (2004 NPS).

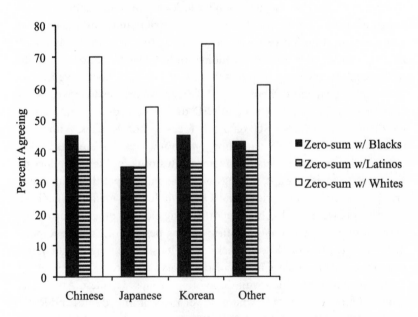

FIGURE 2.3B Asian American racial attitudes by nationality, continued (2004 NPS).

This raises the biggest problem for anticipating the impact of nationality on racial identity: the impact of nationality is highly contingent on how long a person has been in the United States. Japanese Americans, for example, may feel closer to other groups or less linked fate because most of them have been American citizens for several generations. Nationality will be far more important for those who have lived in the United States for only a brief time. For second- and third-generation immigrants, nationality should be far less decisive a predictor of their racial attitudes.

To examine these possibilities, figure 2.4 depicts a replication of the analysis in the tables above, only substituting various measures of immigrant status for nationality. For the MCSUI data, incorporation was gauged by whether the respondent was a citizen and by an additional measure of whether the respondent was interviewed in Spanish; for the NPS data, incorporation was measured in terms of citizenship, whether the respondent was raised in the United States and interviewed in Spanish. Unlike with nationality and racial self-identification, the various measures of incorporation have a consistent effect on Latinos' racial views and ethnic self-identification: Latinos who are noncitizens, who were raised abroad, or who were interviewed in Spanish are consistently more negative in their views of other races and express a higher degree of solidarity with other Latinos. In the NPS data, less incorporated Latinos are much less likely to report feeling close to other races, are much more likely to sense zero-sum competition with Asians and blacks, and have a stronger sense of linked fate. For instance, roughly half of Latinos raised abroad expressed feelings of zero-sum competition with Asians or blacks, compared with only a third of those raised in the United States. In the MCSUI data, Latino noncitizens or those interviewed in Spanish had the highest negative stereotype scores (particularly toward blacks) and were far more likely to prefer Latino neighbors.

There are three central explanations for why unincorporated Latinos are more racially antagonistic. First, Latino noncitizens typically have lower educational and income levels than citizens, particularly compared with second- and third-generation residents.[15] As education is an important predictor of racial attitudes, the higher racial hostility of noncitizens may simply be a reflection of their lower educational levels. Second, noncitizens may be less assimilated into American culture, be less familiar with norms of racial equality, and feel a stronger sense of in-group identification. Finally, Latino respondents interviewed in Spanish may feel more

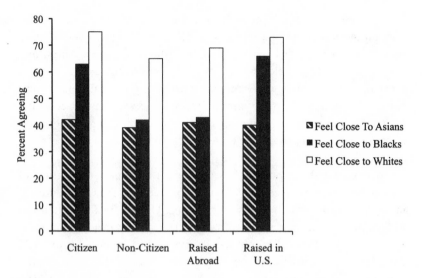

FIGURE 2.4A Latino racial attitudes by citizenship, where raised, and English proficiency (2004 NPS).

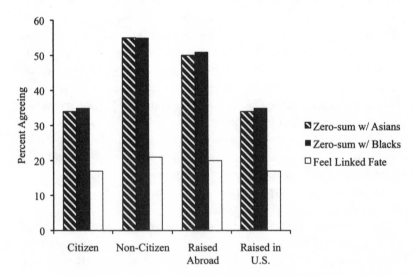

FIGURE 2.4B Latino racial attitudes by citizenship, where raised, and English proficiency, continued (2004 NPS).

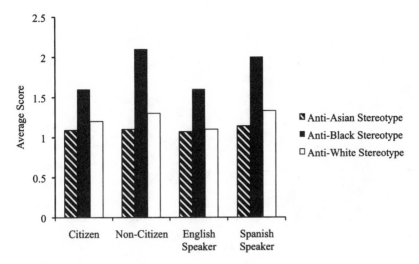

FIGURE 2.4C Latino racial attitudes by citizenship, where raised, and English proficiency, continued (2004 NPS).

comfortable confiding latent racial resentments to a person they consider
a coethnic than to an out-group member.

   Multivariate regressions demonstrate that all of these factors are possibly at work, although none completely explain the results. When the various measures of racial attitudes were regressed on variables measuring education, age, nationality, citizenship, interview language, and where the respondent was raised, each of the estimators of incorporation showed a significant relationship. For example, even when controlling for age and education levels, Latino NPS respondents who were interviewed in Spanish were far less likely to report feeling close to either blacks or whites and to express a feeling of linked fate, while noncitizens were more likely to express feelings of zero-sum competition. In the MCSUI sample, those who were interviewed in Spanish had consistently higher scores on the negative stereotype scales and were more likely to prefer Latino neighbors. In fact, across the board, the greatest explanatory factor of Latinos' racial attitudes was whether they were interviewed in Spanish—the equations predict that Latinos interviewed in Spanish score a quarter-point higher in their antiblack and antiwhite stereotypes than those interviewed in English. The magnitude of this difference is larger than any other factor, including education and age. Similar results occur for the measures of neighborhood preference. Although noncitizens, the less educated, and

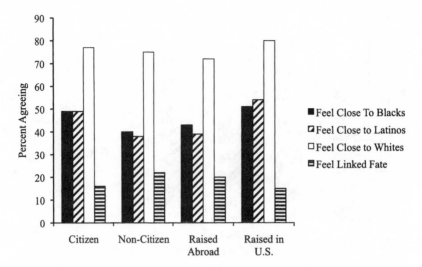

FIGURE 2.5A Asian American racial attitudes by citizenship and where raised (2004 NPS).

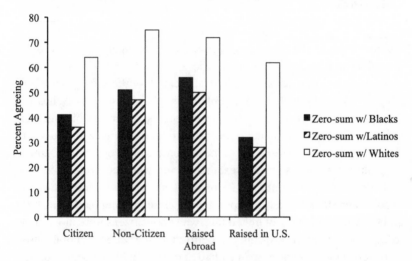

FIGURE 2.5B Asian American racial attitudes by citizenship and where raised, continued (2004 NPS).

younger Latinos all prefer more Latino neighborhoods, the most powerful predictor of neighborhood preference was whether the respondent was interviewed in Spanish.

Asian Americans also demonstrate strong differences in racial attitudes according to their levels of incorporation. Figure 2.5 depicts the percent of Asian Americans in the NPS sample who report feeling close to other groups, a strong sense of linked fate with other Asians, and zero-sum competition with other races by their citizenship status and whether they were raised in the United States. As with Latinos, Asian noncitizens or Asians who were raised abroad express much greater out-group racial alienation than either citizens or their counterparts raised in America. For instance, Asian noncitizens were about 10 percent less likely to report feeling close to blacks or Latinos (although there were no differences with respect to whites) and were over 10 percent more likely to report feelings of zero-sum competition. Even greater differences occurred by virtue of where an Asian respondent grew up. Not only were those raised abroad consistently less likely to report feeling close to other races, they were much more likely to express feelings of zero-sum competition. Over half of foreign-raised Asian respondents felt zero-sum competition with blacks and Latinos compared with less than a third of American-raised Asian respondents.

These patterns are not attributable to levels of age or education, although some of them do arise from nationality. Unlike Latinos, Asian Americans are not dramatically younger than whites or blacks, nor are there large differences in age by levels of incorporation. Nor do the statistics in figure 2.5 arise because Asian immigrants are less educated; in fact, Asian noncitizens and those raised abroad in the NPS sample have higher average education levels. The only factor that accounts for some of these findings are the particular attitudes of Chinese American respondents regarding questions of feeling close to other races. When the racial attitude measures are regressed on a set of variables including age, education, citizenship, nationality, and place where one was raised, Chinese respondents are much less likely to report feeling close to other groups compared with what other nationalities report, a factor that accounted for the incorporation differences. However, for measures of zero-sum competition, particularly with blacks, the measure of where one was raised continued to be a strong and robust predictor of racial attitudes.

The final factor to consider with regards to Latinos' racial attitudes is their own racial self-identification. As noted above, when asked to identify their own race, Latinos tend to divide between a substantial number who see themselves as white, a small minority who identify as black, and a large portion who classify themselves as a racially distinct other. Given that the racial heritage of many Latinos, particularly those from Mexico, is a mixture of European and indigenous peoples, the reluctance to accept the standard American racial classifications is understandable. But does this racial identification influence Latinos' views toward other races or their own feelings of ethnic solidarity? Examining the MCSUI and SCCBS data, I find few consistent differences in Latinos' racial attitudes toward other groups, even by their own racial self-identification. Across the battery of measures, Latinos who identify as white and as other are statistically indistinguishable. Considering that more than 90 percent of Latinos place themselves in these two racial categories, one can conclude that differences in racial self-identification are not significant for the vast majority of the Latino population. Even in the small minority of Latinos who identify as black there is little difference with other groups. For example, in the SCCBS sample, the percentages of Latinos opposed to interracial marriage with Asians, blacks, and whites all stay within a 3-percentage-point range across all three Latino racial categories: 14 percent of self-identified white Latinos oppose interracial marriage with blacks, but so do 13 percent of self-identified black Latinos, as do 11 percent of those in the "other" racial category. Self-identified black Latinos reported a higher sense of belonging from their ethnicity in the SCCBS data and a lower sense of linked fate in the MCSUI data, but beyond these differences, their scores are very similar to the Latino average. In short, the diversity in the racial self-identification of Latinos does not correspond to any systematic differences in their racial attitudes toward other groups or their feelings of ethnic solidarity.

In sum, these results suggest that many of the differences among Asians and Latinos in terms of nationality and race that are important in economic domains are not as important when it comes to their racial attitudes. The only major factor that systematically differentiates Asians' and Latinos' racial views and feelings of panethnic solidarity is their level of incorporation into American society (and nationality for Chinese Americans). Latinos who speak only Spanish or were raised abroad are far more negative in their views toward Asians, blacks, and whites and are far more likely to feel a strong sense of ethnic solidarity. This is not to imply that all foreign-born Asians or Latinos are identical in their racial attitudes or their sense of ethnic belonging. Many particular Asian and Latino groups have distinct experiences related to their race or nationality that affect their self-conception and attitudes of other racial groups. Rather, the analysis above simply says that the only factor by which Asians and Latinos can be systematically differentiated with large survey instruments is their level of incorporation.

These results have two important implications for the inquiry of this book. First, despite the tremendous diversity by nationality, race, and immigration status, it is still possible to make generalizations about Asians and Latinos as a group with respect to their racial attitudes and feelings of ethnic solidarity, as long as one takes into account their immigration status. When thinking about the racial attitudes of these populations as a whole, most differences by nationality and by race are relatively unimportant factors compared with issues of linguistic isolation and social status. The one exception occurs among Chinese respondents, who appear more alienated from other groups. Second, because Asians and Latinos who are linguistically isolated are also more likely to be socially isolated, it is important to incorporate this factor into the examination of segregation and racial attitudes. Asians and Latinos who are less incorporated into American culture will probably be more likely to seek ethnic enclaves in which to live. Any relationship that may be found between the racial composition of the neighborhood and the individual's racial attitudes needs to take this level of incorporation into account.

Conclusion

Can we tell much about the attitudes among Asians, Latinos, and blacks based upon theories of white racial prejudice? From the findings in this chapter, the answer to this question would seem to be a qualified yes. In terms of negative stereotype scores, whites exhibit similar racial biases toward all minority groups and with few significant differences in their views of Latinos and Asians compared with their view of blacks. Although there may be some instances of "black exceptionalism," whites feel similar levels of difference with Latino populations as they do with black populations. From these data we should expect that whites will react to nearby Latino populations in the same way they do to blacks.

Similarly, the lack of differences between minorities and whites in general racial attitudes means that nonwhites too are likely to respond to racial contexts in similar ways, although once again some particular qualifications will need to be considered. For example, blacks are just as likely to embrace negative stereotypes of other groups and are more likely to view other minorities as competitors for political and economic resources than are whites. Indeed, blacks are more likely to see immigration as a threat to their political and economic standing than are whites. Thus one might expect larger Latino and Asian populations to heighten black perceptions of racial threat and competition.

Latinos and Asian Americans also embrace racial biases at levels that are generally similar to other groups. Asian Americans record some of the highest negative stereotype scores of blacks and Latinos (although not of whites) and are more likely than whites to see themselves as competitors with other minorities. Latinos too hold negative stereotypes toward other groups (particularly blacks) and were the most likely to experience zero-sum competition with Asians and blacks.

In short, negative feelings toward other races are not the sole charge of any group in the United States; the data here show equal amounts of racial resentment among all groups. But this does not mean all groups have identical perspectives on race. Racial minorities, particularly blacks, have much stronger feelings of racial solidarity and are more likely to perceive a linked fate with other members of their group. These feelings of racial solidarity may influence the relationship between social environments and racial attitudes, particularly if feelings of racial solidarity are heightened in more segregated neighborhoods. Important divisions also exist among Latinos and Asian Americans with respect to levels of incorporation and nationality. Latinos' racial attitudes varied sharply depending on whether they were interviewed in Spanish or English, with those interviewed in Spanish expressing more negative racial views. Similarly, strong national differences existed among Asians by virtue of nationality, with Chinese Americans expressing more alienation from other groups.

Consequently, when examining the geographic contours of Americans' racial beliefs, it will be important to take these racial and ethnic differences into account. Feelings of solidarity may be more important for minorities than for whites, linguistic differences are important for Latinos, and national differences and incorporation levels are important for Asian Americans. Nevertheless, such groups should be subject to the same types of environmental forces that influence whites' perceptions of blacks. As no group is immune to perceptions of racial competition or feelings of racial animosity, so no group should be immune to the influences of their social environments. It is to this environmental pressure that we next turn.

CHAPTER THREE

Neighborhood- and Metropolitan-Level Differences in Racial Attitudes

There are two incontrovertible facts about race and segregation in the United States. First, America's different racial groups are highly segregated from each other—Asian Americans and whites live mostly apart from Latinos and African Americans and are somewhat separated from each other; Latinos and blacks live more apart than together as well. Second is the fact that feelings of racial resentment and competition are not the sole possession of any one racial group. As we saw in chapter 2, Asian Americans, blacks, Latinos, and whites all share misperceptions and feelings of competition with other racial groups. Each group generally harbors stereotypes toward the other that are less favorable than perceptions of their own groups, and each group sees itself in varying degrees of alienation with others. In short, no matter what one's own ethnic background, race continues to be an important delineator of self-perception and community in the United States.

What remains unclear, however, is how these two facts are related. As noted in chapter 1, the existing scholarship leads us to two contradictory expectations about how racial environments shape racial attitudes. Those who see racial diversity as generating racial conflict will expect increased racial animosity in diverse settings; those who see diversity as promoting contact and mutual understanding expect greater racial tolerance in diverse settings. Each of these expectations makes reference to particular units of geography—conflict over political power and resources may be more important with respect to larger areas, such as metropolitan areas, than with respect to smaller ones, such as neighborhoods. Opportunities for interracial contact are more likely to relate to the composition of an immediate social environment such as a neighborhood rather than a larger metropolis. In addition, the findings of chapter 2 would lead us to expect that such patterns should generally apply for all four racial groups. Although some asymmetries may exist between whites and nonwhites because of their different population sizes and among Asians and Latinos by their incorporation levels, the general impact of geography should hold universally. In other words, the impact of living around Latinos should be roughly the same for blacks as it is for whites. But past research has not examined whether this is the case. Consequently, it is important to establish here whether racial geography affects all racial groups in an equal way.

This chapter examines differences in racial attitudes across neighborhoods and metropolitan areas. Two general patterns are evident: first, racial resentment is consistently higher in metropolitan areas that are more racially diverse, particularly among whites and blacks—the larger the percentages of minorities in the metropolis, the more likely black and white respondents express racial animosity toward other groups; second, racial resentment is consistently lower in more racially diverse neighborhoods, a pattern that, once again, is largely similar for all racial groups. In short, racial attitudes vary in predictable and consistent ways across racial environments; their direction, however, depends on what type of environment is being considered. To see how this occurs, let us examine each racial group in isolation.

Whites and the Racial Environment

Does living around minorities make whites more or less racially hostile? The answer to this question can be found by looking first at how whites' racial attitudes vary with the most immediate racial context—the neighborhood. Figure 3.1 displays the predicted changes in summary scores of whites' negative stereotypes toward blacks and Latinos by the percentage of each of those groups in the neighborhood, as defined by the census tract (for full description of the variables see chapter 2). In other words, it measures what difference living among more of a particular group has in relation to whites' attitudes toward that particular group. The lines in Figure 3.1 are depictions of coefficients from ordinary least squares (OLS) regression analyses, where the negative stereotype scale was re-

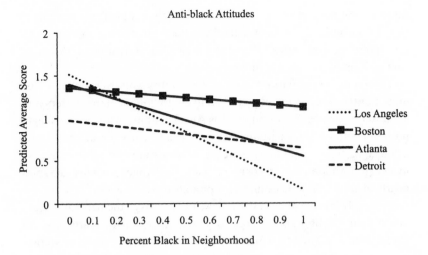

FIGURE 3.1A Predicted whites' scores on negative stereotype scales by the percent of the out-group in neighborhood (1992–1994 MCSUI).

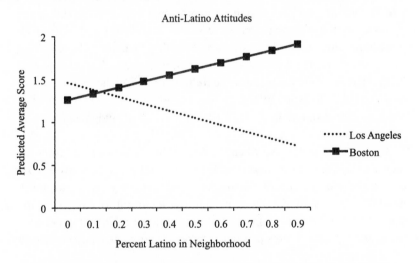

FIGURE 3.1B Predicted whites' scores on negative stereotype scales by the percent of the out-group in neighborhood, continued (1992–1994 MCSUI).

gressed on a measure of the racial composition of the neighborhood along with a number of other individual-level variables that might also predict a person's racial attitudes such as his or her education, age, length of residence, homeownership, and political ideology.[1] In addition, a variable controlling for the economic conditions of the neighborhood (as measured by the percent of residents with more than a high school degree) was also included. From these equations, the predicted average scores on the stereotype scale were calculated for each increment along the racial composition of the neighborhood.[2]

The regression equations predict that whites who live in close proximity to other races generally are less likely to hold negative stereotypes about those groups. For example, Los Angeles whites who live in a neighborhood with no blacks are predicted to score nearly a point higher, on average, on the four-point negative stereotype scale than whites who live in a neighborhood that is 70 percent black. Los Angeles whites also show nearly as large differences in their opinions of Latinos—whites become considerably less negative in their views of Latinos as the percent of Latinos in their neighborhood increases. Differences nearly as large also occur for whites in Atlanta: whites in neighborhoods with no blacks average nearly a point higher on the negative stereotype scale than those in neighborhoods over 90 percent black. The differences in white attitudes toward blacks across neighborhoods in Boston and Detroit, while significant in size, are not as great. For instance, there is only a four-tenths difference predicted in the stereotype scores of whites in the least and most black neighborhoods. Latinos in Boston are the only group not to benefit from racial proximity. The equations predict that whites who live in neighborhoods that are 80 percent Latino score half a point higher than those in neighborhoods with no Latinos. Unlike with every other group, proximity to Latinos does not make Boston's whites less racially judgmental, but in fact more so.

These same results hold when looking at the impact of racial isolation on whites' views toward minorities. Figure 3.2 replicates the analyses conducted above only it substitutes the out-group percentage in the neighborhood with a measure of in-group percentage, while still controlling for the standard set of predictors. In short, it measures the relationship between living among more whites in a neighborhood and whites' perceptions of other groups.[3]

As would be expected, the results in Figure 3.2 largely mirror the findings in Figure 3.1. Just as white respondents in Atlanta and Los Angeles were all less likely to harbor negative out-group stereotypes when there were more minorities in their neighborhood, they were more likely to express such sentiments when there were more whites in their neighborhood. Among residents of Los Angeles and Atlanta in particular, whites in predominantly white neighborhoods score much higher in their negative stereotypes of Asians, blacks, and Latinos than those in neighborhoods with fewer whites. For example, the equations predict that Atlanta's whites living in an all-white neighborhood score eight-tenths a point higher on the negative stereotype scale about blacks and Latinos than those living in neighborhoods with few whites. And, once again, whites in Boston show slightly different patterns: the differences in attitudes about Asians and

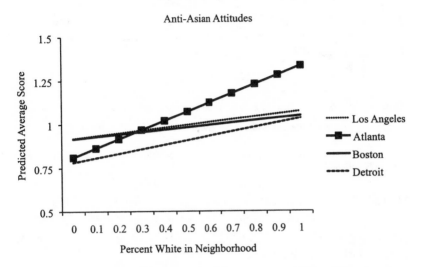

FIGURE 3.2A Predicted whites' negative stereotype scores by the percent white in the neighborhood (1992–1994 MCSUI).

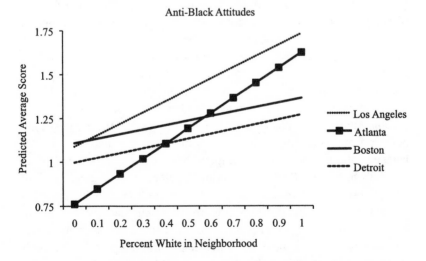

FIGURE 3.2B Predicted whites' negative stereotype scores by the percent white in the neighborhood, continued (1992–1994 MCSUI).

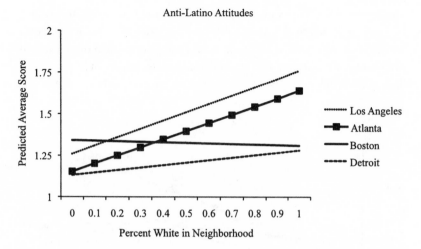

FIGURE 3.2C Predicted whites' negative stereotype scores by the percent white in the neighborhood, continued (1992–1994 MCSUI).

blacks between whites in all-white and nonwhite neighborhoods are not as great as in the other metropolitan areas, and attitudes toward Latinos are actually better in all-white neighborhoods, although these differences are not statistically significant.

Similar patterns also occur for whites' perceptions of interracial competition, in the predicted relationship between whites' racial surroundings (measured by the percent white in the neighborhood) and their feelings of competition with other minority groups and feelings of immigrant threat with the same set of individual-level controls.[4] The findings show that the greater the percentage of whites within the neighborhood, the greater the sense of zero-sum competition with minority out-groups and the greater the perception of threats from immigration, although this effect varies across metropolitan regions and by reference group. Whites in predominantly white Los Angeles neighborhoods feel the greatest competition from Asian Americans, while whites in predominantly white Atlanta neighborhoods feel more competition with blacks. Whites in Boston generally have lower feelings of intergroup competition, and the effects of living in predominantly white neighborhoods are lower, on average, than in Atlanta or Los Angeles. For whites, the economic status of their neighborhood is also a consistent predictor of their sense of competition with minority groups: those in higher status neighborhoods perceive less zero-sum competition with all minority groups and less threat from immigration than whites living in lower status neighborhoods.[5]

The differences between feelings of zero-sum competition and negative stereotype scores across racial environments is consistent with the expectations from chapter 1. Among whites, negative group affect (measured by the stereotype scales) is highly sensitive to neighborhood racial context, with the strongest differences occurring relative to the most ostracized group (that is, African Americans). Perceptions of zero-sum competition, however, relate more to regional differences. Whites in Los Angeles, the area with the largest immigrant population, have the highest perceptions of zero-sum competition, particularly from immigrants. On the neighborhood level, however, there is less difference in feelings of zero-sum competition, particularly from more marginalized groups. It is only when a group has some power, such as among Asians in Los Angeles or blacks in Atlanta, that white perceptions of zero-sum competition change with their neighborhood racial environment. It is also important to note that neighborhood social class is an important predictor of interracial competition—whites in less educated neighborhoods are far more likely to report perceptions of zero-sum conflict.

Similar results are also evident in national data that sample from a large number of metropolitan areas. Figure 3.3 lists the percent of whites expressing opposition to interracial marriage by the percent of whites in both their metropolitan area and neighborhood (as measured by zip code) as reported in the SCCBS data. Across most metropolitan areas and zip codes, white opposition to interracial marriage is about 17 percent for blacks, 10 percent for Latinos, and 7 percent for Asians. However, in areas where the racial composition of the neighborhood differs from that of the metropolitan areas, there are sharply divergent results. Whites who live in racially mixed neighborhoods within mostly white metropolitan areas are far less opposed to interracial marriage than the national average. In these places, only 6 percent of whites are opposed to interracial marriage between whites and blacks and less than 3 percent are opposed for Latinos and Asians. For whites living in all-white neighborhoods in racially mixed metropolitan areas, the results are the opposite: over 25 percent are opposed to interracial marriage between whites and blacks and over 11 percent are opposed for Latinos and Asians.

In other words, whites who live in a racially mixed part of a metropolitan area like Bloomington, Indiana (which is mostly white), should generally have far lower rates of opposition to interracial marriage than the national average. Conversely, whites who live in an all-white neighborhood in a racially mixed metropolitan area like Chicago should have far higher rates of opposition to interracial marriage. As with the stereotype scores above,

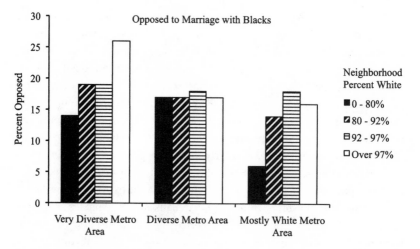

FIGURE 3.3A White opposition to interracial marriage by the percent white in the neighborhood and metropolitan area (2000 SCCBS).

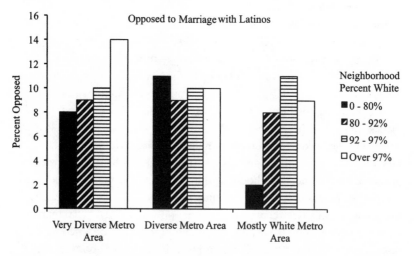

FIGURE 3.3B White opposition to interracial marriage by the percent white in the neighborhood and metropolitan area, continued (2000 SCCBS).

the highest rates of racial animosity occur among whites who are locally most isolated from larger minority populations in the metropolitan area.

Nearly identical results also occur for white opinions about immigrants. As with white opinions about interracial marriage, opinions about immigrants also vary with the racial composition of both the metropolitan area

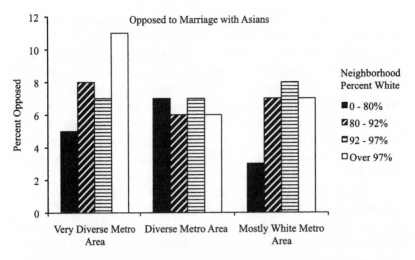

FIGURE 3.3C White opposition to interracial marriage by the percent white in the neighborhood and metropolitan area, continued (2000 SCCBS).

and neighborhood. Whites who lived in the most racially mixed metropolitan areas were, on average, the most in agreement about immigrants "getting to pushy." However, within each metropolitan area there are also consistent results across neighborhoods—the higher the white percentage in the neighborhood, the more white respondents feel that immigrants are too demanding. And, once again, the highest levels of discomfort with immigrants are in the mostly white enclaves within racially mixed metropolitan areas. Over 40 percent of whites in these all-white neighborhoods feel immigrants are getting too pushy, compared with a 32 percent national average. Whites in racially mixed neighborhoods, particularly in mostly white metropolitan areas, are the least threatened by immigrants, with only 24 percent agreeing with the anti-immigrant statement.

In sum, these results demonstrate that racial environments are important predictors of whites' racial attitudes. In many instances, the sizes of the predicted differences between residents of all-white and racially mixed neighborhoods are larger than differences based on individual age, education, or ideology.[6] As previous research on whites' attitudes has illustrated, whites in more racially diverse metropolitan areas are more racially resentful. In the SCCBS data, whites in more diverse metropolitan areas are more opposed to interracial marriage and are more threatened by immigrants. Similarly, the MCSUI data show racial resentment is higher in diverse Los Angeles, Detroit, and Atlanta than in more homogeneous

Boston. However, in neighborhoods, a much different pattern is evident: the greater the percentage of minority neighbors, the lower the negative stereotyping toward that group; the greater the percentage of white neighbors, the higher the negative stereotyping. Moreover, there appears to be an interaction effect between neighborhood and metropolitan racial diversity. The effects of neighborhood racial isolation on whites' racial attitudes are highest in the metropolitan areas with the largest minority populations. In other words, living in an all-white neighborhood in a largely white metropolis does not have the same impact of living in an all-white neighborhood in a metropolis with a large minority population.

These results have two important implications. First, racial diversity corresponds with racial attitudes in different ways at different levels of geography. Diversity at the neighborhood level corresponds with less white racial intolerance; diversity at the metropolitan level, with more. This means that racial environments might be simultaneously influencing racial attitudes in different ways, ideas that will be tested further in subsequent chapters. Second, the relationship between social environments and racial attitudes is largely consistent no matter which out-group is in question. Although whites' attitudes toward blacks demonstrate the largest differences across social environments, whites' perceptions of Latinos and Asian Americans also change in large and systematic ways. In particular, for whites living in predominantly white neighborhoods within diverse metropolitan areas, the average level of racial resentment is much higher no matter what the target group. Having established this basic pattern among whites, our attention now turns to whether it is also evident for other racial groups.

Blacks and the Racial Environment

At first glance, the major hypotheses about the relationship between racial attitudes and social environments seem relatively race neutral. In other words, there is no reason to believe that perceptions of intergroup conflict, threats from competition, or the benefits of interracial contact will be any different for whites than they will be for blacks or Latinos, and thus one should expect very similar patterns in blacks' and whites' racial attitudes across these geographic units. This expectation, however, may be unsettled by two facts: blacks are a much smaller percentage of the national population and live in conditions of hypersegregation. These considerations may alter the relationship between racial environments and racial attitudes. For blacks, like for other minority groups, living in America means living in a predominantly white society. Consequently, attitudes toward whites might not vary as much across metropolitan areas as attitudes toward other minority groups. A black person in Dallas and a black person in Seattle are both likely to encounter whites fairly regularly; whether or not they encounter Latinos or Asians, however, will vary considerably.

In addition, the high level of neighborhood segregation for African Americans means there may be nonlinear relationships between racial attitudes and neighborhood racial composition. In the United States, the difference between a neighborhood that is 20 percent black and a neighborhood that is 50 percent black is far greater than the difference between a neighborhood that is 50 percent black and a neighborhood that is 80 percent black. Nevertheless, if these considerations are taken into account, the hypotheses from chapter 1 should still hold, and the differences in blacks' racial attitudes should be roughly the same as they were for whites.

And, indeed, this is what the data show. Regression equations predicting the change in blacks' scores on negative stereotype scales show that, as with whites, blacks who live around more people of other races tend to have less negative views of those groups.[7] With one exception, the MCSUI data show consistent results: as the percentage of an out-group in a black person's neighborhood increases, the likely score on a negative stereotype scale about that group diminishes. The biggest neighborhood differences are in black Atlantans' views toward whites and black Los Angelenos' views toward Asians. The equations predict that black Atlantans who live in predominantly white neighborhoods will score over a half a point lower on the four-point negative stereotype score than those who live in neighborhoods with many blacks. Blacks who live in heavily Asian neighborhoods in Los Angeles score over one and a half points lower on the anti-Asian scale than blacks who live in neighborhoods with no Asians.

Similar differences are evident in blacks' views toward whites in Los Angeles and Boston (those who live in whiter neighborhoods tend to have less negative stereotypes of whites) and toward Latinos in Los Angeles. The only exception to this trend is among blacks' attitudes toward Latinos in Boston. Like whites in Boston, black Bostonians who live in neighborhoods with more Latinos have more negative stereotypes toward this group, although this difference is not statistically significant. Yet, barring this one case, the trend among blacks seems remarkably similar to that among whites—sharing neighborhoods with people of other races corresponds with fewer negative views toward these groups.

Like whites, blacks who live in racially isolated settings tend to be much more negative in their views of other racial groups. Figure 3.4 depicts the predicted average score on the negative stereotype scale among black respondents with the percent black in their neighborhood.[8] These estimates are derived from full equations that control for the social status of the neighborhood as well as the individual-level characteristics of the respondents.

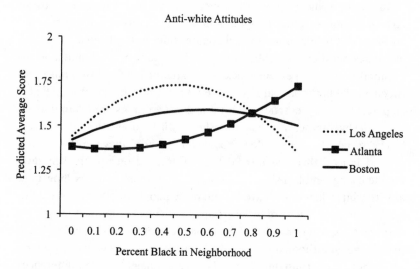

FIGURE 3.4A Predicted scores among African Americans on negative attitude scales toward other races (1992–1994 MCSUI).

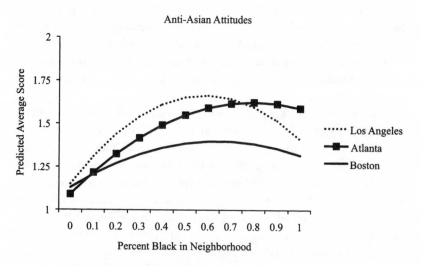

FIGURE 3.4B Predicted scores among African Americans on negative attitude scales toward other races, continued (1992–1994 MCSUI).

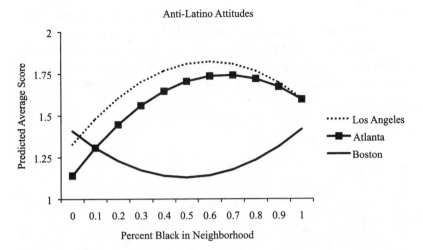

FIGURE 3.4C Predicted scores among African Americans on negative attitude scales toward other races, continued (1992–1994 MCSUI).

Just as blacks and whites who live among other races tend to be less averse to those groups, blacks who live in predominantly black neighborhoods are more negative in their views about other races, although, once again, this varies across the three cities. Unlike whites' attitudes, blacks' racial attitudes do not change as a linear function of the percent black in the neighborhood but tend to level off once a neighborhood is about 50 percent black. For example, in Atlanta and Los Angeles, blacks who live in neighborhoods with few blacks score over half a point lower in the negative views of Asians compared with those who live in neighborhoods that are at least 50 percent black; however, blacks in neighborhoods that are more than 50 percent black generally do not score higher in their negative stereotypes and, in Los Angeles, actually become less averse to Asians. Similarly, in Atlanta and Los Angeles, blacks' negative views of Latinos tend to peak in neighborhoods that are 50 percent black as do blacks' negative views of whites in Boston and Los Angeles.

In fact, there are only two exceptions to this trend: first, the regression equations predict that blacks in Boston will be least negative about Latinos in neighborhoods that are 50 percent black and most negative toward Latinos in neighborhoods that are either all black or entirely nonblack; second, blacks in Atlanta become increasingly negative toward whites as the percent black in the neighborhood increases above 50 percent.[9] These two exceptions notwithstanding, the trend across black neighborhoods is the same: as a neighborhood moves to being 50 percent black, its black residents become increasingly negative in their stereotypes about out-groups; after this point, negative views either hold or decrease slightly.

A similar type of pattern emerges for other measures of racial atti-tudes. Figure 3.5 depicts the predicted score on measures of feelings of zero-sum competition that blacks feel with Asians and Latinos as well as

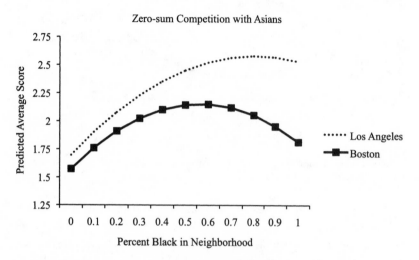

FIGURE 3.5A Predicted scores among African Americans on measures of zero-sum competition and perception of immigrant threat by percent black in neighborhood (1992–1994 MCSUI).

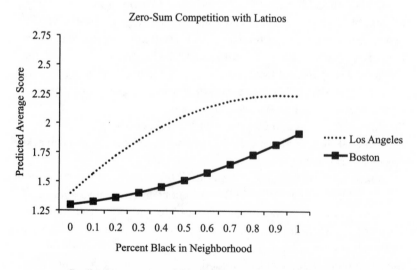

FIGURE 3.5B Predicted scores among African Americans on measures of zero-sum competi-tion and perception of immigrant threat by percent black in neighborhood, continued (1992–1994 MCSUI).

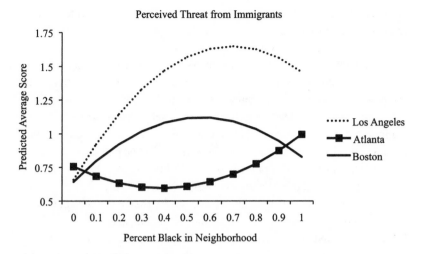

FIGURE 3.5C Predicted scores among African Americans on measures of zero-sum competition and perception of immigrant threat by percent black in neighborhood, continued (1992–1994 MCSUI).

the level of threat they feel from increased immigration.[10] The zero-sum question was a measure of how much they thought gains in jobs and political influence for Asians or Latinos would come at the expense of blacks.[11] The immigrant threat question measured the extent they believed blacks would lose "political influence" and "economic opportunity" if immigration continued at its present pace.

As with negative stereotypes, blacks who live in racially isolated neighborhoods express more feelings of racial threat and competition from Asians and Latinos. For example, in Los Angeles, the regression equations predicting feelings of zero-sum competition with Asians increase nearly a point (on a four-point scale) between nonblack neighborhoods and half-black neighborhoods and increase eight-tenths a point for feelings of competition with Latinos. The equations predict similar patterns for blacks in Boston—feelings of zero-sum competition with Asians increase between nonblack and half-black neighborhoods, although they then drop off in mostly black neighborhoods; feelings of competition with Latinos rise uniformly as the percent of blacks in the neighborhood rises. A similar pattern is also evident in feelings of threat from immigration among blacks in Los Angeles: blacks who live in neighborhoods that are at least half-black are predicted to score nearly a point higher in their feelings of threat from continued immigration than those in nonblack neighborhoods. In Atlanta, feelings of immigrant threat, as with negative views about whites, grow faster in neighborhoods that are over 50 percent black. In Boston, neighborhood differences in feelings about immigrants do not vary beyond a half-point range.

Black feelings of racial solidarity, measured by how much they perceive a linked fate with blacks in general, also follow this curvilinear pattern. The regression equations predict that black agreement with the survey measure of linked fate rises and falls with the percent black in the neighborhood in a manner that is very similar to the measures of negative racial views of other groups.[12] Blacks in neighborhoods that are in the 40–60 percent black range recorded the highest levels of racial solidarity; blacks in neighborhoods with few blacks or in neighborhoods that were almost entirely black indicated the lowest levels of feeling a linked fate with other African Americans. These patterns were most pronounced in Los Angeles and Atlanta but were largely attenuated among the Boston sample, once again due to the skewed distribution of African Americans across the Boston metropolitan area. Interestingly, outside of individual age, social environments were the only variables in the equation that predicted changes in perceptions of racial linked fate. Like other racial attitudes, black feelings of racial solidarity vary consistently according to the racial characteristics of a person's neighborhood.

Data from the SCCBS national sample give results that are somewhat similar but not quite as clear. Black SCCBS respondents were asked about their opposition to interracial marriage between blacks and members of

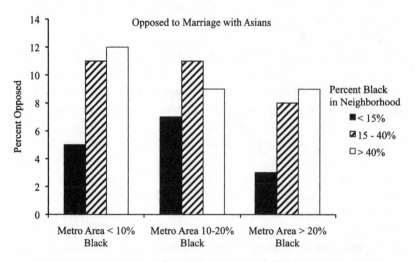

FIGURE 3.6A Opposition among African Americans to interracial marriage by the percent black in the neighborhood and metropolitan area (2000 SCCBS).

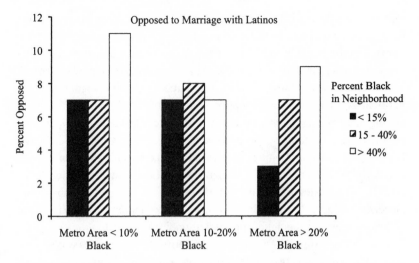

FIGURE 3.6B Opposition among African Americans to interracial marriage by the percent black in the neighborhood and metropolitan area, continued (2000 SCCBS).

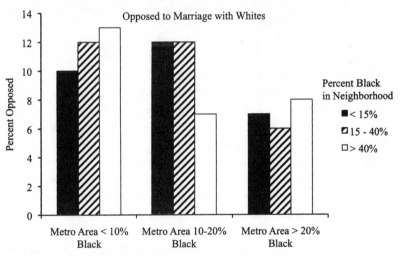

FIGURE 3.6C Opposition among African Americans to interracial marriage by the percent black in the neighborhood and metropolitan area, continued (2000 SCCBS).

other racial groups (those who responded as "somewhat" or "very" opposed were considered opposed and counted as one group). The findings are depicted in Figure 3.6. Although there are no simple patterns in blacks' opposition to interracial marriage for all three other racial groups, there are a few notable findings. The highest levels of opposition to interracial marriage are among blacks in disproportionately black neighborhoods (at least 40 percent black) in metropolitan areas with few blacks, irrespective of whether the target group is Asian, Latino, or white. For instance, over 12 percent of blacks in these places oppose interracial marriage between blacks and both whites and Latinos, which is 4 percentage points higher than the national average. Conversely, opposition to interracial marriage is lowest among blacks living in neighborhoods with fewer blacks that are in metropolitan areas with a higher proportion of blacks. Only 3 percent of blacks in these neighborhoods oppose interracial marriage with Latinos or Asians, compared with a 6 percent national average. Considerable variations exist in all the other categories of neighborhoods that defy easy summarization. Nevertheless, as with whites, black misgivings about interracial marriage are highest in segregated neighborhoods within diverse metropolitan areas.

Another measure in the SCCBS data about racial attitudes was a question on whether the respondent believed that "immigrants are getting too pushy in their demands for equal treatment." Although this question does not ask about a particular ethnic group, it might tap into more latent resentment toward Asians and Latinos. Blacks in predominantly black neighborhoods within more multiracial metropolitan areas express much higher levels of resentment toward immigrants than blacks in either less black neighborhoods in the same metropolitan areas or blacks in metropolitan areas with fewer Asians and Latinos. On average, approximately 30 percent of blacks in metropolitan areas that contain few Asians or Latinos believe that immigrants are getting too pushy (which is roughly equivalent to the national average). However, the rates are significantly higher in metropolitan areas with higher numbers of Asians and Latinos, particularly in predominantly black neighborhoods. Over 45 percent of blacks in neighborhoods that were at least 15 percent black expressed anti-immigrant sentiments, and nearly 50 percent felt this way in neighborhoods that were over 40 percent black. Thus, with respect to both feelings about interracial marriage and anti-immigrant sentiments, the results in the SCCBS data are consistent with the findings in the MCSUI data: blacks who live in black enclaves in largely nonblack regions are more racially averse than average; blacks who live in integrated neighborhoods within areas with high numbers of blacks are less racially averse than average.[13]

Taken together, the results of both the MCSUI and SCCBS data confirm many expectations about how social environments correspond with blacks' racial attitudes. Like whites, blacks' attitudes toward other groups vary with the racial composition of both the neighborhood and metropolitan area. Blacks who live in neighborhoods that are disproportionately black tend to have more negative views of other racial groups: those in neighborhoods that are between 40 and 60 percent black are more likely to embrace negative stereotypes of other groups (particularly Asians and Latinos), feel greater competition with Asians and Latinos, experience greater threat from immigration, and be the most opposed to interracial marriage. Blacks in these neighborhoods also demonstrate the highest levels of racial solidarity. These neighborhood differences vary considerably, however, with the racial composition of the metropolitan area. In the MCSUI sample, neighborhood differences are highest among blacks in Los Angeles and Atlanta and lowest among those in Boston. The greater racial diversity of the former corresponds with higher differences across neighborhoods and a generally higher level of out-group animosity. Although the effects of neighborhood composition are different between blacks and whites— blacks' attitudes typically show the greatest change occurs between neighborhoods that are 0–50 percent black—this is most likely a function of differing racial proportions in the general population. In other words, a neighborhood that is 50 percent black is, in most areas, disproportionately black, and thus the strongest levels of group effects occur in this range.

That geographic difference noted, the most remarkable aspect of these findings is similarities in the patterns of blacks' and whites' racial attitudes. Racial isolation in the context of regional racial diversity corresponds with the highest levels of racial resentment for blacks just as it did for whites.[14] Despite being a small portion of the population and living with a legacy of white racial subjugation, blacks' racial attitudes are influenced by social environments in a manner that is remarkably similar to whites: living in metropolitan areas with people of other races corresponds with increases black racial resentment toward those groups (particularly other minorities); living in neighborhoods with people of other races corresponds with decreases in racial resentment.

Latinos and the Racial Environment

Our attention now shifts to whether these same patterns emerge for another large minority group, Latinos. Once again, from either the contact or conflict hypothesis, there is no reason to believe that the patterns of racial attitudes among Latinos should be any different than those for whites. Yet, like African Americans, Latinos are a minority of the American population, and thus metropolitan-level differences in their racial attitudes should not be quite like the white majority. Furthermore, it is important to remember that Latinos are highly differentiated by race, nationality, and levels of incorporation into American society and that this last factor, as noted in chapter 2, was an important feature in shaping their racial perceptions. When examining the differences in Latinos' racial attitudes across social environments, such factors, particularly the level of incorporation, will need to be considered.

In general, the geographic distribution of racial attitudes among Latinos is similar to that of whites and African Americans. Once again, the regression equations predict that Latinos who live among other racial or ethnic groups will report lower average negative stereotypes of those groups, while Latinos who live in mostly Latino neighborhoods report higher average negative stereotypes.[15] In Los Angeles, Latinos who live in neighborhoods with more Asians, blacks, or whites all report lower negative stereotypes. Latinos who live in neighborhoods that are over 90 percent white are predicted to score half a point lower on the four-point negative stereotype scale than Latinos who live in neighborhoods with no whites. The opposite trend occurs for Latinos living among other Latinos: living in a predominantly Latino neighborhood corresponds with more negative stereotypes of other groups, particularly African Americans. Latinos in all-Latino neighborhoods are predicted to score over half a point higher on the negative stereotype scale than Latinos in neighborhoods with few Latinos.

Many immigration scholars attribute a higher level of racial antagonism between Latinos and other groups to competition for economic and political resources (Bobo and Johnson 2000; Olzak 1989). As more Latinos arrive in an area, they putatively cause more grievances among whites and blacks. With time, Latinos respond with their own negative racial attitudes. Thus, presumably, the higher levels of racial resentment among Latinos in Los Angeles arise from the dynamics of ethnic and racial competition that arise from the larger Latino population. But this scenario rests on an important assumption that Latinos are identifying themselves as a distinct group that is different and in opposition to both whites and blacks. In other words, the reason that Los Angeles Latinos who live in predominantly Latino neighborhoods are more racially hostile is because they have a greater sense of group identity in opposition to other racial groups.

Interestingly, however, the data provide only a little evidence to support this assumption. On the one hand, nearly all the variation in Latinos' racial attitudes across racial context occurs among incorporated Latinos (that is, those interviewed in English). Figure 3.7 depicts the results of regression equations estimating Latino negative stereotype scores by the percentage of the out-group in the neighborhood, interaction terms for English language ability, and controlling for the standard set of predictors. Although Latinos who were interviewed in Spanish generally have higher average negative stereotype scores, there is very little variability in their attitudes

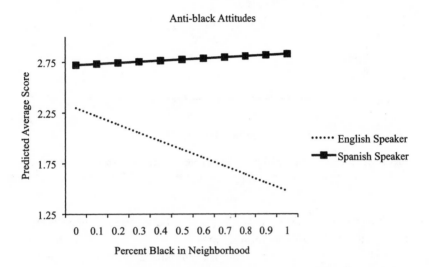

FIGURE 3.7A Negative stereotypes of other races among Latinos by language spoken and percent of that group in the neighborhood (1992–1994 MCSUI, Los Angeles portion).

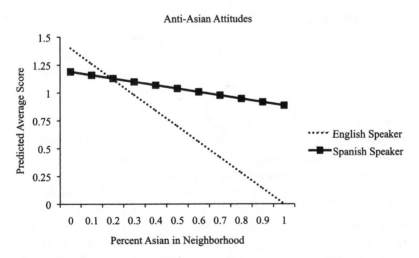

FIGURE 3.7B Negative stereotypes of other races among Latinos by language spoken and percent of that group in the neighborhood, continued (1992–1994 MCSUI, Los Angeles portion).

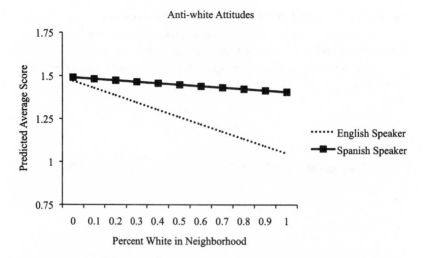

FIGURE 3.7C Negative stereotypes of other races among Latinos by language spoken and percent of that group in the neighborhood, continued (1992–1994 MCSUI, Los Angeles portion).

across social contexts. In other words, the only Latinos who exhibit sensitiv-
ity to their racial environments are those who are more incorporated. This
finding lends support to the idea that as Latinos become more incorporated
into American life, they develop a stronger sense of group identity.

On the other hand, equations measuring scores on the linked fate, zero
competition with Asians and blacks, and perceptions of discrimination
against "Hispanics" scales give inconclusive results about the effect of racial solidarity (see online appendix B, table B7). In no instance does either
a sense of linked fate or feeling of zero-sum competition vary with Latino
percentage in the respondents' neighborhoods for either English or Spanish interviewees in the MCSUI data. Although Latinos who do express a
greater sense of linked fate with other Latinos are also more likely to see
zero-sum competition with blacks and Asians, this still does not change the
fact that Latinos' feelings of in-group solidarity (as measured by a sense of
linked fate) or racial competition with other minorities varies little across
their surroundings. The only measure of racial solidarity that does change
with the neighborhood environment is the perception of discrimination.
In Los Angeles, Latinos who live in predominantly Latino neighborhoods
were more likely to agree that discrimination hurts Latinos in the job
market.[16] But for all the other measures, the data indicate that the differences in Latinos' racial views across neighborhoods are therefore not
related to feelings of racial competition or a feeling of linked fate. As we

will see in the chapters to follow, the extent of ethnic solidarity that occurs in Latino neighborhoods is related as much to the high proportion of non-English-speaking immigrants as to being surrounded by more Latinos.[17]

In the SCCBS data, similarly complicated patterns are evident. Regression equations were estimated to gauge the effects of racial contexts on opposition to interracial marriage.[18] For Latinos in the nationwide sample, opposition to interracial marriage with Asians does not change with the racial composition of either the metropolitan area or their neighborhood but does change with respect to blacks and whites. The OLS coefficients indicate that Latinos who live in predominantly Latino neighborhoods are more opposed to interracial marriage with blacks, as are Latinos who live in metropolitan areas with more blacks. Conversely, Latinos who live in metropolitan areas with more whites are less opposed to interracial marriage with whites, particularly when the Latino composition of their own neighborhood is not considered.

From these two studies it appears that Latinos' racial attitudes are influenced by social environments in some ways that are similar to blacks and whites and in some ways that are unique. First, Latinos' negative stereotypes about out-groups, particularly blacks, vary most sharply across neighborhoods. These differences, however, are almost entirely among incorporated Latinos. Latinos who speak little or no English have very negative views of other groups but exhibit little variation across racial environments. Second, in places with a larger proportionate white population, Latinos exhibit less negative views about whites. For instance, Latinos who live in metropolitan areas with a higher percentage of whites are less opposed to interracial marriage; meanwhile, in Los Angeles, with its relatively small white population, Latinos' views of whites are considerably less negative than other groups. Finally, outside of Los Angeles, Latinos' opinions of Asians are relatively unaffected by racial environments, which most likely comes from the limited exposure between Latinos and Asians. In Los Angeles, where Latinos and Asians do have greater contact, Latinos' attitudes about Asians follow the pattern of their attitudes toward other groups—social isolation corresponds with more negative views.

Asian Americans and the Racial Environment

So far, a consistent relationship has been shown to exist between racial contexts and attitudes. Among whites, blacks, and Latinos, metropolitan racial diversity contributes to a greater sense of racial competition and a heightened racial animosity. Conversely, at the neighborhood level, racial integration corresponds with less antagonism toward other races, although this varies somewhat depending on the group in question. And, despite some slight differences between these groups, the pattern is remarkably consistent. From the limited research on Asian Americans' racial attitudes, there is no reason to suspect that they will be affected differently by their racial environments in any different way (Bobo and Johnson 2000; Lee 2000). If the conflict and contact theories of racial attitudes follow through, a similar pattern should emerge for Asian Americans: metropolitan-area racial diversity should correspond with greater racial animosity; neighborhood racial diversity should correspond with greater racial tolerance.

The difficulty with testing these ideas, particularly at the metropolitan level, is the small and uneven geographic distribution of the Asian American population. Most Asian Americans are concentrated in a handful of states, and within these states in just a few metropolitan areas. In fact, nearly 65 percent of Asian Americans live in just six states (California, Hawaii, Texas, New York, New Jersey, and Illinois), and over 55 percent live in one of six metropolitan areas: Los Angeles, New York, San Francisco, Honolulu, Chicago, and Washington, D.C. Given this skewed disbursal, it is difficult to measure how Asian Americans respond to metropolitan-area differences in population as most live within multiethnic areas. In fact, it is simply difficult to get sufficient numbers of Asian Americans in any national survey sample.

Such limitations mean that empirical tests about Asians' racial attitudes will have to be limited to the neighborhood level using MCSUI data from Los Angeles. At first glance, the equations predicting Asian Americans' racial attitudes seem to offer results that are contrary to the dominant trends for other racial groups.[19] For Asian Americans as a single population, there are no significant differences in racial attitudes across their neighborhoods. In other words, Asian Americans in heavily Asian neighborhoods were no more likely to score higher on any measure of negative stereotypes than those in heavily integrated neighborhoods.

Yet as with the general racial attitudes described in chapter 2, there are significant differences by language of interview. According to the estimations, respondents who were interviewed in Korean were much more likely to report negative stereotypes of other groups, particularly blacks and whites, even when their individual-level education and age were also considered. The equations predict that the average Korean interviewee would score over six-tenths of a point higher on the negative black stereotype scale and nearly a half point higher on the negative white stereotype scale than an Asian American interviewed in English. These differences are larger than any other individual-level predictor including education and age.[20] Yet this is not simply a phenomenon of being interviewed in one's native tongue. Respondents interviewed in Chinese actually scored lower on the black and Latino negative stereotype scales than respondents interviewed in English. These are not a precise measure of ethnicity (many ethnic Koreans and Chinese were interviewed in English), but they are an approximation of a combination of ethnicity and incorporation.[21]

Because of these significant differences by language of interview, the effects of neighborhood racial environment need to be considered separately for each group.[22] When neighborhood effects are considered separately by language, sharp differences emerge in the patterns of racial attitudes across the social environment. For Asian Americans interviewed in English, the effects of neighborhood surroundings are much like they are for other racial groups. English-speaking Asian Americans who live in predominantly Asian neighborhoods are more likely to hold negative views of other races than those who live in integrated settings. The equations predict that an English-speaking Asian American who lives in an all-Asian neighborhood will, on average, score over six-tenths a point higher on the negative stereotype scale for all three other racial groups. The largest differences are in their views of whites—English-speaking Asian Americans in all-Asian neighborhoods score nearly an entire point higher in their negative stereotypes of whites than those who live in mostly non-Asian settings. As with whites, blacks, and Latinos, English-speaking Asians who are racially isolated tend to have the most negative views of other groups.

A much different finding emerges, however, with respect to Korean- and Chinese-speaking interviewees. Korean interviewees who live in largely Asian neighborhoods are actually much less negative in their views of blacks than those who live in non-Asian neighborhoods, a difference that is over one point on the four-point negative stereotype scale. It should be noted, however, that the Asians who live in non-Asian neighborhoods are not necessarily living around more blacks, but, given the high Asian-black segregation, they are more likely to be living around whites or Latinos. In other words, it is not residential exposure to blacks that is making Koreans more negative in their views but residence in a non-Asian setting.[23] There are no significant differences in their attitudes toward Latinos or whites across this scale, on average, but Korean interviewees still have more negative views of these groups than other Asians.

Among Chinese interviewees, a different pattern emerges. Across different neighborhoods there are no significant differences in their attitudes toward blacks or Latinos, but there are big differences in their views of whites. Chinese interviewees who live in more predominantly Asian neighborhoods are less negative in their views of whites than those who live in

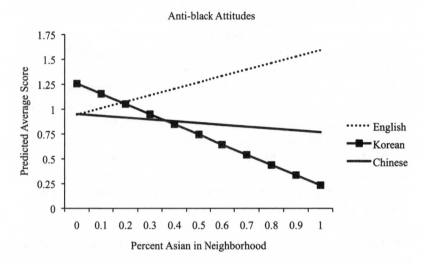

FIGURE 3.8A Negative stereotypes of out-groups among Asian Americans by nationality and percent Asian in neighborhood (1992–1994 MCSUI, Los Angeles portion).

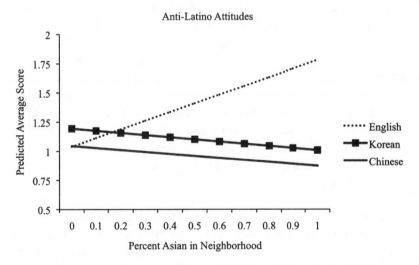

FIGURE 3.8B Negative stereotypes of out-groups among Asian Americans by nationality and percent Asian in neighborhood, continued (1992–1994 MCSUI, Los Angeles portion).

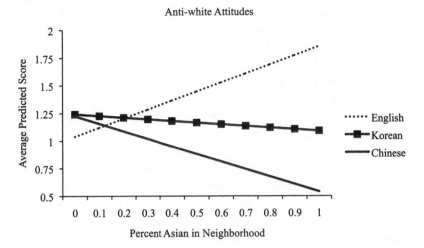

FIGURE 3.8c Negative stereotypes of out-groups among Asian Americans by nationality and percent Asian in neighborhood, continued (1992–1994 MCSUI, Los Angeles portion).

more integrated settings. As most Chinese interviewees who do not live in Asian neighborhoods tend to live around more whites, it is integration with whites that contributes to more negative feelings.[24] In short, among Chinese interviewees, racial isolation tends to promote a more positive view of whites than living in more integrated neighborhoods.

Given that Asians are more likely to be integrated in white neighborhoods than any other minority group, it is also important to consider separately what effect living among whites may have on their racial attitudes. To consider this proposition, the same regressions were reestimated, only with the percent white in the neighborhood substituted for the measure of percent Asian and for the interaction terms (see online appendix B, table B12). Once again, these equations estimate the effects of living among a greater number of whites on Asian respondents' views of other groups while holding constant individual-level factors such as education and age.

For English-speaking Asian respondents, living among more whites corresponds with lower overall levels of racial resentment. All three equations predict that English-speaking Asian interviewees in neighborhoods that are all white will score at least half a point lower on the negative stereotype scales than those who live in neighborhoods with no whites. There is no change in this effect for Korean interviewees, but there is for Chinese interviewees. In all three equations, the interaction term between Chinese interview and the percent white in the neighborhood is quite large and positive. What this means is that for Chinese interviewees, living among more whites corresponds with greater racial animosity toward other groups, especially toward whites. In the equation predicting negative stereotypes of whites, Chinese interviewees in all-white neighborhoods scored over one-point higher on the negative stereotype of whites scale than those in neighborhoods with few or no whites.

Similar patterns are also evident for other measures of racial attitudes such as feelings of zero-sum competition with blacks and Latinos and feelings of linked fate with other Asians (see online appendix B, table B13). Measures of these items were regressed on measures of racial context, interview language, and the standard set of individual-level controls. As with their general racial attitudes, Asian Americans who live in neighborhoods with a higher percentage of Asians feel a greater sense of zero-sum competition with blacks and Latinos than those who live in neighborhoods with fewer Asians, although the difference with regards to Latinos is not large enough to be considered statistically significant. As with the earlier results, Korean interviewees also expressed greater feelings of zero-sum competition with blacks and Latinos, while there were no differences between Chinese interviewees and the rest of the sample. The attitudes of Korean interviewees about zero-sum competition with blacks and Latinos also varied less across contexts. And while Korean interviewees expressed stronger feelings of linked fate with other Asians, there were no other strong contextual or national differences in Asian Americans' feelings of group solidarity. The feelings of interracial competition that occur in more predominantly Asian neighborhoods do not appear to arise from stronger feelings of ethnic solidarity in these places.

Two important results emerge from these findings. First, among Asian Americans who speak English, the effects of neighborhood racial context are somewhat similar to those for other racial groups. English-speaking Asian Americans who live among more Asians tend to have more negative views of other races than those who live in integrated settings, and those who live among more whites tend to be less racially hostile across the board. From these findings, it appears that Asian Americans who are more incorporated into American society also adopt patterns of racial attitudes that are similar to those of white Americans.

Second, among Asian immigrants with limited English skills, the effects of social environments vary significantly by nationality. For Korean interviewees, neighborhood diversity corresponds with more animosity toward blacks but has no effect on their attitudes toward other groups. Chinese interviewees, typically less racially resentful than other Asians in the MCSUI sample, nevertheless feel more negative about whites when they live in more predominantly white neighborhoods. For these less incorporated groups, integration corresponds with more negative feelings toward other races.

Conclusion

In looking across all of these findings, one cannot help but be struck by the similar patterns in the geographic distribution of attitudes among America's different racial groups. Irrespective of whether the person identifies as white, black, Latino, or Asian, those who live in neighborhoods that are prominently same race tend to be more hostile in their racial attitudes toward other groups. This trend usually also holds across a host of different measures including negative stereotypes, opposition to interracial marriage, or feelings of political and economic competition. Living in a neighborhood with more people of a particular minority group, be they black, Asian, or Latino, generally corresponds with less racial animosity toward that group. With a few notable exceptions (such as among Spanish or Chinese interviewees in the MCSUI data), these results show remarkable consistency in neighborhood effects: integration at the neighborhood level corresponds with less racial resentment.

The greatest neighborhood differences in racial attitudes occurred in the most racially diverse metropolitan areas. For example, the SCCBS data, which sample from over two hundred metropolitan areas, show that the highest levels of opposition to interracial marriage and anti-immigrant sentiments are in metropolitan areas that are the most racially mixed. Similarly, the highest levels of racial animosity among all four MCSUI cities were in Los Angeles, which is the most racially diverse.[25] Although the MCSUI data do not sample from enough metropolitan areas to draw any firm conclusion about the effects of metropolitan diversity on overall levels of racial hostility, the results are consistent with the national SCCBS data.

Both data sets show a sharp interaction between neighborhood and metropolitan racial contexts: racial hostility and feelings of competition were greatest in predominantly same-race neighborhoods within racially mixed metropolitan areas. For example, white opposition to interracial marriage with blacks was absolutely highest among residents of neighborhoods

that were over 97 percent white, but only in the most racially mixed metropolitan areas. Similarly, in the MCSUI data, the greatest effects of neighborhood racial composition on racial attitudes were in Los Angeles and
Atlanta, metropolitan areas with both high percentages of minorities and
more fluid boundaries between minorities. Unlike Boston, which has a
very small minority population, and Detroit, where spatial boundaries
between blacks and whites are more firmly defined, Los Angeles and Atlanta are areas where all-white neighborhoods are far more contested and
subject to infiltration by minority groups. Consequently, these highly segregated neighborhoods within the very heterogeneous metropolitan areas
tend to have the highest levels of racial animosity.

Together, these findings shed new light on the seeming contradictions
in past research on social environments and racial attitudes. Many scholars have explained the high levels of racial antagonism among whites who
live in areas with high proportions of minorities by making reference to
economic and political conflict (Quillian 1995; Taylor 1998). Economic
and political competition in diverse locales quickly becomes "racialized"
as the percent of minority groups, and their potential power, increases.
The racial resentment that has consistently appeared in past research
among whites living in diverse metropolitan areas is also found here. This
is consistent with the notion that racial diversity generates racial animosity, probably because of increase racial competition for political and economic resources.

But while evidence of economic and political competition can be found
at the metropolitan level, it does not seem to occur at the neighborhood
level: neighborhood racial diversity corresponds with less racial resentment and not more. If the effects of racial diversity were uniform across all
levels of geography, then one would find greater racial tension in neighborhoods as well as in metropolitan areas. This, however, does not occur, and,
upon further reflection, the different pattern at the neighborhood level
makes intuitive sense. After all, it is typically larger geographic places that
are arenas of competition for jobs, political offices, and other resources.
There are few such resources that can be contested across a neighborhood
because, if someone wants a different job, then all he or she has to do is
travel a few miles to a new place.

It is essential to remember that a racially diverse environment does
not always lead to heightened racial tension. Across all four racial groups,
people who live among people of a different race are more favorable
about the people of that race. Typically these neighborhood differences

are greatest in metropolitan areas with the highest levels of racial diversity. For example, neighborhood differences were far greater in multiethnic Los Angeles than they were in the predominantly white Boston metropolitan area. Interestingly, it is those people who live furthest away from the other races in their metropolis that feel the most competition and most negative about other groups.

The next logical question is what accounts for these patterns. In general the results are consistent with the expectations of the contact hypothesis, that is, people who share neighborhoods with people of other races are more favorable about other races because they are more likely to have a racially diverse set of friendships and social bonds. However, before this idea can be tested, a more succinct, alternative explanation needs to be explored—that the neighborhood differences in racial attitudes are not the result of environmental causes but merely reflect the geographic sorting of people according to their racial attitudes. It is this explanation that we turn to next.

CHAPTER FOUR

Geographic Self-Sorting and Racial Attitudes

From the previous chapter, it is clear that racial attitudes vary in consistent ways across different social environments. Racial diversity at the metropolitan level corresponds with greater racial tension—whites, blacks, and Latinos who live in more racially diverse metropolitan areas exhibit higher levels of interracial competition and resentment. At the neighborhood level, an opposite pattern is typically evident—people who live in racially diverse neighborhoods are much more racially tolerant, while those in homogeneous neighborhoods show more racial mistrust and resentment. These neighborhood differences also tend to be highest in the more diverse metropolitan areas and less pronounced in predominantly white ones.

While past research provides a solid account for the higher levels of racial resentment in more diverse metropolitan areas (greater racial competition), the lower levels of racial resentment in diverse neighborhoods are subject to competing explanations. One explanation, which will be explored in chapter 5, is that the greater interracial contact and exposure among residents in integrated neighborhoods alleviates ethnic animosity and misperception. Before examining this possibility, however, a more self-evident and plausible explanation needs to be considered: geographic self-selection.

According to the self-selection explanation, the reason why people in integrated neighborhoods are more racially tolerant is that racially tolerant people are, by definition, more willing to live in racially diverse settings, while racially intolerant people will seek to live in more segregated places. Indeed, one might see the hypersegregation across neighborhoods as indicative of the contours of racial attitudes and animosities within a metropolitan area. In other words, the large differences across neighborhoods reveal the geographic sorting according to levels of racial animosity.

This explanation has a profound implication for understanding contemporary American race relations. For if the self-selection hypothesis is correct, it would also imply that the high levels of racial segregation in America's metropolitan areas indicate a virulent, latent racism among most of America's racial groups. Despite the professed commitment of most Americans to norms of racial equality, the fact that Americans who choose racially segregated neighborhoods do so from some aversion to other racial groups would suggest that, in practice, racial equality is not a reality most Americans would embrace. In fact, the persistence of segregation over time only shows how deeply engrained American racial mistrust really is.

Before jumping to this rather dark conclusion, it is worth examining how well it holds up to empirical scrutiny. The copious body of previous research on the causes and consequences of racial segregation offer a host of competing explanations for why whites, blacks, Asians, and Latinos continue to live apart. These include white avoidance of minority areas, white discrimination against minorities, institutional discrimination in real estate practices and lending practices (such as redlining), and in-group neighborhood preferences among minorities and recent immigrants. What most studies show is that whites have a very low tolerance for any neighborhood with more than a tiny minority population, while blacks, Latinos, and other minorities often seek neighborhoods that are more racially mixed. What is not clear from this research, however, is how much these preferences are driven by hostility to other races versus other factors such as a desire for in-group solidarity or economic considerations, particularly in multiethnic areas.

This chapter explores how much the relationship between racial attitudes and social environments found in chapter 3 is the result of people's neighborhood racial preferences. The findings indicate that most of the differences in racial attitudes cannot be attributed to self-selection. For minorities, there is no correlation between their neighborhood racial preferences and their views about other groups. Blacks, Latinos, and Asians may exhibit preferences for same-race neighborhoods, but this does not correspond with their animosities toward other races. This type of geographic racial self-selection is only evident among whites. A small portion of the geographic variation in whites' racial attitudes can be attributed to their expressed neighborhood racial preference. Yet, even when this preference is considered, whites who live in same-race neighborhoods still demonstrated much higher levels of racial animosity. While undoubtedly people with racially intolerant views are likely to seek racially homogenous settings, this does not seem to be the primary or sole factor explaining why racial intolerance is so much higher in racially segregated neighborhoods.

Race and Neighborhood Choice

The concept of neighborhood racial self-selection is relatively straightforward: when seeking a neighborhood to live in, people with strong racial biases will look for neighborhoods with few members of other races. Thus racist whites will seek all-white neighborhoods, racist blacks will seek all-black neighborhoods, and so forth. According to this hypothesis, the geographic distribution of racial attitudes found in the past chapter is largely the result of this sorting according to racial preference: higher racial animosity is found in segregated neighborhoods because people with strong racial priors are choosing to live in such places.

American residential patterns of the past century give strong credence to this account, at least for whites. At the end of the 1800s, as American cities began to swell with southern blacks and Jewish and Catholic migrants from eastern and southern Europe, American cities began to become more stratified along racial and ethnic lines. Prior to this time, most American cities were surprisingly integrated, at least by today's standards. This was because most large American cities such as New York, Philadelphia, and Chicago had relatively small minority populations and many of these lived in the same quarters as their employers (the notable exception to this were Chinese immigrants who were sequestered in San Francisco and other western towns). Integration was also helped by the fact that most people had to live within walking distance of where they worked, thus forcing various groups into closer proximity.

However, with the advent of the streetcar and the commuter railroad and the great migration to the burgeoning industrial cities of the north, more definitive racial and ethnic neighborhoods began to materialize. Sometimes this was through self-selection. As new immigrants arrived in cities like New York or Chicago, they would often find help acclimating to their new surroundings from people who shared their background.

But often, segregation was imposed by America's white Anglo-Protestant majority. Through discriminatory real estate practices, restricted deed covenants, redlining, and outright violence, blacks, Asians, Jews, Italians, and many other ethnic groups were often relegated to sharply defined neighborhoods. For example, many white suburbs often had explicit deed restrictions prohibiting ownership by minorities and Jews. African Americans who were able to acquire homes in white neighborhoods often faced scorn and intimidation, as when singer Nat Cole found a burning cross in his front yard after moving into a Beverly Hills mansion (Massey and Denton 1993).

Hypersegregation was also caused by white avoidance of racially mixed neighborhoods. As the African American population swelled in many cities, traditionally black neighborhoods became overcrowded, and blacks began to find housing in nearby areas. Such black expansion often led to "white flight," wherein whites in integrated neighborhoods, fearful of black neighbors and declining property values, sold and moved en masse, often to nearby growing suburban neighborhoods. Such rapid racial turnover increased dramatically after World War II when white veterans took advantage of government housing assistance and made use of the growing interstate highway system to relocate out to suburbs. African Americans were often barred from this migration through government policies that forbade lending to minorities in certain suburban areas and thus often sought to move out of overcrowded ghettos into the neighborhoods that whites were vacating. Although such restrictions were eliminated with the 1968 Fair Housing Act and although minorities are becoming more suburbanized, the vast majority of suburban communities continue to be overwhelmingly white, while most central cities and inner-ring suburbs continue to have a disproportionate number of minorities.

But while the legacy of America's racist past still echoes in its current segregation patterns, it is unclear how much current feelings of racial mistrust, animosity, or in-group cohesion are responsible as well. There is considerable evidence that racial attitudes are important determinants of neighborhood choice, although scholars still debate whether segregation arises from simple self-selection, white discrimination, or both. On the one hand, demographer William Clark has examined the residential preferences of different races in Los Angeles and found that individual choices to live in same-race neighborhoods were a big determinant of residential location among all groups but particularly among whites. Clark concludes, "the unwillingness of groups to prefer and/or to choose combinations that do not include large proportions of their own race is a significant force in creating separate racial and ethnic areas" (Clark 1992, 442). Other research, however, has argued that racial self-sorting is not a phenomenon uniform across races; rather, discriminatory practices in the real estate market have fostered and sustained segregation particularly toward African Americans (Galster and Hill 1992). Some argue that segregation is primarily the consequence of white racial animosity: whites' negative views of other races, particularly blacks and Latinos, create incentives for whites to seek all-white neighborhoods; similarly, these negative views also create a process of "white avoidance" among blacks and Latinos who, knowing they will be unwelcome in white neighborhoods, end up in more same-race locales (Massey and Denton 1993; Farley et al. 1993). Others argue that minorities are far more open to integration than whites and it is white racial discrimination among residents and real estate that perpetuates segregation (Bobo and Zubrinsky 1996).

These different explanations highlight the importance of negative racial attitudes toward other groups in the process of self-selection. If the self-selection explanation is true, then people must be making their residential choices on the basis of an aversion to other groups. In other words, if the neighborhood patterns described in chapter 3 (that is, residents of segregated neighborhoods being more hostile in their racial attitudes) are the result of negative self-selection (that is, people moving to a same-race neighborhood to avoid minorities), then there should exist a strong correspondence between neighborhood racial preference, negative racial attitudes toward other groups, and the actual racial composition of where people live. For example, if Latinos in predominantly Latino neighborhoods are more resentful of blacks or Asians because biased Latinos do not want to live near other races, then a strong correlation should exist between their racial attitudes and their neighborhood racial preferences. The self-selection hypothesis does not hold if people are simply choosing same-race neighborhoods because of an in-group affiliation. The patterns described in chapter 3 all deal with hostility toward other groups that occurs in same-race neighborhoods. If, however, blacks, Latinos, or Asians are seeking same-race neighborhoods as a means of avoiding white discrimination or are looking for support from a coethnic community, it does not mean that there will be higher racial discrimination in such places because residents of segregated minority communities are choosing their neighborhood from an in-group affiliation (or a fear of discrimination) rather than from a hostility toward another group.

Neighborhood Racial Preference

To sort through these competing conceptions of self-selection, I start by first examining ethnic difference in neighborhood racial preference. Respondents in the MCSUI were given a series of five cards depicting a group of fifteen houses with different levels of integration between the respondent's race (whose home was in the middle) and one of three other races (see online appendix B, table B14, for an example). These sets of cards thus presented the respondent with a series of neighborhood choices. Respondents were asked to arrange the neighborhoods from most to least attractive.[1] From these responses, a five-point scale was constructed that measures how much they would prefer to live in an all same-race or predominantly same-race setting versus a racially mixed or largely non-same-race neighborhood.[2]

The majority of people, irrespective of their own race, prefer all or largely same-race neighborhoods, however, there are significant differences along racial lines. Figure 4.1 lists the percentage of respondents, by race, indicating their first preference for a residential neighborhood. Across all four racial groups, the majority prefers a neighborhood that is at least 80 percent of their own group, but this varies greatly by individual race. A large majority of Asians and whites are more likely to prefer

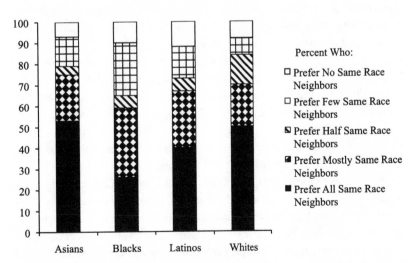

FIGURE 4.1 Distribution of neighborhood racial preference by individual race (1992–1994 MCSUI).

same-race neighborhoods: 53 percent of Asians and 50 percent of whites choose an all-Asian or all-white neighborhood as their first preference (an additional 22 percent of Asians and 20 percent of whites prefer a mostly Asian or mostly white neighborhood). Latinos are slightly less likely to prefer an all-Latino neighborhood (only 40 percent) but are slightly more likely to prefer a mostly Latino neighborhood (27 percent). Blacks are the least likely to prefer same-race neighborhoods (only 26 percent prefer an all-black neighborhood) but are slightly more likely to prefer a mostly same-race neighborhoods (33 percent of blacks prefer a mostly black neighborhood).

On the other side, blacks and Latinos were much more open to living in more integrated neighborhoods or even as the only member of their race in a neighborhood than whites or Asians. Twenty-five percent of blacks and 15 percent of Latinos prioritized a neighborhood with few blacks or Latinos and 10 percent of blacks and 12 percent of Latinos chose neighborhoods with no blacks or Latinos. Roughly one in three Latinos or blacks would choose a largely non-Latino or nonblack neighborhood. Conversely, only 21 percent of Asians and only 17 percent of whites would choose a neighborhood with few or no members of their own race.

From these findings, it is apparent that most Americans, regardless of their own race, prefer neighborhoods that are racially tilted toward their own group, although how tilted depends on the person's race. Upon further investigation, it is also clear that these neighborhood preferences correspond with the actual racial percentages within a person's neighborhood. I calculated the average score on the same-race neighborhood preference scale by the actual racial composition of the respondents' neighborhoods. The neighborhood preference scale is scored from zero (for those who prefer non-same-race neighborhoods) to four (for those who prefer all same-race neighbors)—the higher the average score, the greater the preference a respondent has for same-race neighbors. In short, this simple statistic measures how much people's preference for neighbors of their own race matches the reality of their own neighborhoods.

With the exception of blacks, people who live in more segregated neighborhoods tend to express a preference for more segregated neighborhoods. For example, among Latinos and whites who live in neighborhoods that are under 50 percent Latino and white, respectively, the average score on the same-race neighborhood preference scale is only 2.5, among the lowest of any group. Among Latinos and whites who live in predominantly Latino or white neighborhoods (over 94 percent of their group), the average score is roughly 3.4, nearly a single point higher on the neighborhood preference scale. Similar differences also occur for Asians—Asians who live in the least Asian neighborhoods score nearly a point lower on the same-race neighborhood preference scale than those who live in all-Asian neighborhoods. Indeed, the only group whose neighborhood preferences do not correspond to their actual surroundings are African Americans. Blacks who live in integrated neighborhoods have, on average, roughly the same scores on their same-race neighbor preference scales as those who live in predominantly black places.

At first glance, these findings would seem to support the self-selection explanation for the neighborhood differences in racial attitudes. On the aggregate level, most Americans are segregated along neighborhood lines by race, and from the survey data most Americans also prefer largely segregated neighborhoods. Furthermore, on the individual level, there is a strong correspondence between a person's neighborhood preferences and his or her actual neighborhood patterns—people who live in segregated neighborhoods, on average, are more likely to prefer segregated neighborhoods.

But if the self-selection hypothesis is correct, then another important factor needs to be considered—aversion to other races. In other words, if people who choose segregated neighborhoods are doing so because of their racial biases, then there should be a strong correlation between neighborhood racial preference and racial antipathy toward other groups. Otherwise, one might attribute the findings above to simple in-group affiliations, which do not always imply hostility toward other races. For example, Latinos and Asian Americans, which are groups with large immigrant populations, may seek Latino or Asian neighborhoods because they offer more cultural amenities that are familiar to them, not because they dislike other racial groups. Similarly, the choice of an all-black or all-Latino neighborhood may come from a sense of group pride or a fear of discrimination that might arise from living among more of some other group, particularly if it is a white majority.

In examining the data, the link between neighborhood racial preference and actual racial antipathy toward other groups appears only for whites. Table 4.1 lists the average score on the negative stereotype scales toward all three out-groups by the neighborhood racial preference measure for each of the four races in the MCSUI data. In other words, this table depicts how much a preference for living in a segregated neighborhood actually corresponds with negative racial views toward another group. Among

TABLE 4.1 **Average score on negative stereotype scales by neighborhood racial preference**

	Prefer all same-race neighbors	Prefer most same-race neighbors	Prefer half same-race neighbors	Prefer few same-race neighbors	Prefer no same-race neighbors
Asians:					
Antiblack	1.7	1.8	1.5	1.6	1.9
Anti-Latino	1.5	1.5	1.3	1.4	1.7
Antiwhite	.97	.90	.68	.88	.85
Blacks:					
Anti-Asian	1.2	1.1	.77	1.0	1.1
Anti-Latino	1.2	1.2	.90	1.1	1.3
Antiwhite	1.3	1.2	.94	1.1	1.2
Latinos:					
Anti-Asian	1.1	1.1	.98	1.1	1.1
Antiblack	2.0	1.7	1.4	1.7	1.9
Antiwhite	1.3	1.2	1.1	1.3	1.2
Whites:					
Anti-Asian	.67	.60	.72	.62	.59
Antiblack	1.8	1.7	1.6	1.3	.92
Anti-Latino	1.4	1.4	1.3	1.1	.90

Source: 1992–1994 MCSUI.

nonwhites, there is virtually no correspondence between a preference for a same-race neighborhood and negative attitudes toward other groups. For example, blacks' racial attitudes toward other groups do not correspond with a preference for having black neighbors. In fact, some of the highest average negative stereotype scores are among blacks who prefer neighborhoods with the fewest blacks. Blacks who prefer neighborhoods with few or no other blacks score, on average, over 1.2 on the negative stereotype scale across all other racial groups. These scores are higher than those of respondents who prefer neighborhoods that are half or mostly black and roughly equivalent to the scores of respondents who prefer all-black neighborhoods. Similarly, among Asian Americans and Latinos there are no clear patterns linking racial attitudes toward other groups to their own neighborhood racial preferences.

It is only among whites where one finds a relationship between racial hostility and neighborhood racial preference. Whites who prefer mostly white or all-white neighborhoods have more negative stereotypes of blacks and Latinos than whites who prefer racially mixed neighborhoods. For instance, whites who prefer all-white neighborhoods score, on average, nearly a point higher on the four-point antiblack stereotype scale and half a point higher on the anti-Latino scale than whites who prefer mostly nonwhite neighborhoods. Interestingly, negative stereotypes toward Asian Americans do not vary across the neighborhood racial preference scale.

Much of white aversion to residentially integrated neighborhoods is primarily related to negative feelings about African Americans and Latinos.

Further tests show that the relationship between nonwhites' racial attitudes and their neighborhood racial composition are not influenced when their neighborhood racial composition is taken into consideration. For example, controlling for blacks' neighborhood racial preferences does not affect the relationship between their neighborhood racial settings and their racial attitudes. Including the controls for neighborhood racial preferences had virtually no effect on the relationship between the percent black in the neighborhood and the negative stereotypes toward Asians, Latinos, and whites. Blacks who live in predominantly black neighborhoods were still more negative toward other groups even when their preference for living in a black neighborhood was considered. Blacks who live in predominantly black neighborhoods are more likely to express an affinity for black neighbors, but this in-group preference does not explain their out-group animosities. Blacks who prefer black neighbors are no more racially resentful toward Asians, Latinos, or whites than blacks who prefer racially mixed neighborhoods. Although whites may be sorting themselves geographically according to their racial aversion to out-groups, blacks seem to sort themselves more from a position of in-group favoritism rather than out-group denigration.

Similar findings are evident for Latinos. I ran equations measuring the effect of Latinos' neighborhoods on their negative stereotypes of other groups with the measure of neighborhood racial preference added to the control group of variables. Once again, these equations, in effect, measure how much variance in Latinos' racial stereotypes can be accounted for by the racial composition of their neighborhood once their neighborhood racial preference is held constant. For Latinos, having a preference for Latino neighbors is not related to negative attitudes toward other groups. In none of the equations is there a significant difference in the racial attitudes toward other groups between Latinos who score high and and those who score low on the scale for Latino neighbor preference. Moreover, adding the controls for neighborhood racial preference has no effect on the relationship between the percent Latino in the neighborhood and the negative stereotype scales. Latinos who live in predominantly Latino neighborhoods still exhibit more negative stereotypes about non-Latinos, even when their neighborhood racial preference is taken into account.

Asian American respondents show a slightly different trend. Regression equations predict that preferring a predominantly Asian neighborhood does not correspond with animosity toward other minority groups. In the equations measuring negative stereotypes toward blacks and Latinos, the addition of the Asian neighborhood preference measure does not alter the equation either in it having any direct relationship to the measure of racial attitudes or in it changing the relationship between the measure of the actual racial environment and the racial attitudes. In short, the higher levels of negative stereotyping of blacks and Latinos in predominantly Asian neighborhoods are not the consequence of self-selection. Interestingly, however, neighborhood preferences do correspond with racial attitudes toward whites. The equations predict that those who prefer Asian neighborhoods are more likely to hold negative stereotypes about whites than those who do not. The inclusion of the neighborhood preference measure, however, does not alter the relationship between the percent of Asians in the respondents' real neighborhood and their negative feelings toward whites—English-speaking Asian respondents who live in predominantly Asian neighborhoods are still more negative in their feelings of whites even when their neighborhood preferences are considered. There are no different effects from Chinese- or Korean-speaking Asians either.

In sum, there is no evidence from these data that Asian Americans, blacks, or Latinos are segregating themselves into predominantly same-race neighborhoods because of an aversion to any other minority group. In this regard, they differ from whites. Many nonwhites, such as Asian Americans, may be sorting themselves into predominantly minority neighborhoods from a feeling of aversion or mistrust of whites, which may explain some of the higher levels of animosity among Chinese-speaking Asians who live in predominantly Asian neighborhoods. This is one of the few cases in which a minority group has negative feelings toward whites that shape their desire to live in a predominantly minority neighborhood. Nevertheless, on the whole, the neighborhood differences in racial attitudes among minorities cannot be accounted for by geographic self-selection.

Whites and Self-Selection

Considering the high correlations between whites' racial attitudes and their neighborhood racial preferences, it is possible that much of the relationship between neighborhood racial contexts and racial attitudes depicted in the last chapter is the result of self-selection. Whites who choose white neighborhoods generally view minorities less favorably than whites who choose integrated neighborhoods. But is this process of self-selection really driving the relationship between neighborhood racial composition and racial attitudes? And, if so, then how do we account for the fact that whites who prefer all-white neighborhoods vary more in their feeling toward some minority groups than toward others, while whites who live in all-white neighborhoods are consistently more hostile to all minority groups?

One way to answer these questions is to see how much the relationship between the racial composition of a neighborhood and a person's racial attitudes changes once his or her neighborhood racial preferences are considered. If residents of all-white neighborhoods are more hostile to minorities because people with racial biases are more likely to choose such places, then the strong relationship between neighborhood racial composition and racial attitudes should diminish once whites' neighborhood preferences are factored into the equation. To test this, the MCSUI data are used to compare the scores on racial stereotype indices by the percent white in the neighborhood across all four metropolitan areas.[3] Interestingly, controlling for neighborhood racial preferences has little impact on the effect of neighborhood racial composition on whites' attitudes toward Asians and Latinos—the changes in racial attitudes toward Asians and Latinos between white residents of all-white and nonwhite neighborhoods are virtually unaffected by the controls for neighborhood racial preference. Whites who live in all-white neighborhoods are still more negative toward Latinos and Asian Americans even when their preexisting preferences to live in all-white neighborhoods are considered. The increasing levels of white resentment toward Latinos and Asian Americans that appear as a neighborhood becomes more white are not attributable solely to racially biased neighborhood preferences.

Moreover, even the effect on whites' attitudes toward blacks is not solely attributable to their self-sorting into segregated neighborhoods.[4] Even when controlling for neighborhood racial preference, whites who live in all- white neighborhoods are still more likely to hold negative attitudes toward African Americans. Although the effects of neighborhood racial composition on negative out-group attitudes diminish slightly, particularly in Atlanta and Boston, they do not lose most of their size or statistical significance. And, among Detroit residents, controlling for neighborhood racial preferences actually increases the extent of the relationship between neighborhood racial composition and negative attitudes toward blacks. Once Detroit's whites' neighborhood preferences are considered, a greater difference in racial attitudes between residents of nonwhite and all-white areas actually exists.

These findings suggest that self-selection is undoubtedly a small contributing factor to the higher levels of white racial resentment in all-white neighborhoods. Whites who have a strong aversion to minorities are going to express this aversion in their residential choice. But self-selection is not the sole reason why more negative attitudes toward minorities exist in all-white neighborhoods. It probably is not even the most important reason. Whites' neighborhood racial preferences still do not account for most of the differences in whites' racial attitudes across neighborhood settings. Self-selection effects are greatest among whites' attitudes toward blacks. Not only is the relationship between a preference for white neighborhoods stronger with the measure of antiblack affect than with the measure of anti-Asian or anti-Latino affect, but the attenuating effect of controlling for white neighborhood preferences is stronger on the relationship between neighborhood racial composition and attitudes toward blacks. Simply put, whites who live in all-white neighborhoods are partly there because of their racial hostility, but it is a racial hostility aimed primarily at African Americans. The comparatively high level of racial resentment among whites in all-white neighborhoods toward Latino and Asian Americans as well as blacks must come from some other source.

Conclusion

People who live in segregated neighborhoods are more likely to be racially hostile toward other races but, among nonwhites, this is not because racists are disproportionately sorting themselves into same-race neighborhoods. Indeed, for most minorities, the preference for a same-race neighborhood does not always correspond with animosity toward other groups. Among minorities, the choice of a predominantly minority neighborhood may result from an avoidance of white racism, a desire for ethnic solidarity, or simply a limited choice of housing options in a racially biased real estate market. The fact that racial attitudes vary in systematic ways across environments, despite the absence of a clear rationale for self-selection, suggests that some other factor must be linking nonwhite attitudes to the social composition of their neighborhood.

The only group whose geographic distribution of racial attitudes can be explained by self-selection is whites. Among whites, the choice of an all-white neighborhood does typically correspond with a greater aversion toward minorities. Furthermore, much of the difference in racial attitudes between whites in segregated versus integrated neighborhoods can be explained by their residential preference, particularly with respect to their views of African Americans. In other words, once whites' racial neighborhood preferences are taken into account, there is less of a sharp relationship between living in a segregated neighborhood and having more negative racial views about blacks, although a similar effect does not occur for whites' views about Latinos or Asians. Self-selection accounts for part of the geographic differences in whites' attitudes, although it seems to occur only with respect to their views of blacks. From the data available, it does not explain the differences in racial attitudes found among any of the other groups.

For advocates of racial harmony, these findings provide a reason for hope. After all, if the self-selection hypothesis is correct, then the deep levels of racial segregation across most American metropolitan areas would belie a tremendous level of latent racial hostility. As most Americans may realize the prohibitions of expressing racial hostility in public, the self-selection notion would see them expressing their racially negative views in their residential choice. For the most part, however, this is not the case. Even though people who live in segregated neighborhoods tend to be more racially negative, this is not simply a reflection of a geographic sorting among people by virtue of their racial attitudes. The high levels of segregation, particularly among different minority groups, are often as not more strongly related to a sense of in-group affiliation. They may also arise from minorities seeking to avoid white hostility. There may be a strong undercurrent of racial animosity in the United States today as some suggest, but high levels of segregation by themselves are not proof of its existence.

CHAPTER FIVE

Interracial Civic and Social Contact in Multiethnic America

If geographic self-selection does not explain completely why people who live in integrated neighborhoods are less racially averse, then what can? Adherents of Gordon Allport's hypotheses about racial contact may feel they have the answer: positive social contact with people of other races. People who live in racially mixed neighborhoods may be more tolerant of other groups because their daily social experiences and interactions offset their socially learned prejudices. Although the contact hypothesis has been much criticized, recent studies have demonstrated positive effects of interracial contact on whites' attitudes toward minority groups (Forbes 1997; Jackman and Crane 1986; Dixon 2006; McLaren 2003). Presumably, these same processes will work for other races as well, particularly on the relationship among Asians, blacks, and Latinos. From this perspective, contact with the newly emerging racial groups may be a crucial mechanism for offsetting the inevitable tensions that will arise with America's growing racial diversity.

In this regard, racially integrated neighborhoods may be an ideal setting for promoting better racial understanding. Living in close proximity with people of other races will mean that people have greater opportunities for social interactions with one another. With time, the theory goes, neighbors get a chance to know each other, develop friendships, and share an identity as residents of the same place. For example, residents of integrated neighborhoods such as Hyde Park in Chicago or Fort Greene in New York may develop a common identity as neighbors that may transcend their previous feelings of ethnic or racial difference. In an increasingly diverse America, as people come to be surrounded by neighbors of other races, such racial misconceptions and stereotypes may begin to recede.

And indeed this is what some research suggests. In perhaps the most authoritative study of neighborhood contexts and whites' racial attitudes, political scientist Susan Welch and her colleagues find that as the racial mix of a neighborhood increases, so does the likelihood that whites will have both casual interracial contact as well as close friends who are of different races (Welch et al. 2001). They find that whites living in racially integrated neighborhoods are less likely to adhere to racially hostile stereotypes or be opposed to interracial marriage than those who live in all-white neighborhoods. Finally, and most importantly, they report that many of the differences in whites' racial attitudes across neighborhoods are attributable to their levels of interracial social contact. Once the higher level of interracial contact among whites in racially mixed neighborhoods is considered, the differences in levels of racial hostility across neighborhoods diminish significantly.

This research is very suggestive about the geographic patterns of racial attitudes that are evident in the preceding chapters.[1] If the same processes that Welch and her colleagues found in Detroit are applicable for all races, then the higher levels of racial tolerance in integrated neighborhoods found in chapter 3 may be the consequence of more integrated patterns of social contact. People in integrated neighborhoods may be more racially tolerant because people in integrated neighborhoods are more likely to have interracial social ties.

But while this interpretation of the data has obvious appeal, in reality, tracking the impact of interracial contact in a multiethnic society like the United States is a very difficult matter. The biggest weakness in many studies linking interracial contact and racial tolerance is in specifying what kind of contact is taking place. Take, for example, the Welch et al. study. Despite its robust findings, it did not specify or measure where, exactly, the interracial contact was taking place; rather the authors simply infer that exposure to other groups promotes racial understanding. Many social psychologists would disagree with this conclusion, noting that simple contact with other races will not necessarily generate racial understanding and, in some cases, will exacerbate racial tensions; rather, they argue that interracial contact needs to be under very specific conditions for it to have its beneficial effects, conditions that include people being in positions of equal status, having shared goals, and maintaining repeated interactions over time. Otherwise, interracial propinquity may simply cause greater tension (Forbes 1997; Pettigrew 1998). For example, a recent study of Indian ethnic relations concluded that simply having high levels of interethnic socializing did not reduce ethnic hostility (Varshnay 2001). Instead, it was the participation in integrated civic associations that was the key factor in preventing ethnic strife.

If interracial contact only works under very specific circumstances, then it is essential to identify what types of contact most Americans are having with people of other races and whether that contact is affected by their racial surroundings. And, if interracial contact truly is a crucial mechanism for promoting racial understanding in both integrated neighborhoods and the nation at large, then we need to identify just what types of interracial contact various groups in the United States are having with each other, how this contact is shaped by their racial surroundings, and what impact it has on their views of other groups.

This chapter examines the types of interracial contact among America's four major racial groups and how they are affected by a neighborhood's racial composition. Residents of more integrated neighborhoods are more likely to have interracial friendship groups and belong to more interracial civic associations, particularly if they are white. Furthermore, among whites, these patterns of contact account for some of the geographic differences in their racial attitudes. But these findings also raise many important questions about the extent and nature of interracial contact in the United States, questions that lead to many uncomfortable conclusions regarding the future of its race relations.

Measuring Interracial Contact in a Multiethnic Society

Although the idea that interracial contact can promote understanding has a very strong normative allure, wide-scale evidence in support of this proposition has been an elusive quarry. Most studies of interracial contact have been based on psychological experiments with rather small groups of participants and it is difficult to know whether their results hold outside of laboratory-like conditions. Part of the problem arises from the variety of social interactions that take place in a large and complex society. Most people experience a wide assortment of social interactions that can range from short and fleeting to complex and intimate, from positive or life changing to negative and mundane. In one setting, I may meet a person who confounds all my negative expectations about his or her particular group only to have such new perspectives clouded by a negative experience with someone else. The greatest difficulty is determining a threshold for which one might consider a particular social interaction to be meaningful enough to influence one's previously held conceptions and worldviews.

In response to this problem, social psychologists have added a host of additional specifications to Allport's original theories about under which circumstances contact will be beneficial. Some claim, for example, that initial views of other groups must not be too severe, while others suggest that contact in some contexts does not work as well as in others (Brewer and Miller 1988). In his review of the literature, psychologist Thomas Pettigrew specifies the most crucial conditions under which social contact must occur for a transformative process to take place: both parties must be of an equivalent social position, both parties must be working together in pursuit of a common end, the contact should be voluntary and long in duration, and the contact should be meaningful and extend beyond the immediate situation (Pettigrew 1998). Thus, for example, casual contact between a black customer in a hardware store and a Latino salesclerk should not have an effect on their racial views because the parties are not equal and the contact not voluntary nor long lasting; conversely, a black woman and a Latina playing together on a softball team would presumably be in an ideal setting for overcoming previous prejudices toward each other's group.

This, however, leads to a second problem: how should we measure the levels of interracial social interaction that most Americans experience in their daily lives? Although other researchers have used national survey data to measure patterns of social interaction, the indicators usually have been limited to one dimension of contact, such as listing how many friends or acquaintances of other races a person has. Such items are rough measures at best, and it is not always clear how much they are capturing the dynamics of contact among different groups; yet with survey methodology, it is hard to obtain more accurate depictions of people's social interactions than relying on their own self-reports, and any measurement of the interracial social life of the average American is thus highly constrained.

These methodological issues become even more complex when we consider the patterns of multiethnic growth in the United States. The fastest growing minority populations, Latinos and Asian Americans, are not evenly distributed across the country but tend to be most heavily concentrated in the Southwest, on the West Coast, or in a handful of metropolitan areas like New York, Miami, and Chicago. As a result, opportunities for contact among these different groups tend to be skewed: whites in South Dakota have few opportunities to encounter Asian Americans, blacks in

Alabama have little exposure to Latinos, Cubans in Miami see almost no Filipinos or Mexicans, and so on. Similarly limited opportunities for contact occur at the neighborhood level. Remember, most Americans live in predominantly same-race neighborhoods: the overwhelming majority of whites live in neighborhoods that are at least 85 percent white, and most African Americans live in neighborhoods that are usually more than 60 percent black. Latinos and Asian Americans may be slightly more integrated into white society, although many are sequestered in ethnic enclaves and barrios.

Such segregation patterns may have a profound influence on the likelihood of having meaningful interracial contact. After all, for most people, social contact begins literally in their backyard: people with school-aged children, for example, often tend to socialize with other parents in their neighborhood as their children play together; community groups, churches, and other types of civic associations draw their memberships from their immediate surroundings; and even many workplaces are staffed with people in close proximity. Cumulatively, this means that most folks who live in segregated neighborhoods or suburbs have few opportunities, at home, at church, in their civic lives, or even at work, for positive interracial contact. Much of their exposure to people of other races would either be incidental contact in public places or through the media, which itself might generate a host of negative consequences. Like studying racial attitudes, studying patterns of interracial contact makes little sense unless one also takes into account the makeup of people's racial environments.

Finally, the opportunities for interracial contact also vary considerably by individual differences in employment, education, English-language ability, and race. The number of friends, the likelihood of joining a voluntary organization, employment, and place of residence all vary as a direct result of education. Similarly, new immigrants to America who lack English language skills will be highly constrained in their ability to mingle with people outside of their own ethnic groups. Most importantly, a person's race is the biggest predictor of what type of contact he or she may have. For many whites in America, particularly those in states with few minorities or in segregated areas, contact with people of other races is uncommon; meanwhile, among minority groups in America, some level of interracial contact is all but inevitable. Contact among minorities or between whites and minorities can vary considerably by region and ethnicity. Asians, as a much smaller minority, are far more likely to encounter blacks or Latinos than vice versa. Given the asymmetric sizes of various ethnic groups in the United States, we should also expect to see similar asymmetries in the patterns of social interaction.

In short, trying to measure overall patterns of interracial contact in a society as large and diverse as the United States, much less their effects on people's racial attitudes, is a difficult proposition. We must look at different venues of contact, at different levels of geography, and at differences among the various racial groups. Most importantly, we need to take into account the racial composition of people's neighborhoods and metropolitan areas. Our first step, therefore, is to determine not only where and how Americans are interacting with other races but how these patterns vary with the racial composition of people's neighborhoods. To this we can look to data from national surveys.

Interracial Contact in Multiethnic America

Our empirical investigation starts with some general statistics on the levels of interracial contact occurring among the four major racial groups in the United States. Figure 5.1 lists the percentage of respondents in the NPS and CID surveys who report having interracial contact in four different contexts: among friends, among people they interact with at work, in their neighborhood, and in civic organizations. For each of these venues,

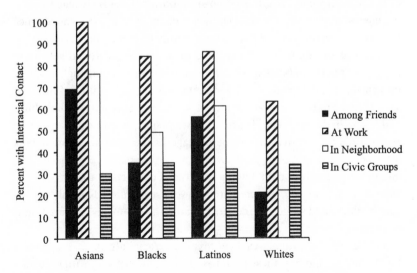

FIGURE 5.1 Interracial contact in various contexts by individual race (2005 CID).

the survey respondents were asked to estimate whether they were mostly of one race or different races (which they could specify). Although this measure is highly subjective, it can provide a rough indicator of the diversity across different social settings.

There are substantial differences in interracial contact that occur not only by individual race but by venue as well. Looking at differences by racial group, whites have the lowest levels of racial diversity in their social contacts. Only 22 percent of whites report having more than one in ten of their friends or neighbors as being of another race, compared with over 70 percent of Asian Americans, 35 percent of blacks, and 56 percent of Latinos. Among employed whites, substantially more (63 percent) have interracial contact at work. Among minorities, Asians and Latinos have substantially higher percentages of interracial contact among friends and neighbors than African Americans, although all have very high levels of interracial contact at work sites. Interestingly, all four racial groups have very similar levels of interracial contact among their civic organizations: roughly one in three respondents from each group belonged to a club or organization with more than 10 percent of its members from another race. Most importantly, whites, the largest racial group in America, are far more racially isolated than any minority population. In the CID survey, 12 percent of the white respondents reported no interracial contacts in any of the four venues listed above, compared with less than 3 percent of Asians, blacks, or Latinos. As we will see, this finding is important because it suggests that the biggest impact of interracial contact is likely to be among whites, since this is the group afforded the least opportunity to meet other races.

In terms of venue for contact, the most integrated social setting in America appears to be at work, although minorities report high levels of interracial friendship and neighbor contacts. Large majorities of the CID sample reported interracial contact at work, and only half of the whites and blacks in the NPS sample said their work sites were mostly same race. Interestingly, a relatively small percentage of the sample report having interracial experiences in their civic lives—in no instance did a third of any racial group reporting having interracial contacts in their voluntary associations. Similarly, churches are also very segregated. Roughly 70 percent of blacks and whites attend mostly same-race churches, a figure that is 60 percent for Latinos and nearly 50 percent for Asian Americans.

Given how important social context is for racial attitudes, it is important to understand how these patterns of social contact vary with the racial composition of people's neighborhoods. Although the NPS data do not

TABLE 5.1 **Interracial friendship patterns by neighborhood racial percentages**

	Has Asian friend	Has black friend	Has Latino friend	Has white friend
Whites in a neighborhood that is:				
<80% White	50	69	57	
80%–95% White	41	66	49	
>95% White	30	55	33	
Blacks in a neighborhood that is:				
<15% Black	33		52	79
15%–40% Black	30		44	78
>40% Black	24		41	70
Latino citizens in a neighborhood that is:				
<15% Latino	45	70		85
15%–40% Latino	40	62		76
>40% Latino	38	60		73
Latino noncitizens in a neighborhood that is:				
<15% Latino	21	33		54
15%–40% Latino	17	24		52
>40% Latino	18	22		50
Asian citizens in a neighborhood that is:				
<5% Asian		62	53	83
6%–20% Asian		53	56	81
>20% Asian		54	52	71
Asian noncitizens in a neighborhood that is:				
<5% Asian		45	25	72
6%–20% Asian		40	30	69
>20% Asian		46	33	67

Source: 2000 SCCBS.

have geographic markers and the CID data do not offer enough cases to track the changes in social contact for all four groups, the SCCBS data do have one item, friendship patterns, that allow for contextual analysis. Table 5.1 lists the percent of whites, blacks, Latinos, and Asian Americans in the SCCBS data set claiming to have a "personal friend" of another race by the percent of their own group in their neighborhood. Because minorities make up differing portions of the population, the neighborhood racial percentages are not identically scaled. In addition, because of the heavily immigrant portion of the Latino and Asian populations, they are divided among citizens and noncitizens.

Looking at friendship patterns across neighborhoods, it is clear that the color of one's neighbors has a strong relationship with the racial diversity of one's friends. For all four racial groups, significant differences exist both in their levels of interracial friendship and in the friendship patterns across neighborhoods—people who live in more racially mixed neighborhoods tend to have more interracial friendship ties.[2] For example, there are tremendous differences in whites' interracial friendship patterns by the percent white within their neighborhood. Those living in neighborhoods that were under 80 percent white were nearly twice as likely in some instances to report having a friend of another race than those in neighborhoods over 95 percent white. In addition, 50 percent of whites in a racially mixed neighborhood reported having an Asian friend, compared with only 30 percent in a segregated neighborhood; for those with Latino friends, there was a difference that was similarly large (57 versus 33 percent). Whites' friendship patterns with blacks also varied by these patterns of segregation, although the difference is not as great. Sixty-nine percent of whites in diverse neighborhoods report having a black friend, versus only 55 percent of whites in predominantly white neighborhoods, results that are similar to what occurs across metropolitan areas. Nevertheless, the trend is still the same: the whiter the neighborhood, the less likely its white residents will have a friend who is a minority group member.

The SCCBS data also show similar differences in blacks' interracial friendship patterns. Blacks who live in neighborhoods with a lower percentage of blacks (under 15 percent black) are much more likely, on average, to have interracial friendship ties. For example, in this group, 33 percent of blacks reported being friends with an Asian American, 52 percent reported a Latino friend, and 79 percent reported having a white friend. By contrast, among blacks in predominantly black neighborhoods (over 40 percent black), only 24 percent reported an Asian friend, 41 percent a Latino friend, and 70 percent a white friend.

What is most striking about just these two groups are notable differences in interracial friendship patterns: whites are more likely to have Asian friends than blacks, blacks are more likely to have white friends than vice versa. These differences in friendship patterns make sense given the patterns of racial segregation between the groups. Whites and Asian Americans are both highly segregated from African Americans and are relatively integrated with each other. Similarly, the United States is nearly 70 percent white and only 13 percent black, thus blacks are going to have many more opportunities for contact (and friendship) with whites. Indeed, this will be the case with all minorities in the United States; by virtue of the size of the white majority, Asians, Latinos, and blacks will all have more opportunities for interracial contact than the white population does.

Latino friendship patterns also vary according to their racial surroundings, although, as one might expect, there are considerable differences also by virtue of citizenship. Among Latino citizens who live in neighborhoods with fewer Latinos (under 15 percent), 45 percent report an Asian friend, 70 percent report a black friend, and 85 percent report a white friend; among Latino citizens in predominantly Latino neighborhoods, these percentages are 38, 60, and 73, respectively. However, among Latino noncitizens, the neighborhood differences are much smaller (for example, only 4 percentage points in the percentages reporting Asian or white friends); more importantly, the rates of interracial friendship are also much lower than among Latino citizens. On average, 41 percent of Latino citizens report having an Asian friend compared with only 19 percent of noncitizens; 68 percent of citizens report a black friend compared with only 27 percent of noncitizens; and 79 percent of citizens report a white friend compared with only 52 percent of noncitizens. While neighborhood racial segregation is important for Latinos' interracial friendship ties, their levels of citizenship (that is, incorporation) are much more important.

This same pattern is also evident for Asian Americans. Small differences exist in Asians' interracial friendship patterns by the percent Asian in their neighborhood. Among Asian American citizens, those who live in neighborhoods with small percentages of Asians are more likely to have interracial friendship ties across all groups than those who live in neighborhoods that are at least 20 percent Asian. Yet these differences pale in comparison with those between citizens and noncitizens. Asian American citizens were nearly twice as likely to have Latino friends and much more likely to have black and white friends than noncitizens.

Clearly then, people who live in more racially diverse neighborhoods are more likely to have interracial friendship ties. Although there are differences by individual races and particularly large gaps between citizens and noncitizens among Asian Americans and Latinos, the patterns here are consistent with the expectations of the contact hypothesis. Moreover, multivariate analyses also show that these patterns are not the result of individual-level differences either. When the measures of interracial friendship are regressed on a set of predictors that include the percent Latino in the neighborhood as well as controls for individual-level education, age, homeownership, length of residence, political knowledge, citizenship, and neighborhood income, the effects of neighborhood racial status persist. For whites, blacks, and Latinos, as the percent of their own race in their neighborhood increases, the likelihood that they will report an interracial friendship declines.

A similar pattern is also evident when the racial composition of people's civic life is considered. Selecting respondents in the SCCBS who say they belong to a voluntary organization, I compared the percent who say their organization has an interracial membership with the percent of their own race in their neighborhood.[3] People who live in more racially diverse neighborhoods are far more likely to report belonging to an integrated civic association. Forty percent of civically active whites in diverse neighborhoods belong to an integrated organization, as opposed to only 23 percent in segregated neighborhoods. For blacks, these percentages are 54 and 43; for Latinos, they are 62 and 47; and for Asian Americans, they are 73 and 64.[4] Irrespective of the individual's race, the pattern is remarkably similar—people who live in integrated neighborhoods are much more likely to have interracial civic ties than people who live in more segregated places.

In sum, most Americans have some regular level of interracial contact, although the extent of this contact and where this contact occurs depend largely on their race and where they live. Among Asian American and Latino citizens, interracial friendship and work contact with whites is more the rule than not; in both cases, a majority report having at least one friend of the other three major ethnic groups. Among noncitizens, contact is much lower, particularly with other minority groups. Yet, for Asians and Latinos, incorporation into American society via citizenship corresponds with a very integrated social life. The same cannot be said, however, of blacks and whites. Although a significant portion of African Americans report having at least one white friend and some interracial contact at work, most black friendship and neighbor contacts are largely black. Whites are even more racially isolated. Although a slim majority of whites claim to have at least one black friend, the social diversity of whites' friendship and neighborhood contact remains much lower than among minority groups. Partly this is attributable to the relatively large size of the American white population, but much of this is demonstrably linked to their higher levels of neighborhood segregation. The fact that whites who live in integrated neighborhoods are at least 15 percentage points more likely to have a friend of another race indicates the massive impact that racial segregation has on white contact with people of other races.

Contact and Racial Attitudes

Americans who live in more integrated neighborhoods are more likely to have meaningful interracial contact, but is this what makes them less racially hostile? The answer to this question depends on whether this contact then corresponds with lower levels of racial animosity. After all, social psychologists are quick to point out that mere contact is not sufficient for reducing racial animosities. There are plenty of places, such as schools and prisons, where high levels of interracial contact lead to greater mistrust and hatred. If the neighborhood differences in social contact are behind the differences in racial attitudes, then we need to first ascertain whether contact is making people more racially tolerant.

Unfortunately, here is where we run into the limitations of survey data. Although the data from these surveys are consistent with the idea that contact makes people more racially tolerant, they cannot provide conclusive evidence of a causal linkage. Consider, for example, the relationship between interracial friendships and opposition to interracial marriage as found in the SCCBS data. People without interracial friendships are significantly more opposed to interracial marriage, a level that is often twice as high as it is for those who have friends of other races: 25 percent of Asian respondents without black friends are opposed to someone in their family marrying a black person, compared with only 11 percent of those with black friends; 15 percent of blacks with no white friends are opposed to interracial marriage with whites, compared with only 8 percent of those with white friends. Such differences were evident across all racial groups. In nearly every case, people without interracial friendship ties are nearly twice as likely to be opposed to interracial marriage. Yet is impossible to know from these data whether the interracial friendship is responsible for lowering one's opposition to interracial marriage or whether racially tolerant people are simply more likely to be open to or report having friends of other races. After all, if a person is opposed to having a family member marry someone of another race, it seems likely that such a person would also be resistant to forming friendships with that group as well.

Another reason to be suspicious of these findings is that interracial contact seems to make people more racially tolerant in general rather than toward any specific group. For example, according to the SCCBS data, people with interracial friendships are also less opposed to interracial marriage as well. Asians, Latinos, and whites all express the highest levels of opposition to interracial marriage with blacks; yet among these groups, opposition to interracial marriage with blacks is much less for those with interracial friendship ties, even if they are not black. Asians and Latinos with white friends are far less opposed to interracial marriage with blacks as are whites with Asian and Latino friends. These findings indicate that simply being friends with someone of another race is strongly predictive of one's racial views across the board. This trend toward a more generalized racial liberalism among those with interracial friendship ties, however, does not necessarily conform to the expectations of the contact hypothesis, which is based on attitudes toward specific groups. In other words, the contact hypothesis suggests that being friends with a white person is supposed to only change your attitudes about whites, not necessarily about other groups.

Slightly better evidence in support of the contact hypothesis can be found in the CID and NPS data, although once again they are not definitive. From the CID data, I examined how agreement with racial stereotypes varied according to the diversity in someone's friendship groups, workplace and neighbor interactions, or their organizations.[5] Looking at blacks, Latinos, and whites, a strongly consistent pattern is evident— people who have integrated contact, irrespective of whether it is at work, at home, or in their voluntary organizations, also report lower levels of negative traits associated with other groups. Among whites, the greatest differences occurred between those in integrated versus homogenous civic groups: whites in homogeneous organizations report the highest negative stereotype scores, on average, while those in integrated organizations report the lowest. Among Latinos, a similar pattern exists—Latinos who have integrated friendship groups, workplaces, and neighborhoods all express less negative views of other minority groups, particularly in regards to African Americans. Among African Americans, a slightly more complicated pattern was evident. Diverse friendship groups only relate to more positive attitudes about whites but have little relationship toward attitudes about Asians or Latinos. The venues in which interracial contact seems to have the most salutary relationship with black attitudes toward other groups are workplaces and civic organizations. As with whites, blacks who interact with other races at work or who belong to integrated civic groups have far more positive attitudes about other groups, particularly other minorities, than those in racially homogeneous settings.

The NPS data also have findings that are consistent with the contact hypothesis. Table 5.2 lists the percentage of respondents reporting feeling close to racial groups and zero-sum competition with other groups (these measures are described in chapter 2), comparing those with racially diverse and homogeneous friendship networks. With no exceptions, respondents with diverse friendship groups and work settings were more likely to feel close to other races or report less zero-sum conflict with other groups. For instance, 68 percent of Latinos with diverse friendships

TABLE 5.2 Comparative perspectives on racial closeness, competition, solidarity, perceived discrimination, and immigration-related issues among racial groups by interracial friendship patterns

	Asians (percent)		Blacks (percent)		Latinos (percent)		Whites (percent)	
	Only Asian friends	Racially mixed friends	Only black friends	Racially mixed friends	Only Latino friends	Racially mixed friends	Only white friends	Racially mixed friends
Feel close with Asians	87	85	39	48	36	46	51	64
Feel close with blacks	39	52	92	90	47	68	65	83
Feel close with Latinos	41	50	65	73	—	—	54	74
Feel close with whites	65	83	52	71	65	79	94	91
Zero-sum competition with Asians	—	—	49	47	47	33	22	15
Zero-sum competition with blacks	50	39	—	—	47	35	24	15
Zero-sum competition with Latinos	45	35	49	44	—	—	25	18
Zero-sum competition with whites	78	61	75	63	65	58	—	—
N	447		720		716		873	

Source: 2004 NPS.

reported feeling close to blacks, compared with only 47 percent of Latinos with same-race friends; 74 percent of whites with racially mixed friendships reported feeling close to Latinos, compared with only 54 percent of those with only white friends. Even more interesting, those who worked in settings that had specific members of other groups were typically more likely to report feeling close to that group. For example, only 56 percent of whites reported feeling close to either Asians or Latinos if they worked in an all-white workplace, compared with the 80 percent who work in places where Asians or Latinos work.

Finally, the NPS data allow us to further examine the impact of contact by comparing racial attitudes among Asians and Latinos by virtue of their levels of incorporation. Figure 5.2 depicts the percent of Asians and Latinos who report feeling close to other groups by whether they have same-race friends and if they were raised abroad, for Asians, or if they were interviewed in Spanish, for Latinos. The effects of incorporation on racial attitudes are clearly mediated by levels of interracial contact. For example, Asians who were raised abroad and have only Asian friends have the lowest rates of feeling close to other groups, while Asians raised in America with diverse friendships report the highest rates. These trends are not surprising. However, Asians who were raised abroad but have interracial friendships tend to feel closer to blacks and whites than Asians raised in America with homogeneous friendship ties. In other words, having racially mixed friends seems to be more important for Asian perceptions of blacks and whites than being raised in the United States. The same pattern holds for Latinos. Having friends of other racial groups corresponds more strongly with feeling close to those groups than whether one was interviewed in English or Spanish.

On the whole, all of these findings show a strong correlation between interracial contact and racial tolerance. By and large, people who live in more integrated neighborhoods, work in more integrated jobs, or have integrated friendship networks generally feel closer and exhibit lower levels of racial animus toward other groups. Undoubtedly, many of these findings reflect patterns of self-selection. People with liberal racial views, by definition, are going to be more open to having friends of other races, joining racially integrated civic organizations, and generally entertaining more racially diverse experiences.[6] Yet the difference in racial attitudes across work sites would speak against the idea that these patterns are purely an expression of self-selection. Most people do not choose their place of work based on how much contact they have with people of other races. The fact that people in integrated work sites are consistently less hostile

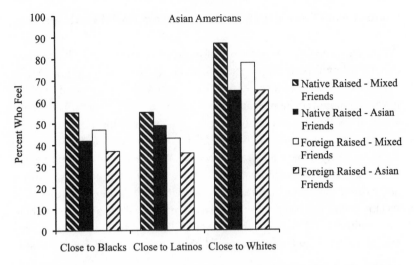

FIGURE 5.2A Feelings of closeness to other racial groups by incorporation levels and inter-racial friendship patterns for Asian Americans and Latinos (2004 NPS).

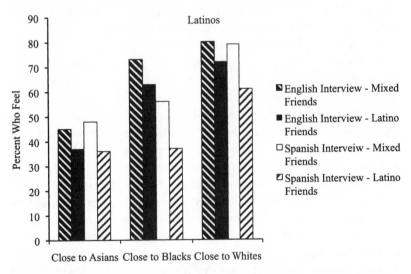

FIGURE 5.2B Feelings of closeness to other racial groups by incorporation levels and inter-racial friendship patterns for Asian Americans and Latinos, continued (2004 NPS).

to other races lends strong credence to the idea that regular contact lowers racial misperception. So given our confidence that racial contact may be affecting people's racial attitudes, our next question is whether contact is behind the neighborhood differences in racial attitudes we found in chapter 3.

Contact and Differences in Attitudes across Racial Environments

As we have seen so far, residents of integrated neighborhoods are more racially tolerant than those in segregated ones. According to the contact hypothesis, this is because people in integrated places are more likely to have meaningful social interactions with people of other races. The results above show that residents of integrated neighborhoods, no matter what their own race, are more likely to be friends with people of other races and are more likely to have interracial civic ties. We have also seen that people with interracial friendship patterns and people in integrated associations and workplaces and who interact with neighbors of other races are more racially tolerant. Thus if these patterns of interracial social ties are behind the neighborhood differences in racial attitudes, it would provide confirmation of the benefits of interracial contact that come from integrated settings.

But do these greater levels of interracial contact among residents of racially mixed neighborhoods contribute to their greater level of racial tolerance? Or, conversely, does the absence of interracial contact among residents of racially isolated neighborhoods fuel their greater racial resentment? The answer to these questions hinges on the idea that interracial contact and civic ties correspond with greater racial tolerance. Unfortunately, the data sets available for this book cannot provide an adequate test for this proposition, particularly among minority groups.[7] We simply do not have a large enough sample of minorities in the CID data set or an adequate selection of measures in the other data sets to estimate how much the relationship between racial contexts and racial attitudes is affected by structured contact for all races. Consequently, to test this claim any further, the analysis will have to focus solely on whites.

Looking just at whites, we can try to estimate how much neighborhood differences in racial attitudes are affected by taking into account their interracial social contacts in the SCCBS data. To estimate this I ran ordinary least squares (OLS) regressions estimating the effects of neighborhood and metropolitan racial composition on opposition to interracial marriage, along with a set of controls for individual-level variables such as education, age, homeownership, and so on, before and after additional measures for whether the white respondent has a black friend and belongs to a racially mixed civic association.[8] As with the cross tabulations presented in chapter 3, white opposition to interracial marriage with all minority groups increases with the percent of whites in the neighborhood and decreases with the percent of whites in the metropolitan area. However, once the friendship and associational ties of the white respondent are taken into account, these trends attenuate. Across all three equations, the difference in white opposition to interracial marriage between residents of all-white and racially mixed neighborhoods shrinks once the personal and associational contacts with other races are considered. For example, before the interracial social contact is controlled for, the OLS equations predict a 12-percentage-point difference in opposition to interracial marriage between residents of the least and most white neighborhoods. After controlling for interracial contacts, this difference is only 7 percentage points. Although there is still greater opposition to interracial marriage in all-white neighborhoods even with the controls for social contact, the difference in attitudes is not nearly as great. In the instance of attitudes toward interracial marriage with Latinos, the difference is no longer statistically significant.

Interestingly, however, controlling for social contacts has no effect on the differences across metropolitan areas in opposition to interracial marriage. In regards to white opposition to interracial marriage with all three racial groups, whites who live in racially mixed metropolitan areas are still more likely to oppose interracial marriage even when their interracial social contacts are considered. And this is consistent with both the hypotheses and earlier findings. The effects of interracial contact are relative to microcontexts, such as neighborhoods and voluntary organizations. Interracial contact, either as friendships or within voluntary organizations, varies significantly across neighborhood racial contexts but not so much by metropolitan area. Although whites in racially mixed metropolitan areas were slightly more likely to have interracial contacts than those in predominantly white metropolitan areas, these differences were not nearly as great as they were across neighborhoods. The effects of interracial contact mediate only the differences in racial attitudes that occur across neighborhoods because neighborhoods themselves are the primary geographic unit that influences interracial social patterns.

Conclusion

The findings in this chapter provide evidence that is consistent, if not conclusive, with the hypothesis that interracial contact may underlie some of the differences in racial attitudes between people in racially mixed and all-white neighborhoods. As we would expect, people who live in more racially diverse areas have a more racially diverse set of social contacts. The extent of this interracial social exposure varies in relation to the relative sizes of each racial group. For the smallest and most integrated minority group, Asian Americans, exposure to whites and other minority groups occurs quite regularly, particularly for those who are culturally incorporated. A majority of Latinos also report extensive interracial social contacts, although this too varies: incorporated Latinos have much higher levels of interracial contact than unincorporated Latinos. The biggest differences in levels of social contact occur among blacks and whites. Unlike other minority groups, blacks are relatively more isolated in their social contacts—they are less likely to report interracial contacts at work or in their neighborhoods, and, compared with Asian and Latino citizens, they are less likely to report interminority friendships than vice versa. Whites too are less likely to report interracial experiences than minority groups, although much of this is a function of their relative population size. Nevertheless, in spite of these baseline asymmetries, a common trend occurs for all groups: the more segregated their immediate environment, the less likely they have interracial friends or interracial contact in their neighborhoods, work sites, or civic groups.

But while these findings are consistent with the contact hypothesis, we cannot ascertain whether these geographic differences in interracial social contact are causing changes in the geographic patterns of racial attitudes. First, because of data limitations, we can only test in the racial attitudes of whites. Among this group, there are reasonably consistent results: whites who are racially isolated in their neighborhoods are less likely to have interracial friendship ties or participate in interracial civic associations, and this absence of interracial contact accounts for some of their higher levels of opposition to interracial marriage. When the differences in interracial contact between neighborhoods are taken into account, much smaller differences in whites' racial attitudes come as a result of the racial composition of their neighborhood. The increased social contact between whites and minorities that occurs in integrated neighborhoods appears to be a significant factor correlated to the reduction of whites' negative racial attitudes; however, because these are cross-sectional survey data, this does not provide a very good test of causality.

The data for nonwhites are even less conclusive. On the one hand, Asians, Latinos, and blacks who live in predominantly same-race neighborhoods are far less likely to have friends of other races and are less likely to participate in integrated civic associations. As with their white counterparts, neighborhood racial isolation translates into more racially segregated socializing patterns. Because of the limitations in the available data, the question remains whether these differences in social contact are responsible for the higher levels of racial resentment toward other groups. However, if their racial attitudes are affected by racial environments in the same way as with whites (and the findings above give every indication of this), then it seems quite likely that at least part of the geographic difference in minorities' racial attitudes can be attributed to the higher levels of social isolation in racially segregated neighborhoods. Having fewer cooperative contacts with people of other races, minorities in segregated neighborhoods may have fewer opportunities to correct negative views of these groups and to continue to harbor racial resentments.

The patterns of racial contact among nonwhites might also explain why minorities' racial attitudes do not vary nearly as much across geography. As we saw in the findings above, a large majority of blacks and Latino and Asian American citizens report substantial contact and friendship levels with people of other races, much more so than whites. Even the most segregated minority member, by living in a predominantly white society, is likely to have more interracial contact than a similarly segregated white person. Consequently, the near inevitability of interracial contact for most minorities means that, if the contact effect is occurring, their racial attitudes will be less sensitive to geographic differences than will those of whites.

Taken together, these findings are very suggestive about the detrimental effects of segregation, particularly for whites, in promoting racial understanding. If we assume that the contact patterns above are causally affecting people's racial attitudes, then one key issue in understanding the impact of segregation on racial attitudes is the way that neighborhood isolation creates a racially segregated social and civic life. Segregation is pernicious not simply because of its disparate impact on the health, education, and economic opportunity of minorities but because it socially isolates Americans from one another and contributes to greater misunderstanding among different groups. Segregation would seem to reinforce racial differences as it reinforces an apartheid of social and civic connections. If people only socialize or congregate with people of their own race or ethnicity, they enjoy few opportunities (and have few incentives) to correct their negative views of other groups. It appears that residential integration can foster more positive racial views, in part by cultivating a more integrated social world. However, even if one were to draw such inferences from what are admittedly inconclusive data, the issue of integration still needs to be considered in greater detail. As will be demonstrated in the next chapter, residential integration is a complicated phenomenon with many unintended by-products.

CHAPTER SIX

The Civic and Social Paradoxes of Neighborhood Racial Integration

Integration is a seductive concept. For most Americans, the image of different races and ethnicities peacefully coming together as a single community is enormously appealing. It epitomizes such classically liberal values as individual respect, justice, and equality before the law; segregation, by contrast, bespeaks of racism, apartheid, and centuries of injustice. But beyond this, integration seems to have some practical benefits, particularly in a multiracial country like the United States. People who live around other races are more tolerant, more likely to have interracial friendships and social contacts, and would seem to be better equipped to live in a larger, multicultural society. Given the high levels of residential segregation and mistrust among America's four major racial groups, integration may seem like a palliative for solving its many racial problems. Indeed, many commentators have suggested that the integration of neighborhoods and civic life is the best way to avoid racial confrontation in the future (Varshnay 2002; Welch et al. 2001). An integrated society, some believe, is not just peaceful, but a civically vibrant community as well.

But before rushing to this conclusion, we need to understand the complexity of integration, particularly in the United States. Since whites remain the largest racial group in the United States, integration inevitably will involve a great deal of minority penetration into predominantly white areas. Integration, under such circumstances, will mean different things for different people: for whites, integration means accepting a larger portion of neighbors as nonwhite; for most Asians, blacks, and Latinos, integration means leaving their own ethnic enclaves and moving into white neighborhoods.

   This type of integration, however, is rarely peaceful or easy. Historically, America's white population has fiercely resisted minority encroachment, and while the cross burnings, lynchings, and other violent measures perpetrated against minorities have declined significantly over the past decades, most whites, as illustrated in chapter 4, are still unwilling to accept all but a small number of minorities as neighbors (Meyer 2001). Consequently, for many minorities, moving into a white neighborhood often means facing ostracism, threats, and intimidation (Kryson and Farley 2002; Bobo and Zubrinsky 1996). In the face of such racial animosity, many minorities are quick to abandon white areas and seek same-race neighborhoods that are more welcoming (Clark 1992). In situations in which minorities do not leave, whites often depart, making neighborhoods "tip" racially from all white to all black or all Latino within a short period of time (Wilson and Taub 2006).

   The issue of integration is further complicated by the cultural and linguistic differences among its fast-growing Latino and Asian American populations. Since many Latinos and Asian Americans are immigrants with limited English language skills and different norms of social engagement, their interaction with American society may be quite limited or simply restricted to their own ethnic enclave. For instance, past research on ethnic differences in civic participation finds much lower levels of participation among Asian Americans and Latinos, which is often related to their language skills and familiarity with American cultural norms (Leighley and Vedlitz 1999; Wong 2006). In addition to being stymied by linguistic and cultural barriers, immigrants' community involvement may be reduced by the strong ties to the country of origin among many first-generation immigrants (Jones-Correa 1996). And just as the linguistic and cultural isolation of many immigrants provides incentives to segregate themselves geographically, these same factors may also inhibit their social incorporation even within more integrated settings. Some may even resist a greater social and civic incorporation for fear of losing their own distinct ethnic identity.

   In addition, we must consider the larger context of where and how different races in America live. A disproportionately large percentage of blacks and Latinos live below the poverty line, are concentrated in central cities, and have little financial capital. For these groups, housing options are highly limited, and the most likely paths of integration are through economically disadvantaged white neighborhoods or through Latinos migrating into black enclaves. Yet, even more than in middle-class neighborhoods, such migration patterns have been met with either violence, organized resistance, or massive white flight (Rieder 1987; Wilson and Taub 2006). The challenge of integration is further exacerbated by the suburbanization of the metropolitan population, where many predominantly white communities use zoning laws and other restrictions to keep lower income residents out. And, even if minorities are able to penetrate white, suburban neighborhoods, their efforts to find community may be further stymied by the unique social and civic dynamics that affect suburban civic life. Suburban neighborhoods are more likely to be dominated by antisocial architectural forms, be highly segregated by social class, and have relatively lower levels of civic interaction (Oliver 2001). If racial integration means moving to predominantly white areas, it also means the movement into suburban areas, areas that by virtue of their design, economic composition, and political homogeneity may limit the venues for meaningful social interaction and fostering community.

But perhaps the most important problem with our romantic notions about integration is that we have little understanding of how it works in practice, particularly for people's feelings of community and belonging. If our primary concern is building a sense of connection and shared purpose among America's different racial groups, then one of our crucial points of attention should be on how people in integrated settings experience community life. Yet this is a topic for which little research exists. Social scientists have largely overlooked whether civil society is affected by people's racial surroundings. Although a few studies have examined how blacks' feelings of group solidarity and civic involvement change with the racial composition of their environments, researchers have generally not examined whether feelings of community and civic attachment vary for all racial groups (Bledsoe et al. 1995; Cohen and Dawson 1993). As a result, many important questions remain unanswered. Are people in integrated neighborhoods more or less active in community affairs? Do Latinos and Asians who live in segregated barrios feel less tied to American civil society? Do feelings of community exacerbate or mitigate the higher feelings of racial animosity that exist in segregated neighborhoods?

This chapter examines how people's racial environments shape their involvement in community life. As with racial attitudes, feelings of community and civic engagement vary with a person's racial surroundings. But, unlike with racial attitudes, the impact of integration seems largely negative. Whites who live in integrated neighborhoods are less civically active, are less trusting of their neighbors, and feel a weaker sense of community than their counterparts in segregated places. Similarly, African Americans also express greater alienation as the percent of whites in their surroundings increases, although this is less the case for Asian Americans and Latinos, whose civic participation is shaped less by their social surroundings than by their levels of incorporation into American society—citizens and English speakers are far more active in their communities than noncitizens. These findings demonstrate that integration is a complicated process whose implications depend as much on one's individual racial identity as one's incorporation into a predominantly white American culture.

How Our Racial Environments Affect Our Feelings of Community and Civic Life

Over the past decades, Americans have become preoccupied with their civic life, or at least its putative decline. According to political scientist Robert Putnam's now famous argument, Americans are no longer joining civic organizations as they once did and America's stocks of social capital, the resources that amass from our connections with other people, are beginning to wane (Putnam 2000). With the growth of television, commuting times, and dual-income households, Americans are spending less discretionary time in community activities and more time by themselves. In Putnam's words, Americans are no longer joining bowling leagues but are now "bowling alone." This increasing social isolation putatively brings with it a host of negative consequences such as declining levels of interpersonal trust, social norms of respect for community, and sustained commitments to democratic ideals. This erosion of social capital is seen as a threat to both the health and integrity of American democratic society.

Interestingly, one factor that has gone unnoticed in the hoopla over America's diminishing social capital is its growing racial diversity. America may be a country where people are now bowling alone, and it may be a country made up of a larger number of racial and ethnic groups, but few people have sought to ask whether these phenomena are related. Most published research on the relationship between community heterogeneity and civic participation has come from economists using formal models to generate predictions about the relationships between social environments and individual behavior (e.g., Alesina and La Ferrara 2000). Although such mathematical models offer strong predictions, they provide very little information about the causal mechanisms linking context and behavior.

For instance, these models are usually based on the assumption of a social preference for being around people of similar races; in other words, social diversity imposes "costs" because individuals "prefer to interact with others like them because of shared interests, socialization to the same cultural norms, and greater empathy toward individuals who remind them of themselves" (Costa and Kahn 2003, 104). Yet this research provides no detailed evidence to justify these assumptions. The fact that heterogeneity corresponds with less civic engagement is simply taken as proof that the operating mechanisms are at work. This approach is unsatisfactory—not only does it preclude other explanations, but it is not grounded in any theory about civic participation or community life.

To understand how the racial composition of a social environment might affect people's participation in their communities, we must determine why people become involved in local affairs in the first place. In their authoritative study of civic participation in the United States, political scientists Sidney Verba, Kay Schlozman, and Henry Brady identified three factors that determine whether people get involved in local civic activities: resources, interest, and mobilization (Verba, Schlozman, and Brady 1995). People are far more likely to be active in their communities if they have more resources like time and money, if they are interested in a particular set of issues, or if they are asked by others to get involved.

From this perspective, we can see how America's growing racial diversity might affect its civic participation. First, people's feelings about their communities are likely to be shaped by their racial environment. As people live among more people of their own ethnicity or race, particularly in contrast to neighboring different groups, they are likely to have stronger feelings of group affiliation, what scholars commonly refer to as a sense of "ethnic community" (Bobo and Zubrinsky 1996; Dawson 1994). For example, a Latina may have little sense of ethnic community in her home country but feel a strong sense of ethnicity in a barrio of Los Angeles (Jones-Correa and Leal 1996). Researchers find that blacks who feel a greater sense of ethnic community are more likely to be active in volunteer organizations (Guterbock and London 1983). Conversely, people who feel racially ostracized or alienated from their neighbors may withdraw socially and keep to themselves. Feeling less in common with her neighbors, the resident of a heterogeneous community would be less interested in local or community affairs, feel less bound by community norms that encourage civic involvement, and be less motivated to join a local organization (Campbell 2006). Thus one of the first things we would need to consider is whether people in diverse settings have different perceptions of their community than people in homogeneous settings.

Second, racial diversity may constrain the social connections between neighbors and thus limit their opportunities to be mobilized into neighborhood life. Given the high levels of racial mistrust in the United States, people living in diverse settings may have fewer social bonds with their neighbors, which can, in turn, reduce the opportunities to become recruited for a local group. The importance of these social networks cannot be overstated; after all, most people get involved in local voluntary organizations because they are asked at some point to do so (Verba et al. 1995]). If people in diverse places are less familiar with their neighbors, the likelihood they will be recruited to join anything from a neighborhood association to the Rotary club will be significantly lower. When looking at the impact of racial surroundings on local organizational involvement, it is essential, therefore, to also look at the informal social ties between residents.

The other factor to consider when thinking about racial environments and community perceptions is the impact of an individual's race. Not all racial and ethnic groups in the United States perceive their communities or involve themselves in civic affairs in the same way. Past research has indicated that Latinos and Asian Americans are typically less engaged in many types of civic activities than whites and blacks (Wong 2006). Few studies, however, have sufficiently explained why such differences exist, whether these differences would translate across all community activities (or if they are simply relegated to political activities), or whether they are differentiated by other factors such as English language ability or citizenship.

Therefore, before going any further, it is important to examine some comparative data on levels of civic and social engagement by individual race and citizenship. Figure 6.1 displays the average scores by these criteria on four indicators of local social and civic activity in the NPS data. The local activities include an index measure of civic participation, an index score of informal social behavior, the percent of respondents who reported belonging to a neighborhood-based group or association, and the percent who reported working on a neighborhood project during the past year.[1]

Significant racial differences exist in rates of civic and social participation, although these vary significantly by citizenship and the type of activity in question. There are relatively minor differences among racial groups in terms of informally socializing with neighbors. Whites and minority citizens have slightly higher average informal social activity scores than

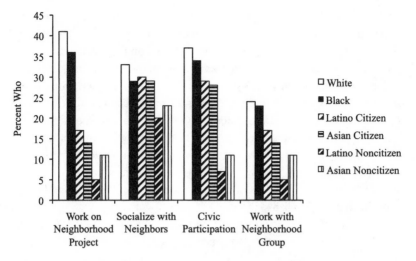

FIGURE 6.1 Civic participation rates by race and citizenship (2004 NPS).

minority noncitizens, but the interethnic differences are not very large. Given that this measure gauges mere informal socializing, we should not expect large differences across racial groups.

However, significant differences occur in more formal civic activity across racial groups. Whites and blacks tend to participate in civic activities at much higher rates than Latinos and Asians, particularly compared with noncitizens. For example, roughly 24 percent of blacks and whites reported participating in a neighborhood group, compared with only 16 percent of Latinos and 14 percent of Asian citizens. Whites and blacks scored over 8 percentage points higher, on average, on the civic participation scale. However, when compared with noncitizens, these differences grow quite substantially. Latino noncitizens score only at one-eighteenth a point and Asian noncitizens score just over one-tenth a point on the civic participation scale compared with the average scores of over a quarter a point for all citizen groups. Latino noncitizens were also far less likely to work on neighborhood projects or belong to neighborhood civic associations.

Similar patterns also exist when looking at different types of civic and social organizations. For example, the MCSUI study has data on the percent of respondents who reported participating in a neighborhood-based civic organization during the past year by race/ethnicity and English language ability. This could include a parent/teacher association or organization (PTA/PTO), a social club, a neighborhood group, a cultural group, or a political organization. As with the other findings, there are few consistent racial or ethnic differences in civic activities among incorporated respondents but large differences in civic activity based on English language ability. English-speaking Asians, blacks, Latinos, and whites all participated in organizations at roughly the same level, although whites were more likely to belong to social clubs and political groups and Asian Americans more likely to belong to cultural groups. Among non-English-speaking Asian Americans and Latinos, however, rates of most civic activities were far below the other groups. With the exception of PTAs, under 11 percent of non-English-speaking Latinos and Asian Americans reported belonging to a civic organization, rates of participation that were roughly a third of those with good English skills.

Thus many of the differences in the civic and social activity of Latinos and Asian Americans are clearly related to their lower levels of citizenship and English language ability. Yet even when these factors are considered, some racial differences in the social and civic patterns still remain: whites and blacks are slightly more active in local civic activities and more involved in neighborhood affairs than Latinos and Asian Americans, but they are no more active in informal social activities and sometimes less active in many types of social organizations. Other research suggests that Asian Americans and Latinos are much less civically active because of cultural differences stemming from their countries of origin, a feeling of marginalization in American society, and a lack of group-based mobilization (Wong 2006).

Regardless of its source, Americans' involvement in civic affairs depends, in part, on their own racial identity; the question remains, however, whether this affects the way different groups respond to their racial environments. If Latinos and Asian Americans are already less civically active, then neighborhood effects might even be more of a depressant to their involvement. In other words, if living in an integrated neighborhood makes Latinos less likely to be mobilized or less interested in local civic affairs, then we should expect them to be even less likely to be civically engaged. Yet, among Asians and Latinos, there are no differences (at least among citizens) in informal social activities. Since such informal activities provide opportunities for mobilization and may indicate some level of alienation with a person's community, this would suggest that among incorporated Americans, we may not expect any systematic differences. In other words, the biggest differences may not occur by race or ethnicity but by level of incorporation into American society.

The Effects of Neighborhood Racial Segregation on Civic Participation

How much are these differences in civic engagement affected by people's racial environments? To answer this question, let us compare whites and nonwhites. Figure 6.2 depicts the predicted average number of civic activities for white respondents in the CID data by the percentage white in the neighborhood based on a multivariate regression analysis.[2] Each measure of civic participation is based on questions about membership in seventeen associational groups and additional questions on activities in these groups, such as participation in group activities or doing other voluntary works.[3] As expected, whites in predominantly white neighborhoods are far more likely to engage in the activities of voluntary organizations.[4] The equations predict that a white person living in a predominantly white area (whether it is a metropolis or neighborhood) is over twice as likely to belong to an organization, participate in organizational activities, or volunteer for an organizational project.

In contrast with whites, living in a predominantly white neighborhood does not bolster minority civic participation; instead, it corresponds with lower levels of civic engagement, although this varies somewhat by race. Among blacks in the CID sample, overall civic participation did not change

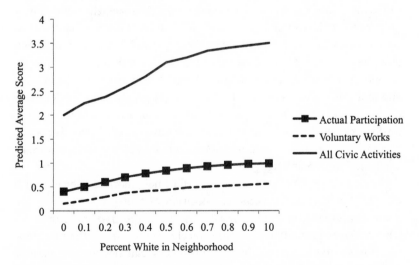

FIGURE 6.2 Predicted rates of white civic participation by the percent white in neighborhood (2005 CID).

with the racial composition of their surroundings, but actual participation and volunteering did decline. The equations predict that as the percentage of whites in a black person's neighborhood increases, blacks' average numbers of participatory or voluntary activities drops from 1.5 to zero. Similar declines also occur for Latinos—actual participation and volunteering declines as the percent of whites in the neighborhood increases. Among Latinos in the CID sample, average rates of civic membership also dropped with the percentage of whites in their neighborhood. The equations predict that Latinos who live in neighborhoods that have almost no whites belong to three civic organizations, a rate that drops to zero once the percentage of whites in the neighborhood goes above fifty.

These same trends are also evident in measures of local civic activities. The SCCBS survey asked a series of specific questions about the respondents' neighborhood civic activities.[5] Significant differences occur in the predicted rates of civic and social participation by the racial composition of people's neighborhoods, although these vary considerably by the individual's race. For whites, living in a predominantly white neighborhood coincides with a lower likelihood of belonging to a neighborhood group, but it corresponds with a higher level of informal social activity. The equations predict that a white person living in an all-white community would be 23 percent less likely to belong to a neighborhood group than if he or she lived in a nonwhite neighborhood; yet this same person would also score 8 percent higher on the informal socializing scale. These findings coincide with other research that shows that predominantly white communities have fewer neighborhood groups, largely because such communities are more likely to be suburban locales with fewer social problems (Oliver 2001). Because integrated neighborhoods tend to be in older and more urban areas, they often present neighbors with a wider array of community issues and a more mature civic infrastructure in which to involve residents. But while whites in integrated neighborhoods may be more likely to participate in neighborhood groups they are less socially connected with their neighbors.

Among minorities, a different pattern of neighborhood socializing is evident. For blacks, the racial composition of the community had few distinctive effects on their civic activity above the baseline effects for whites. The biggest difference among blacks is in regards to their informal social ties—unlike whites, blacks' informal social ties do not increase with the percent of whites in their neighborhood. The equations predict that a black person living in a predominantly white community is no more (but also no less) socially active than a black person in a nonwhite community.[6] Latinos and Asian Americans are less likely to be involved in neighborhood groups (a trend consistent with their overall lower levels of civic participation), but they are only slightly less likely to get involved as the percent white in their neighborhoods increases. Latinos also reported lower average scores on the informal socializing scale, although they are more likely to score higher as the percentage of whites in their neighborhood rises. Among Asian Americans, informal socializing declines with the percentage of whites in their neighborhood.

When examining the effects of social contexts on civic behavior, it is important to consider what influences the measures of the social environment may be capturing. The racial composition of a neighborhood is not simply a measure of all its residents' races but also relates to other factors such as its age, urbanity, and political history. Although the regression equations take the economic status of the community into account, it is quite likely that the measure of a community's racial composition also relates to other political factors that could influence people's civic participation. It is quite telling, for instance, that whites are more likely to be civically active as the percent of whites in their community grows, although less likely to belong to neighborhood groups. This disjunction may be due to a lack of compelling problems in the neighborhood. Many predominantly white areas are in suburbs that effectively use municipal powers to reduce the level of social diversity and political problems, hence diminishing the incentive for neighborhood civic action.

It is important, therefore, to keep these factors in mind when examining the effects of neighborhood racial contexts on minority civic participation. Most minorities score lower on the civic participation scale as the percent of whites in their neighborhood rises. This is may be due to a lower level of compelling civic issues in such areas, but it may also relate to a greater level of social ostracism. Blacks in predominantly white areas are not more socially active than those in nonwhite areas, and Asian Americans are less socially involved. As these minorities who live in predominantly white areas are less socially connected than their white neighbors, they may have fewer invitations to be civically involved. They also might be provided with fewer opportunities for interracial contact. Interestingly, in the one exception to this trend, Latinos and Asian Americans are more likely to participate in neighborhood groups when they live in predominantly white areas. Although the exact reason for this trend is unclear, it may be related to a process of immigrant incorporation—Latinos and Asian Americans who move into predominantly white neighborhoods may do so as a part of incorporating themselves fully into American society, and thus they may become more involved in their neighborhood groups. Nevertheless, on the whole, the findings above would indicate that predominantly white neighborhoods are not the most fertile ground for encouraging the civic and social participation of minority groups.

Another way of gauging the social connectedness of minorities in predominantly white areas is to examine their attitudes about their neighbors. If integration contributes to greater social understanding, then presumably people in integrated settings will develop greater bonds with their neighbors. This, however, does not seem to be the case. The SCCBS data queried respondents about their perceptions of their surroundings, asking them how much their neighbors provided them with "a sense of belonging" and how much they trusted their neighbors.[7] Figure 6.3 depicts the predicted scores on measures of social connection to neighbors by the percent white in the neighborhood from regression equations.

Whites and minorities exhibit sharply different perceptions of their sense of place in their community depending on its racial composition. As the percent of whites in their neighborhoods increases, whites are far more likely to report a sense of trust in their neighbors and a sense of belonging in the community. The OLS equations predict that a white person in an all-white neighborhood would score nearly half a point higher on the neighbor-trust scale than if that same person lived in an entirely nonwhite neighborhood; they would also be 6 percent more likely to report a feeling of belonging in their neighborhood.[8] Whites who live in more segregated surroundings report a greater sense of community and connection with their neighbors than those in less white neighborhoods.

The opposite trend occurs for blacks and Latinos—as the percentage of whites in their neighborhood increases, they are less likely to report trusting their neighbors or feeling like they belong in their community. When considering the baseline effects plus all the interaction terms, the equations predict that a black person living in an all-white neighborhood will feel far less trusting of their neighbors than a white person in that neighborhood and only slightly more trusting of their neighbors than if they lived in a nonwhite neighborhood. The equations would also predict a similar effect for Latinos—those who live in all-white neighborhoods are much less trusting of their neighbors than whites and only slightly more trusting than Latinos who live in nonwhite locales. Both Latinos and blacks are also less likely to report a sense of belonging with respect

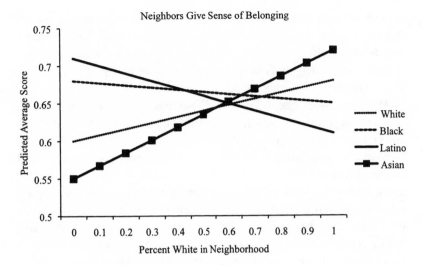

FIGURE 6.3A Predicted levels of neighborhood belonging and trust by the percent white in neighborhood (2000 SCCBS).

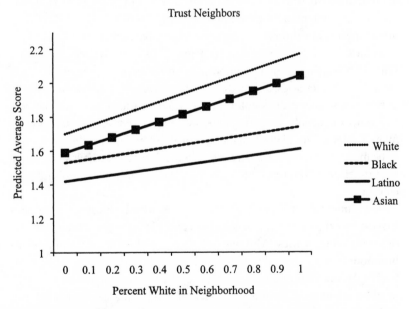

FIGURE 6.3B Predicted levels of neighborhood belonging and trust by the percent white in neighborhood, continued (2000 SCCBS).

to their neighbors as the percent of whites in their surroundings increases. Asians, however, do not appear to be so adversely affected. There were no statistically significant differences between Asian and white respondents in their trust in neighbors or feeling of belonging by virtue of the white percentage in their neighborhood.

The conclusions one draws from these findings depend largely upon which racial group is in question. Minorities have different levels of social and civic involvement and are affected by the racial composition of their surroundings in different ways. African Americans are just as socially and civically active as whites, and, like whites, their civic action declines in predominantly white settings. If there is an encouraging sign from the data it is that blacks in predominantly white neighborhoods are no more civically disengaged than their white neighbors or any more socially alienated than blacks in nonwhite neighborhoods. Integration would not appear to be a major deterrent to black civic engagement or social life.

Latinos and Asian Americans are significantly less civically active than either whites or blacks. However, they are not adversely affected by living in predominantly white areas—Asian Americans and Latinos in predominantly white neighborhoods are just as civically active as those who live in nonwhite neighborhoods and, in some cases, participate more. Latinos, like blacks, are less trusting of their neighbors and are less likely to feel a sense of belonging in their neighborhood as the percent of whites in their surroundings increases, although this is not a factor for Asian Americans. Taken as a whole, it does not appear that integration into white areas is a civically or socially alienating experience for Asian Americans or even many Latinos. The biggest challenge for these groups is in getting them to be more civically and socially active in the first place, which simply may be a function of their unfamiliarity with American society, politics, and culture.

The same cannot be said, however, for whites. Interestingly, the data suggest that the most adverse social effects of integration actually may be experienced by whites. Although whites in predominantly white neighborhoods are less civically active than those in more integrated neighborhoods, this is probably less because of their social connections with neighbors and more because of a lack of compelling issues in predominantly white neighborhoods. Because most predominantly white neighborhoods are located within suburban areas that have fewer social and civic issues drawing citizens into the public realm, it is understandable that neighborhood racial composition would correspond with changing white civic participation. More troubling are the changing social patterns and feelings of community between whites in segregated and integrated communities. Whites in segregated neighborhoods are more socially active with their neighbors and experience greater feelings of neighborly trust and belonging than whites in more integrated neighborhoods. This suggests that as a white neighborhood becomes more integrated, its white residents will become less socially connected with their neighbors. Although whites in integrated neighborhoods may have more opportunities for interracial contact through high levels of civic activity, they may feel less of a sense of community and be less socially connected to people of other races. Paradoxically, it is the social connections of whites that may be most adversely influenced by integration.

Conclusion

Since the issuance of the controversial Moynihan report in the late 1960s, a voluminous amount of research has investigated the social consequences of racial segregation in the United States. Most of this research has focused on the social pathologies and inequities that have accompanied the hypersegregation of African Americans. Segregation, particularly of African Americans, has been linked to higher infant mortality, unemployment, and crime rates and numerous other social ills (for example, see Boger and Wegner 1996; Banfield 1970; Orfield 1988; and Pettigrew 1979). Sociologist William Julius Wilson has argued quite extensively that the social isolation of blacks has disconnected them from job networks and other opportunities for economic advancement and has mired them in a permanent underclass status (Wilson 1985). These studies, like most studies of racial residential patterns, focus almost entirely on the experience of minorities in segregated contexts.

But while there is general agreement that segregation has had many harmful by-products, almost no research has been conducted on the experience of people, either white or nonwhite, in integrated neighborhoods. With the exception of research on the performance of black students in integrated schools and recent writings on the Gautreaux desegregation program and the recent Moving to Opportunity housing experiments, relatively little has been written about the lives of minority adults in integrated or predominantly white residential settings. And, as with many aspects of race relations, there is almost no large-scale, quantitative research on how integration affects the lives of Latinos and Asian Americans.[9] We know that segregation has many adverse consequences, but is integration necessarily a more positive experience?

If interracial civic and social connections are the key factors in promoting greater racial tolerance among people in integrated settings, then the findings in this chapter demonstrate that neighborhood racial integration is not guaranteed to bring simple or even desirable consequences. Since any meaningful integration in America will largely be based on the movement of minorities into predominantly white areas, at least over the short run, it is important to focus on how the social and civic experiences of whites and minorities vary between integrated and segregated places. The findings from this chapter show different results for different groups. Whites who live in all-white neighborhoods consistently demonstrate greater social connections and more affiliation with their neighbors than those who live in integrated settings. For instance, whites who live in racially mixed neighborhoods on average are 5 percentage points lower in their feelings of neighborhood community and levels of trust than those in all-white neighborhoods. For whites, just as with other minorities, racial homogeneity promotes a feeling of community. Integration, while promoting some types of associational membership, does not enhance feelings of linkage with a place. In fact, it produces just the opposite.

Interestingly, integration may have some of the most important social and civic consequences, not just for minorities, but for America's white population. As the previous chapters showed, neighborhood racial integration may be important for promoting interracial understanding, which would, in theory, enhance the community between whites and other racial groups, particularly African Americans and Latinos. Yet in the short run, this type of community may be difficult to achieve. Whites in integrated neighborhoods may be less racially judgmental, but they do not feel as connected or trusting of their neighbors either. Paradoxically, the very integration that helps whites gain better racial understanding may also undermine a sense of trust and community between their neighbors. If integration is essential for promoting a more racially tolerant view of society at large, it may come at the cost of a sense of community and fellowship among one's immediate neighbors. As long as race continues to be a defining characteristic in American society, the relationship between segregation, white racial attitudes, and the strength of community bonds will remain in tension.

The impact of integration on blacks is related to this point. For hundreds of years, African Americans lived in a society that discriminated against them, banned them from public facilities, and relegated them to the bottom of the social ladder. Accepting a sense of community in the larger society meant accepting a denigrated social position. Consequently, the strongest community ties most blacks formed were within a black society. Since the civil rights era, the state-sanctioned segregation has been undone, but the challenge of community still remains. For blacks, integrating into American society as equal members means facing an enormous residue of past discrimination. Many blacks still feel strong ties and a linked fate with other African Americans and derive a greater sense of community from living in segregated spaces.

Yet if neighborhood integration fosters greater racial harmony through greater civic participation, then one might conclude that the way to promote greater racial understanding between blacks and nonblacks is to encourage greater residential integration. Neighborhood integration is important for blacks not because it increases casual contact (in which blacks may experience prejudice, particularly from whites) but because it fosters an integrated civic and social community. The problem with this argument, however, is that black civic participation is lower in predominantly white neighborhoods. Partly this is because white neighborhoods themselves are less civically active but partly this can be attributed to the difference in the social connectedness of blacks in white neighborhoods. When compared against the black racial percentage in their communities, blacks who live in predominantly black neighborhoods derive a greater sense of community from their surroundings. In the SCCBS data, 78 percent of African Americans in largely black neighborhoods felt community with their neighbors, compared with only 71 percent in neighborhoods with few blacks. Herein lies another paradox of segregation: the neighborhood integration that is so important for creating interracial associational ties also diminishes black social involvement; the solidarity and community provided by segregated black neighborhoods may also sustain racial misperceptions by those who live outside of these areas. But if blacks, like whites, want to overcome the continued barriers of racial difference they see with other races, the conundrum of residential integration must be faced.

Latinos and Asian Americans, as diverse ethnic groups composed largely of immigrants, encounter a much different set of issues with respect to civic and social integration. The biggest challenge for these groups may have less to do with the segregation in their neighborhoods and more to do with their much lower levels of social and civic engagement and the question of identity in a new society. Undoubtedly, this is a function of so many being first- and second-generation immigrants to the United States—many of whom have limited English skills, are noncitizens, have stronger ties to their home countries, or simply feel marginalized by American life. And their incorporation into American civic life will undoubtedly coincide somewhat with their integration into white residential areas. Indeed, the findings show that Latinos and Asian Americans who live in white neighborhoods are actually more civically active. However, for many Latinos and Asians, particularly newly arrived immigrants, residence in a predominantly white neighborhood may not be an optimal option for their social and economic well-being. For many there are also concerns of sustaining their indigenous cultural values and identities, something that may be undermined with further integration into white American society. The challenge for these groups will be in balancing their competing cultural identities—their countries of origin, the United States, and their own ethnic or racial self-perception—all while becoming incorporated into American society. Whether these new identities will serve to act as catalysts to further racial antagonism or blur racial and group distinctions remains to be seen. In the meantime, the cultural and linguistic segregation of many Latinos and Asian Americans may actually be the biggest challenge to promoting better race relations between them and other groups in American society.

For all of these reasons, residential integration itself may be an obstacle to civic and social integration—between the social ostracism of minorities in predominantly white areas, the cultural alienation and low levels of incorporation among many Asians and Latinos, and the prevalence of whites in many civically alienating suburbs, the actual experience of integration may preclude the social and civic engagement that is necessary for promoting racial tolerance. Herein lies another paradox of neighborhood integration and racial animosity: the ameliorative effects of integration are based on the idea that people in such settings are civically and socially engaged with their neighbors. Often, however, this is not the case. Not only are minorities who move into predominantly white areas subject to possible harassment and violence, they may find other barriers to social and civic connections with their neighbors. Integration may also alienate whites who see little in common with or feel different from their nonwhite neighbors. Considering these ideas in light of the previous chapters, one might speculate that a cycle of race, segregation, and community continues to operate in the United States: racial animosity in white areas drives minorities to seek community in minority neighborhoods, which further sustains racial segregation; high levels of racial segregation perpetuate more racial intolerance, which, in turn, bolsters further segregation. Ironically, the very integration that can bridge various social chasms seems to be undercutting the bonding experiences that are so important for fostering racial understanding in the first place.

CHAPTER SEVEN

On Segregation and Multiculturalism

The question we Americans need to address, before it is answered for us, is: Does this First World nation wish to become a Third World country? Because that is our destiny if we do not build a sea wall against the waves of immigration rolling over our shores.—Patrick Buchanan, *New York Post*, June 20, 1990

Recently, some very loud alarms have been sounding about America's racial future. Some of these alarms have been triggered by the very fact of its growing diversity. America has a long history of racial division between blacks and whites, and, with the addition of two large minority groups, some fear America may face more strife and social division. Anecdotal evidence from diverse countries around the globe would seem to justify these fears. From the Balkans to Rwanda, from East Timor to Northern India, societies that are more heterogeneous appear to have greater problems in maintaining peace and stability (Horowitz 1998; Cederman and Girardin 2000). If this is true, then America too may fall victim to similar violence and discord as it transforms from a country with a large white majority and relatively small black minority into a country with four sizeable racial groups of which no one is an overall majority.

Other alarms are triggered by the sources of America's growing diversity. According to commentators like Patrick Buchanan and Samuel Huntington, today's immigrants, particularly from Mexico, pose a unique threat to American society and the future of its democratic institutions: unlike previous generations of immigrants who adopted the Anglo-Protestant values that have "defined" American culture and integrated themselves into American society, contemporary Mexican immigrants supposedly are maintaining their indigenous affiliations, refusing to learn English, and remaining on the outside of American civil society. From this perspective, the continued migration and segregation of Latino immigrants will render America asunder: non-Latinos will feel increasingly alienated from Spanish-speaking Americans; Hispanics will maintain allegiances to their home country and fail to embrace an American identity; and large parts of the Southwest may eventually be drained of white populations and turned into Mexican satellites.

Still others see the challenge of diversity arising less from America's growing racial heterogeneity per se and more from the persistence of inequality among its various racial groups. According to this view, racial discord and violence might arise, not because America is becoming more ethnically diverse, but because there is an unequal distribution of resources along racial lines (Smelser, Wilson, and Mitchell 2001). Economically based racial violence has historical precedent—the race riots that hit many American cities in the 1960s have been widely attributed to the limited economic opportunities of African Americans trapped in urban ghettos (Boger and Wegner 1996). Today, economic advancement is not evenly distributed across a multiethnic population: some groups, such as Chinese, Korean, and Indian Americans, have had a great deal of success moving up the economic ladder, while many African Americans and Latinos seem trapped in a persistent underclass. If this is the case, the underlying problem of diversity will come less from the growth of new minorities than from the growing levels of economic stratification that are demarcated largely along racial lines.

Given all these concerns, it is hard not to be pessimistic about America's racial future. It is almost without question that increasing numbers of Asian and Latino immigrants to this country will create greater racial hostility among both whites and blacks, particularly in the areas in which most immigrants are settling. If Asian Americans and Latinos develop a stronger sense of panethnic identity and begin to assert many group-based prerogatives, then whites may respond with more antagonism as their racial preeminence is further questioned and blacks may feel displaced by new groups asserting a higher position in America's racial hierarchy. Already there has been evidence of a growing racial backlash—Texas and California, both states with increasingly diverse populations, have been at the forefront of rolling back affirmative action in university admissions and have contested other issues of immigration policy. If whites and blacks harden in their racial attitudes toward Latinos and Asians, it is difficult to believe that Latinos themselves and possibly Asians will not respond with their own group-based biases. All of these racial problems will be exacerbated by disparities in income and education, particularly among blacks and Latinos. As long as large percentages of these groups have limited opportunities for economic mobility, further racial conflict seems a foregone conclusion.

Those concerned with America's racial future must therefore come to grips with the following questions: how, in light of their growing racial diversity, will Americans relate to their neighbors and avoid future racial conflict? Must diversity lead to greater racial discord, or can it foster greater racial understanding and cooperation? Must Americans meld together within one cultural norm, or can they sustain a host of competing and different cultures and ethnicities?

The preceding chapters demonstrate that one cannot begin to answer these or any questions about America's racial future without some reference to geography. People's views of other races and their own racial identity depend fundamentally on their surroundings—social environments not only define a person's experience of race, but they also make up the arenas in which racial groups contest resources, status, and privilege. Indeed, each of the concerns highlighted above is a geographic concern. Consider, for example, the anxiety over diversity. The United States may be growing more racially diverse as a whole, but many parts of the country remain predominantly white; diversity is far less of a concern in New Hampshire than it is in New Mexico. If there are problems with diversity, they are more likely to be felt in some localities than others. Similarly, the "problem" of Latino assimilation is far more acute in the Southwest than it is in the rest of the country; concerns about dual nationalism are less pressing the further one is away from the Mexican border. Even the problem of economic inequality is geographically specific. According to many scholars, the perpetuation of an underclass is largely sustained by high levels of racial and economic segregation in an urban core that fundamentally limits opportunities for social mobility (see Massey and Denton 1993). Thus, no matter what one's perspective is, the future of race in America is fundamentally tied to place.

In examining the relationship between geography and Americans' racial attitudes, this book's findings offer cause for both concern and hope. Perhaps the biggest source of worry should be in the current patterns of residential segregation that exist across our metropolitan areas. Residentially, America remains a country highly stratified along racial lines. Although most neighborhoods are less homogeneous than they were two decades ago, a majority of Americans still live largely around people of

their own race. Ironically, for minorities, this trend is often most pronounced within a very diverse metropolitan context. In truly multiethnic
cities like Chicago, Houston, Los Angeles, and New York, many ethnic
groups live in same-race neighborhoods that stand in sharp contrast to the
broader racial mosaic.

As we have seen, such patterns of segregation appear to be a recipe
for further racial strife. On the one hand, regional diversity corresponds
with higher levels of animosity and mistrust. In diverse metropolitan areas,
whites feel more racial competition and harbor, on average, more negative
attitudes toward minorities. Similarly, blacks and Latinos in more diverse
cities (that is, places with larger black, Latino, and Asian populations) also
hold other minority groups in a less positive light, seeing them as competitors for political and economic resources. And Latinos in more diverse
areas also have less positive views of whites. If feelings of group competition and the protection of group social position and privilege underlie
people's racial attitudes, then the metropolitan area is one of the most
salient arenas in which racial struggles can take place. On the other hand,
neighborhood segregation also corresponds with greater racial hostility.
People who live immediately around people of their own race, particularly
in contrast with a more diverse metropolitan population, tend to exhibit
the most negative views of other groups. The combination of neighborhood segregation amid metropolitan diversity (the pattern that character-
izes most large American metropolitan areas) is one that correlates with
the maximum amount of racial resentment for nearly every racial group.[1]

What remains unclear is whether these geographic patterns are a cause
or consequence of these racial sentiments. There is clearly a strong case
to be made for the latter: people with negative views of other groups have
strong motivations to live in racially segregated neighborhoods. The fact
that segregation is sustained in such a high degree speaks not just to the
preference of most people to live among their own ethnic group (which
they do) but also to the preferences of whites to live far away from minorities. If this is the case, then our current patterns of segregation merely
reflect Americans' underlying racial animosities (which, by this indicator,
are quite high). Some might even argue that these patterns of segregation,
by physically separating people with the highest levels of racial hostility
from out-groups, actually help to diminish racial conflict.

Neighborhood self-selection alone, however, cannot explain the geographic contours of Americans' racial attitudes. While some degree of
self-sorting is undoubtedly behind the trends described above, there are

several reasons why it falls short as a complete explanation. First, it does not fully account for the geographic differences in whites' racial views (whites in segregated neighborhoods are still more racially hostile even when their neighborhood racial preferences are considered). Second, among minorities, a person's self-reported neighborhood racial preference is not a very good predictor of his of her racial attitudes in general. This is because, for most minorities, an in-group preference does not necessarily mean an out-group animosity. For instance, African Americans' preference for black neighbors does not necessarily arise from a hostility toward whites, Latinos, or Asians but can simply come from a feeling of solidarity with a small minority. Third, in a housing market that is still rife with racial discrimination, minorities face many obstacles in their ability to "self-select" into the neighborhood of their choice. The fact that minorities exhibit similar geographic patterns in their racial attitudes, even though they have limited abilities to self-select, suggests that other factors must underlie the greater racial tolerance in racially integrated settings.

Which leads us to the most intriguing and perplexing part of this study: do more integrated social settings actually promote racial harmony? The evidence suggests this is a possibility. Irrespective of their own ethnicity, people who live in integrated neighborhoods were more likely to report having interracial friendship ties, to belong to integrated civic organizations, and to have interracial contacts at work. Among whites, in particular, having interracial social connections strongly correlates with more positive racial views. It was also a factor linking their racial attitudes to their neighborhood's racial composition. Yet it is important to recognize that the data are not conclusive about whether a transformative process occurs within integrated settings. The data only show a correspondence between positive racial attitudes and the racial composition of neighborhoods, civic associations, and work sites; they cannot reveal or test for the actual transformation of racial attitudes as the result of integration in these settings. Even with these caveats, it is extremely tempting to think that integration has positive benefits for racial attitudes. The concept of integration, after all, embodies our basic principles of fairness and equal treatment before the law. Given its strong normative allure, it is understandable that we would like to find that it also has practical benefits.

Integration, however, is a very complicated phenomenon and carries a host of difficult questions and problematic assumptions. First is the question of where Americans will integrate: is it in their neighborhoods, workplaces, religious and civic institutions? As we have seen, in some of these settings, such as neighborhoods, integration is difficult to sustain and may come with its own costs. Integration can also take many different forms. It can mean sharing a similar language, religion, or other set of cultural values; it can mean living in the same neighborhoods; it can also mean having equal access to jobs, education, and political representation. Depending on one's conception, integration presents a host of highly contested ideas regarding multiculturalism, identity politics, and public policy. Finally, there is the question of how the process of integration occurs: is it an inevitable part of American historical development, or are there systemic barriers that prevent certain groups from fully integrating into the American mainstream? In short, if America's racial future hinges on how well we live together, then we must sift through the myriad of meanings and implications that integration brings.

On Integration and Incorporation

Racial integration is not simply an ideal, it is also a conundrum. On the one hand, a large body of scholarship has documented the negative impact of residential segregation, particularly on the well-being of minority communities. For generations, African Americans and dark-skinned Latinos have been highly segregated in largely urban, poor neighborhoods; ceteris paribus, blacks and dark-skinned Latinos are much more likely to be surrounded by poor neighbors than low-income whites or fair-skinned Latinos (Massey 2001). These patterns of residential exclusion and concentrations of poverty have had serious consequences for their residents' health, employment, education, and economic well-being. The hypersegregation of African Americans has contributed to higher rates of mortality, unemployment, crime, and educational failure (Massey and Denton 1993). Beyond these physical and economic consequences, neighborhood racial segregation has negative effects on racial attitudes as well—as noted above, whites and blacks in segregated neighborhoods express much higher levels of racial resentment than those in integrated places. Looking at these findings and the gross inequalities that exist in many metropolitan areas, it is easy to conclude that racial segregation is a pernicious blight on American society.

On the other hand, it is not self-evident that integration would solve many of America's social ills or even eliminate the persistence of race as a social problem. Part of the problem comes with the fact that, given the current racial distribution of the population (that is, a predominantly white majority), meaningful integration means minority penetration into predominantly white suburbs and neighborhoods. In practice, this type of racial integration rarely comes easily or brings immediate benefits. Historically, African Americans and other minorities moving into white areas have met with violence, hostility, and social ostracism, something that continues today (Wilson and Taub 2006).

Contemporary efforts to encourage integration have also met with mixed results. Take, for example, one of the most ambitious experiments in encouraging integration. In 1994, the U.S. Department of Housing and Urban Development conducted an experiment called "Moving to Opportunity" among 4,200 households residing in public housing in highly impoverished, largely minority neighborhoods. Some families were given no new assistance, some families were offered Section 8 vouchers that allowed them to relocate to new neighborhoods (although these were often other poor places), and some families were specifically relocated in neighborhoods with poverty rates below 10 percent. Five years later, researchers tracked down each family and inquired about their health, employment, and overall economic prospects. In general, families who moved out of impoverished neighborhoods experienced no significant improvements in employment or earnings, nor were they less likely to receive public assistance (Kling et al. 2006). And while adolescent girls experienced some health benefits from moving out of impoverished neighborhoods, their male counterparts actually did worse. For poor teenage boys, relocating to better neighborhoods often brought more encounters with law enforcement, problems in school, and a return to impoverished areas (Clampet-Lundquist et al. 2006). The Moving to Opportunity experiment demonstrates that involuntary integration brings negligible health and economic benefits, at least in the short run.[2]

Then there are the social consequences of integration. One of the most consistently reported experiences of minorities who migrate to predominantly white neighborhoods is a high level of social alienation. For example, a very high percentage of the thousands of black families who participated in the Gautreaux housing program (a court-ordered desegregation program that moved several thousand black families from Chicago housing projects to predominantly white suburbs) reported high levels of loneliness, harassment, and social disconnection in their new, white neighborhoods (Rubinowitz and Rosenbaum 2000). Nor is this social alienation limited to minorities. As reported in chapter 6, people of all races who live in integrated neighborhoods have a weaker sense of community and are less trusting of their neighbors. As the percentage of nonwhites in their neighborhoods increase, whites tend to become less civically active, less trusting, and less involved in community affairs. Conversely, blacks in more integrated neighborhoods also reported feeling less connection to their neighbors and a lower sense of involvement.[3] Ironically, for some groups, neighborhood integration itself can be a deterrent to the very civic participation and community involvement that is supposed provide opportunities for positive interracial contact. Segregation may have negative consequences for African Americans, but it also provides many with a strong sense of place, access to social capital, and a feeling of community in a white-dominated society. In other words, residential segregation may breed contempt, but integration seems to breed alienation.

The problems of integration, alienation, and community life become even more complicated when Latinos and Asian Americans are brought into the picture. At first glance, many Latinos and Asian Americans appear to be successfully integrating into American society: fairer-skinned Latinos and Asian Americans have far lower levels of residential segregation than African Americans, have more friends and social contacts of other races, and have met less resistance penetrating predominantly white domains. But these levels of integration are not consistent for all groups, races, or nationalities. Among Latinos, skin color and English language ability appear to be crucial determinants of their integration into American social and community life (Alba and Nee 1997). For example, sociologist Douglas Massey reports that dark-skinned Latinos experience a much harder time integrating into white neighborhoods (Massey 2001). As noted in the previous chapters, English language ability also foretells Latinos' racial views, their levels of community and civic involvement, and the likelihood they live outside of a Latino barrio. In fact, much of the geographic difference in Latinos' racial attitudes was attributable to their levels of incorporation; unincorporated Latinos, who are more likely to have negative attitudes toward other groups, were also far more likely to live in heavily Latino neighborhoods. New Latino immigrants who are segregated in ethnic enclaves are hindered in their incorporation into American society and may, as a consequence, sustain greater racial animosity.

Given these findings, it is somewhat understandable that many commentators are concerned about how fast Latinos are adopting English language skills and American social customs. But in regards to the anxieties of nativists like Samuel Huntington, the evidence is mixed. As some note, many Latino immigrants come to the United States as "temporary" workers and, given this transience, feel less compelled to learn English, acquire an American education, or adopt American racial norms (Alba and Nee 1997). In addition, around half of all foreign-born Mexican immigrants are unauthorized, and a majority of these lack much of an education; for example, the average foreign-born Mexican immigrant is three times less likely to have a high school degree than the average American (Borjas 1999). A significant portion of Latinos also live in segregated neighborhoods that are linguistically and culturally shielded from mainstream America. Although such immigrant enclaves have historically provided social and economic resources for newcomers, such segregation can also inhibit Latino economic advancement and social incorporation into wider American life (Bean and Stevens 2003). This is particularly the case with American civic and social activities, where Latinos participate at levels far below their black and white counterparts (Oliver 2001). As millions of unauthorized Latinos continue to seek work and other economic opportunities in the United States, there will continue to be a large group of people existing at the social and civic margins of American society.

But among those Latinos who plant roots in the United States, linguistic and cultural incorporation over two and three generations is the norm. Despite the fears of commentators like Huntington and Buchanan, contemporary patterns of Latino immigrant incorporation into the United States seem largely similar to those of the past two centuries (Alba and Nee 1997). Second-generation immigrants from Mexico and Latino America are not significantly different than comparable immigrant groups in the rates in which they adopt English, acquire education, move up the economic ladder, embrace an American identity, and spatially assimilate into nonimmigrant neighborhoods (Portes 2001). While the pathway to incorporation is rarely linear and these statistics generally do not include unauthorized immigrants, the vast majority of Latino immigrants appear to be following a trajectory that is roughly similar to that of generations past, that is, they are becoming a part of the American mainstream.

Although we have fewer data on Asian Americans, they too seem to be successfully incorporating into American society, although here significant differences occur by nationality: some groups, such as Chinese and Indian Americans, have had greater economic success, while others, such as Hmong, Cambodians, and Vietnamese, have had less. Many of these differences can be attributable to education and wealth levels among immigrants. Many Southeast Asians came to the United States as rural-based refugees from the Vietnam War, with limited education and little capital; many Chinese and Indian immigrants, on the other hand, were able to immigrate to the United States precisely because they had high job skills and education. Such variety highlights the difficulty in characterizing Asian Americans in panethnic terms. The tremendous social, linguistic, and cultural diversity among Asian Americans renders suspect any single generalization about people who have immigrated, or whose families have immigrated, from Asia. Not only is it hard to make reliable generalizations about Asian American economic, political, or social life, it is still unclear whether the panethnic identity of "Asian American" has much significance to those who fall under its heading. Recent studies on Asian Americans suggest very sharp differences by nationality among Asian Americans in feelings of panethnic identification and political participation—most Asian Americans are still more likely to see themselves in terms of their nationalities rather than as members of a pan-Asian ethnic group (Lien et al. 2001).

All of this makes it difficult to anticipate the future of an Asian American ethnic identity or the place of Asian Americans as a distinct racial group. The high education levels, economic success, cross-racial adoption, and intermarriage rates of many Asian Americans would suggest that they, like other immigrant groups before, will quickly incorporate into the American mainstream, perhaps diminishing the importance of a panethnic identity. As Asians move into predominantly white neighborhoods, attend largely white universities, intermarry, and enjoy high employment opportunities, it is not evident that they will see themselves as having distinctive interests related to their continent of origin. Yet the strong cultural ties that many Asians continue to have with their home countries, the emergence of particular ethnic neighborhoods and suburbs, and the continually high rates of immigration for certain groups might instill a greater ethnic consciousness, although this is more likely to be based on nationalist identities rather than on any larger perception of shared "Asianness." It also remains unclear whether white racial hostility based on skin tone or other physical characteristics will greatly impede an Asian incorporation into a predominantly white mainstream.

For both Latinos and Asians, the pressures of assimilation present a much larger set of dilemmas regarding their own cultural identities. If residential, social, and civic integration, and hence cultural incorporation, are the keys for reducing racial hostility, then this also implies that cultural and ethnic markers are impediments for eliminating racial differences.

After all, if Latinos or Asian Americans are to be seen as less differentiated from America's white majority, it would presumably require more use of English, adopting more "American" behavioral norms, and deemphasizing much of their previous nationalistic identity.

Yet some may wonder whether integration and incorporation into a predominantly white America also mean assimilation of cultural norms and subservience within a social hierarchy that is still largely defined by race and dominated by a white majority. Integration into white America may help reduce racial misunderstanding, but will it come at the cost of many people's own ethnic and cultural traditions? Does the end of racial strife require that blacks, Asians, and Latinos become more "white," and, if so, just how does this "whiteness" get defined? These questions present one of the core paradoxes of race and segregation in a multiethnic America: how do we, as a country, simultaneously foster an inclusive society with a minimal amount of ethnic tension and hostility while at the same time welcoming an even wider array of ethnic groups that have a right to their own cultural traditions? Can the diversity of different cultures be preserved even as America becomes a more residentially and civically integrated country?

For advocates of multiculturalism, an integrated America would not be culturally homogenous but rather integrated and pluralistic. New groups could incorporate into America, changing their new societies as they themselves change. Already this is evident in the expansion of "hyphenated" identities (for example, Chinese-American, Cuban-American, etc.) or a postethnic American identity forged in a common civic nationality based on core, liberal democratic ideals (Hollinger 2005). From this optimistic perspective, different ethnic traditions can coexist separately yet in harmony as long as they unify under a shared set of political principles.

Many doubt, however, whether this delicate balance between cultural diversity and social cohesion, namely, through dual identities, can be maintained. Historically, the American immigrant experience has meant the movement away from indigenous affiliations: over generations, German, English, Irish, Jewish, and Italians became not just Americans, but white Americans (Roediger 2005).[4] At one level, it seems likely that this type of racial assimilation will also occur for Latinos and Asians because of the power of intermarriage and economic mobility. As more people marry across religious, ethnic, and racial lines, work in diverse areas, and relocate themselves for jobs and schools, they and their children's identities become more fluid and less tied to a preexisting indigenous affiliation

(Lee and Bean 2004). This is particularly the case for Latinos and Asian Americans with higher income and education levels.

Others see this racial assimilation mediated through class and relative social position. Historians who have written on the social construction of a white racial identity observe that whiteness in America has almost always been defined in class terms and relative to blacks. Irish, Jewish, Italian, and Polish immigrants were, throughout much of the nineteenth and early twentieth centuries, seen as nonwhites, at least in relation to America's Anglo-Protestant majority (Ignatiev 1996; Roediger 2005). It was only through their own economic and political incorporation, often defined in opposition to African Americans, that these immigrant groups transformed themselves into "whites."

With the rapid economic incorporation of many Asians and Latinos, there are many possible ways that this economic and racial stratification could become reproduced. One scenario is a growing ethnic stratification among Latinos and Asians. Unlike the previous great wave of immigration that came to an abrupt halt in 1920, today's immigrant groups are continually supplemented with new members. Whereas Italians, Poles, Jews, and other groups had a relatively long period of ethnic isolation to assimilate into the American mainstream, contemporary immigrant groups are more differentiated among themselves in their incorporation levels. As a result, a growing difference is emerging between fully incorporated Latinos and Asians who have been in the United States for generations and those who have just arrived, which is evident in language usage, social practices, economic status, and racial self-identification. Although it is unclear how this stratification will become manifest, it could point to a division between incorporated Asians and Latinos who see themselves as categorically more similar to America's white majority than their ethnic counterparts. In other words, the major social divisions of the twenty-first century may be determined less by race and more by nativity.

Another scenario that is already beginning to arise is a shifting of the traditional color divide. Throughout most of America's history, whiteness has been given a preeminent status as a racial category compared with all other groups. As a result, many Latinos and Asians rightly saw themselves in alignment with African Americans as being legally denigrated minority groups. With the eradication of official sanctions against nonwhiteness and the economic incorporation of many Asians and Latinos, some scholars believe the color line is shifting from white/nonwhite to black/nonblack (Yancey 2003). In other words, Asians and Latinos may see themselves less as a separate minority group subordinate to whites and more as a unified ethnicity with whites in opposition to African Americans.

There is much evidence to validate this assertion. As we saw throughout this book, blacks are viewed more negatively than any other racial group in American society. It is not just whites who express more racial resentment toward African Americans than toward other groups, but Asians and Latinos as well. Another telling statistic comes in changes in the rates of interracial marriage. Over the past forty years, rates of interracial marriage in the United States have rapidly grown, yet the racial balance of exogamy has not been evenly distributed. Interracial marriage rates among Latinos and Asian Americans (typically to whites) are nearly three times as high as those among African Americans (Lee and Bean 2004). If interracial marriage is an indictor of a group's social incorporation, then African Americans are continuing to lag far behind other minority groups. Similarly, African Americans are more residentially segregated than other minorities. This is not from a black desire to be in same-race neighborhoods; if anything, blacks are more eager than other minorities to live among other races. Rather, black segregation continues to be imposed from discriminatory housing practices and social ostracism from whites, and increasingly Latinos, in same-race neighborhoods. Finally, as we saw in chapter 5, blacks are also more socially isolated than other minorities—blacks are significantly less likely to report interracial contacts at work, in their neighborhoods, or in their friendship networks.

Together, these findings lend credence to the idea that the real problem of race in a multiethnic America continues to be its age-old problem: the continued marginalization and denigration of dark-skinned peoples. This suggests that concerns about America's growing diversity or even the sources of diversity are misplaced. After all, if Latinos and Asians are incorporating into the American mainstream, then the simple growth of these populations ultimately means little in terms of overall intergroup relations. The dire predictions of ethnic balkanization among Latinos, whites, and Asians are off base. Indeed, the anxieties of nativist commentators over increases in immigration reveal their own racial biases: if they are truly concerned about racial division in the United States and the continuation of the American democratic ethos, they should worry less about new immigrant groups and more about the chronic marginalization of blacks. The fact that so many commentators seem completely untroubled by the continued isolation of African Americans while wringing their hands about the impact of Latinos belies their own ethnomyopia. The real threat to America's racial future comes less from the antagonisms toward new groups and more from the perpetuation of an insidious racial hierarchy that keeps African Americans at the bottom of the social ladder.

Which brings us back to the paradoxes of segregation in a multiethnic America. How can we demand that Latinos or Asians assimilate themselves into a "racially neutral" American society while such sharp cleavages between blacks and every other group persist? As long as skin color determines where Americans live and as long as residential location constrains economic opportunity, America has a race problem. Segregation not only epitomizes the racial biases within American culture, it reinforces their consequences. This means that America's racial challenge in the twenty-first century is whether it can better address the problems of the twentieth century, namely, a color line that is realized most vividly in the spatial isolation of its poorest and darkest skinned members. Until phenotype becomes a less restrictive determinant of residential location, skin color will continue to inhibit the economic incorporation of its most marginalized groups and America will remain saddled with chronic racial problems.

So where does this leave us? For all their dour implications, the findings in this book also provide some glimmers of hope. Race is a social construct, and, like any such construct, the misinformation that accompanies its use can be undone and undone equally for all. Americans of all races may continue to harbor negative stereotypes of other groups, but they often do so more from ignorance than from experience. Although race may seem to be an indelible difference between Americans, their patterns of racial attitudes are often more alike than different. Racial bias is not the sole property of any racial group, nor is it set in stone. Just as all groups exhibit similar trends in their racial views, all groups can unlearn their biases.

Despite all its problems, residential integration remains one of the best tools available to us for eliminating these racial biases. It provides opportunities for social contact, intermarriage, and the myriad of microinteractions that help erase racial differences. The key for successfully using integration as a tool is to recognize its limitations. Mere integration, by itself, is unlikely to promote social cohesion. Simply plopping poor and dark-skinned peoples in the midst of white, middle-class communities is unlikely to provide many social benefits unless it is coupled with efforts to build both human and social capital. This includes extra efforts for economic incorporation, such as job training, educational outreach, and social counseling. Not only can such efforts help erase the class-race divide in this country, they can help make use of the American workplace, perhaps the most integrated arena of American life, as a venue for building interracial understanding. But for people to make use of this resource, they must have proper job skills, training, and education levels. In practice, this means continuing state efforts at promoting economic and racial desegregation of poor neighborhoods, improving public housing and mortgage assistance, developing better systems of public transit, and advancing education and job training. The problems of segregation are as much economic as they are racial, and, therefore, any efforts at desegregation must tackle both with equal fervor.

Of course, our public institutions alone cannot meet this challenge. Although they may assist in building the human capital necessary to overcome economic disenfranchisement, they cannot sustain the social capital that is so essential for promoting health and well-being. Here is where America's robust civic sector must come into play. Despite its putative decline, American stocks of social capital remain quite high. Churches, professional organizations, and community groups remain a tremendous resource for helping Americans bridge their racial and economic divides. It is incumbent upon us to utilize this resource as a means of narrowing the racial gulfs in the United States. This includes encouraging existing organizations to pursue or continue efforts at interracial outreach, such as recruiting members from other racial or ethnic groups, promoting the development of human capital and providing services in poor areas, and fostering greater efforts at residential integration. The American workplace also can provide a valuable mechanism for building social linkages that cross racial boundaries.

The problems of race in America, despite their magnitude, are not insurmountable. Substantial progress has already been made in many dimensions of American life. Over the past fifty years, there has been a dramatic integration of the American higher educational system, workplaces, media, and the public sphere. Rather than seeing the increasing diversification of the American population as an obstacle to further racial progress, we can actually see it as an opportunity. As millions of Asians, blacks, and Latinos become incorporated into the American mainstream, they already are redefining what the mainstream looks like. While some may remain pessimistic and maintain that American has a dominant racial culture that is defined in opposition to darker skinned peoples, it is hard to believe that the ethnic diversification of America's economic elite will not make the boundaries between races ever more porous. Although such progress will undoubtedly be slow and still requires much political will and social mobilization, the alternative—the racial balkanization and marginalization of dark-skinned peoples—is unacceptable, particularly in a society that prides itself on its commitments to equality of opportunity and treatment before the law.

Appendix A: Data Sources

This book utilizes a combination of census and survey data to analyze the relationship between racial and economic contexts and racial attitudes. It relies primarily on four major surveys and the 2000 U.S. Census. The first is the 1992–94 Multi-City Study of Urban Inequality (MCSUI). The MCSUI data are the product of more than forty researchers at fifteen colleges and universities. A household survey was undertaken of adults over twenty-one years of age, oversampling in census tracts with high proportions of poor and minority residents. Although primarily designed as a study of labor market outcomes, the extensive surveys also had questions regarding racial attitudes and neighborhood choice. The MCSUI is a stratified-area probability household survey from 1994 and 1995 that generated over 8,900 face-to-face interviews with oversamples of blacks, Latinos, and Asian Americans in the metropolitan areas of Atlanta, Boston, and Detroit and in Los Angeles County. Adults twenty-one years and older were interviewed in English, Spanish, Korean, Mandarin, or Cantonese.

The MCSUI oversampled underrepresented minority groups whose small numbers and geographic concentration in the general population often lead to lack of sufficient sample sizes in traditional surveys. The Atlanta sample includes 651 whites, 832 blacks, and forty-five persons who identified with neither group. The Boston sample includes 469 whites, 518 blacks, and 833 Latinos. The Los Angeles sample includes 861 whites, 1,119 blacks, 986 Latinos, and 1,055 Asian Americans. Among the 1,055 Asian Americans surveyed, the majority (nearly 80 percent) were of Chinese and Korean origin, and the remainder of the sample was made up of respondents of Japanese and South Asian descent. The majority (88 percent) of the Asian American sample were foreign-born. Over half of the Los Angeles Latino sample (68 percent) were of Mexican origin. Central Americans, primarily from El Salvador and Guatemala, made up the remainder of the sample. Similar to the Asian American sample, the majority of Los Angeles Latinos included in the study (80 percent) were foreign-born. The overwhelming majority of Latinos in the Boston sample were either Puerto Rican or Dominican in descent. To identify the racial context, the census block group of each respondent was identified and matched with appropriate census data. Each block group varies from several hundred to up to two thousand in population size.

The second major survey is the 2000 Social Capital Community Benchmark Survey (SCCBS). Initiated by Professor Robert Putnam and the Saguaro Seminar at the Kennedy School of Government at Harvard University, the SSCBS was designed to measure various indicators of social capital and community involvement. It entailed surveys conducted in forty-one different communities around the United States as well as a national sample. The national sample of over 3,000 respondents contains an oversampling of blacks and Hispanics, totaling at least 500 blacks and 500 Hispanics in all. This required screening to identify households with black or Hispanic residents. This screening was conducted randomly across the continental United States; areas of higher concentration were not targeted in this design. For each respondent, local geography was measured at both the metropolitan and zip code level and once again came from the 2000 U.S. Census.

The third major data set is the Citizen, Information, and Democracy (CID) Survey conducted in 2004. The CID consists of in-person interviews with a nationwide, clustered sample of 1,001 Americans who answered an eighty-minute questionnaire. The CID contains extensive questions about civic engagement (both informal social activities and activities in formal clubs or organizations), social capital, democratic values, and diversity. For the CID, the metropolitan area and the census tract of each respondent were identified and supplemented with data from the 2000 census.

The final data set comes from the 2004 National Politics Study initiated by the Program for Research on Black Americans and the Center for Political Studies at the University of Michigan's Institute for Social Research and sponsored by the National Science Foundation, the University of Michigan, and the Carnegie Corporation. From September 2004 to February 2005, 3,339 telephone interviews were conducted in the United States with adults and a large oversample of African American, Latino, and Asian American respondents. The survey queried respondents on their voting preferences, party affiliation, organizational membership, and racial attitudes. The public release of these data included no geographic identifiers and, unlike the other data, was not matched with census data.

Notes

Introduction

1. Throughout this book, the terms "white" and "black" will refer primarily to non-Latino whites and blacks, respectively. "Latino" will generally refer to those Americans who have immigrated or whose forebears have immigrated from Latin America. "Asian Americans" will refer to those Americans who have immigrated or whose forebears have immigrated from Asia.

2. The United States can be divided roughly into four sizeable racial groups: non-Latino whites of European descent, who are roughly 69 percent of U.S. residents; African Americans and Latinos, each approximately 13 percent; and Asian Americans, roughly 4 percent (about 1.5 percent of Americans identified themselves as having multiple races in the 2000 census). Of course, these percentages do not include indigenous peoples of North America or the Pacific Islands who, while also distinct racial/ethnic groups, number around 1 percent of the American population; but, because of their small size and high degree of geographic isolation, they are not included in the analysis in this book.

3. The relatively constant segregation rate does not mean that Latinos' integration patterns are holding constant. Some Latinos are integrating into American society, but the high level of immigration and the great population increase are creating larger pockets of heavily Latino areas. As the Latino population grows so quickly, more Latinos are living in integrated settings, but more, particularly new immigrants, are moving into segregated ethnic communities (Frey and Farley 1996).

4. Obviously there are more than four racial groups in the United States, and some may question whether the categories of Latino and Asian American even make sense as racial groupings. To the first concern, I note that most other significant racial categories measured by the census and survey researchers, such as Native Americans or Pacific Islanders, are not large enough portions of the population to adequately research with the data available. The second concern is addressed in more detail in chapter 2.

5. This issue also represents a chronic dilemma at the heart of any social science inquiry: how much of human behavior can be attributed to environmental characteristics versus the individual characteristics of the people in that environment?

6. Some recent excellent works on race in the United States include Fredrickson (2002), Gilens (1999), Kinder and Sanders (1996), Patterson (1997), Sears et al. (2000), and Sniderman and Piazza (1993).

Chapter 1

1. For an exception, see Cumming and Lambert (1997).

2. White perceptions of racial threat also depend upon economic circumstances. Situations of economic duress have been found to exacerbate white feelings of racial vulnerability and thus heighten racial tension. For example, in his classic study of the old South, Key (1949) found that the racial and political differences between counties in Alabama and North Carolina came not just from the presence of large black populations (which were equally large in both places) but from the particular white class arrangements. Whites who were more economically marginalized were much more prone to racial violence than those who were not. In more recent research, both Oliver and Mendelberg (2000) and Quillian (1995) find that economic contexts are just as important as the racial setting in shaping white racial attitudes toward blacks.

3. An important caveat to note about this simple formula is that the relationship between minority population size and white racial attitudes is not static but is time and place sensitive. Racial threat is a dynamic process that comes from the challenge that minorities present to white social predominance; the impact of minority populations on white perceptions of threat will also be related not just to their current position but to their relative position. White attitudes will be affected not only by the size of minority populations but also by the change in population size and by the rigidity of segregation. In other words, whites who live in a metropolis that has been 20 percent black for decades may not feel as threatened as whites who live in a metropolitan area that became 20 percent black only in recent time. Similarly, whites who live in an area where the boundaries of segregation are clearly defined may feel less threatened than those who live in areas where neighborhood racial lines are more fluid.

4. It is also important to consider whether the high levels of racial segregation among neighborhoods and suburbs in most American metropolitan areas allow for racial threat to even exist in smaller geographic areas. Most whites are politically and spatially segregated from African Americans along municipal lines. Given that many public goods and resources, such as schools and housing, are distributed within these municipal boundaries, one may wonder how much competition suburban whites feel from neighboring black populations. In other words, high

levels of neighborhood and suburban racial segregation serve to protect whites from any competition or threat to status no matter how large the proximate black population. While larger minority populations in a county may threaten some types of resources, such as jobs, it is not self-evident that a high percentage of blacks in a unit as large as a county or metropolitan area is a sufficient threat to all privileges. The extent to which whites feel threatened from black populations (assuming the threat hypothesis is true) may hinge on the degree to which they feel their immediate racial context, be it their neighborhood or city, is secure from racial incursion.

5. Some of the benefits of interracial proximity may be related to mere social exposure; according to research in psychology, anxiety and misperception of foreign groups will lessen with more familiarity (Zajonc 1968). Welch et al. (2001) suggest that this theory can be applied to the relationship between integration and racial tolerance. Negative images promoted through the mass media, as well as those triggered by unfamiliar languages or traditions associated with particular ethnic groups, may reinforce the belief that a group is foreign or does not "belong." Such negative attitudes can be countered through increased exposure to different communities. Residents of highly segregated neighborhoods who are never exposed to out-groups save through images in the mass media may have few opportunities to correct or disconfirm erroneous stereotypes (Dyer, Velditz, and Worchel 1989; Lee 2000; Hum and Zonta 2000). Interracial social experiences or simple exposure may alleviate racial animosity, but minority groups need to have the opportunity to be seen before any effects will be felt. Others, however, may doubt this. Pettigrew (1998) argues that exposure and contact under social conditions that do not include equal status and goal sharing can actually exacerbate racial tensions.

6. Some ethnographies (e.g., Rieder 1987) have studied patterns of white racial animosity in integrated neighborhoods, but it is impossible to generalize from this research whether living in an integrated neighborhood in general makes whites more hostile to blacks. It is unclear whether the same levels of racial hostility might also exist in all-white neighborhoods because such places were not studies in comparison.

7. For example, in their otherwise excellent study of racial attitudes in Detroit, Welch et al. (2001) leave out any mention of self-selection in their findings. It is impossible to know whether their hopeful results, that integration fosters greater racial tolerance, is simply the result of people with more racially tolerant attitudes choosing to live in more integrated settings.

8. For possible evidence, see Hood and Morris (1997), Quillian (1995), and Stein, Post, and Rinden (2000).

9. The exit, voice, pass options derive from Albert Hirschmann's theories of organizational behavior and are well articulated in this context by Roger Brown's explanation of social identification theory.

Chapter 2

1. Throughout this book I will use Asian and Asian American interchangeably.

2. Respondents in the 2005 CID were asked a series of questions that started with the following: "Now we would like to ask your opinion about different racial groups in the United States. Would you say you agree strongly, agree, are uncertain, disagree, or disagree strongly with the following statements." The respondents were then read a series of statements about each group and asked how much they agreed or disagreed with each statement. Each italicized term above refers to a particular question.

3. In Los Angeles and Boston, respondents were divided between those asked about blacks and those asked about Latinos. In Detroit and Atlanta, respondents were only asked about blacks. The question was posed as follows: "I'm going to mention several reason for why [blacks/Latinos] have worse jobs, housing, and income than white people. I'd like you to tell me whether you strongly agree, somewhat agree, somewhat disagree or strongly disagree with each reason I mention." The respondents were then asked about "racial discrimination," "most [blacks/Latinos] have less in-born ability to learn," "most [blacks/Latinos] don't have the chance for the education it takes to rise out of poverty," and "most [blacks/Latinos just don't have the motivation or will power to pull themselves up out of poverty."

4. With respect to blacks, the ability and motivation questions correlated at .26 and .39 with the composite negative stereotype scale.

5. Respondents were asked a series of questions with which they could agree or disagree (either strongly or somewhat) for each racial group; these questions included "More good jobs for [OTHER GROUP] means few good jobs for people like me" and "The more influence [OTHER GROUP] have in politics, the less influence people like me will have in politics."

6. Slightly different trends appear in the MCSUI data. In Boston and Los Angeles, whites express the greatest feelings of competition with Asians, slightly lower levels with Latinos, and the lowest levels with African Americans. For instance, whites in Los Angeles score .78 on the Asian competition scale, .75 on the Latino competition scale, and only .66 on the black competition scale. In Atlanta, whites express a higher average rating on the black competition scale, but there are no other ethnic groups to provide a basis of comparison. Nevertheless, in multiethnic Los Angeles and Boston, whites feel a greater sense of racial competition with Latinos and Asians than they do with African Americans.

7. In the NPS survey, respondents were asked, "Do you think what happens generally to [the respondent's race] people in this country will have something to do with what happens in your life?" If they said yes, they were asked to gauge the extent of this as either "a lot," "some," or "not very much." The cell entries in table 2.1 are for those who answered "a lot."

8. NPS respondents were asked, "Some people say the following things are important for being truly American. Others say they are not important. How impor-

tant do you think each of the following is for being truly American, very important, fairly important, not very important, or not important at all? How important is it to have been born in America?"

9. These figures are based on data released by the U.S. Census (http://www .census.gov) and have some limitations because the census allowed for multiple racial identities and 2.5 percent of the population listed more than one race. In addition, the census asks a separate question about whether the respondents indicated whether they were Hispanic or Latino. Consequently, there will be some overlap between the groups. However, these issues are unlikely to alter the fact that Latinos now outnumber African Americans: a significant portion of blacks also consider themselves Latino, and over one-third of the multiracial respondents consider themselves Latino. Consequently, even if the complexities of racial identity could be sorted through, it is unlikely that blacks would outnumber Latinos.

10. Yet not all Asian Americans have achieved this level of incorporation, and many Asian American groups retain persistent gaps in education, income, health, and life status. Some of these differences are due to the circumstances of nationality. The majority of Asian Americans are Chinese, Indian, or Filipino in origin, but a significant number are refugees from Southeast Asia, such as Vietnam or Cambodia. Many of these groups did not arrive with the education or capital of immigrants from other parts of Asia and have shown much lower levels of economic success (Oliver et al. 1995).

11. Over 6 percent of Latinos identified with two or more races, although the vast majority of these were with white and other.

12. In the MCSUI data, Latino respondents were allowed to identify themselves by their own country of origin or the country from which they claimed a heritage. These included, "Mexican," "Mexican-American," "Puerto Rican," "Salvadoran," as well as other ethnic groups. Given the relatively small numbers in the survey coming from other countries, they were lumped together as other. In the SCCBS data, substantial numbers of respondents could list "Mexican," "Cuban," and "Puerto Rican," which were differentiated. All other Latino respondents were grouped in the "other" category.

13. For the negative stereotype scale, the question was worded as follows:

> Now I [the interviewer] have some questions about different groups in our (U.S.) Society. I'm going to show you a 7-point scale on which the characteristics of people in a group can be rated. In the first statement a score of 1 means that you think almost all of the people in that group are "rich." A score of 7 means that you think almost everyone in the group is "poor." A score of 4 means you think that the group is not towards one end or the other and, of course, you may choose any number in between that comes closest to where you think people in the group stand. Where would you rate (GROUP) on this scale, where 1 means tends to be rich and 7 means tends to be poor?

After this question, the following questions were asked and used in the negative stereotype summary score: "Next, for each group, I want to know whether you think they tend to be intelligent or tend to be unintelligent . . ."; "Next, for each group, I want to know whether you think they tend to prefer to be self-supporting or tend to prefer to be on welfare . . ."; "Next, for each group, I want to know if you think they tend to be easy to get along with or tend to be hard to get along with . . ."; and, "Finally, for each group, I want to know whether you think they tend to treat members of other races equally or tend to discriminate against members of other groups." For each of these questions, the respondent was asked about members of all other racial groups. Each of the seven-point scales was recoded so that positive and neutral perceptions were counted as zero and any negative perception as one; then the scores were added to produce a four-point summary negative stereotype score.

14. This difference may be related to regional factors—most of the Mexicans in the MCSUI data are in Los Angeles, while most Puerto Ricans are in Boston.

15. In part, because the vast majority of these immigrants come from Mexico or Central America, Latinos tend to be disproportionately located in the southwestern parts of the United States, with half of all Latinos living in either California or Texas. In addition, the large immigrant component of the Latino population, together with its generally higher fertility, creates great differences in age, length of residence, and region with the rest of the nation. Latinos are much younger than the country as a whole. The median age for Latinos is 25.9 years, compared with 35.3 years for the U.S. population (Bean and Stevens 2003).

Chapter 3

1. Although individual income is often used as a predictor of negative out-group stereotypes, and is related to the place of residence, a significant portion of the MCSUI sample, as with most surveys, refused to answer the household income item. In order to minimize the number of missing cases, individual income was not included in the model. This action seems justified in two respects. First, the individual education and homeownership items as well as the block group education items capture a good deal of the individual's own income and social status level. Second, when the regressions were estimated with income included, the results were generally the same.

2. A longer description of this estimation procedure and the full equations for the figures are listed in online appendix B, table B1. Because of the tiny Asian American and Latino populations in Atlanta and Detroit, there is not enough variance to estimate the effects of the size of these groups in the neighborhood for these metropolitan areas. The same holds for Asian Americans in Boston. Hence the effects of neighborhood context were estimated separately for each metropolitan area.

3. In the OLS equations, as listed in appendix A, the distinct effects of the metropolitan area are measured with dummy variables for Atlanta, Boston, and Detroit plus interaction terms between the dummy variables and the term measuring percent white in the neighborhood, which are all included in the equation along with a standard set of individual-level controls.

4. The racial competition variable was the same one described above in chapter 2. The immigrant threat variable was constructed from two five-point scales asking how much "political influence" and "economic opportunity" people of the respondent's race would have if immigration continues at its current rate. Once again, samples from all three metropolitan areas were pooled with dummy variables measuring residence in Atlanta and Boston and interaction terms between the percent in-group in the neighborhood and the metropolitan dummy variables. In short, these equations predict perceptions of zero-sum competition with specific minority groups and threats to political and economic power by immigrants. The full equation is listed in online appendix B, table B4.

5. These results are also found when examining whites' opinions about affirmative action. Across all three metropolitan areas, whites who live in predominantly white neighborhoods were consistently more opposed to affirmative action policies that benefited minorities than whites in more integrated neighborhoods. And, once again, the economic composition of whites' neighborhoods is also an important predictor of their racial policy views: whites who live in low-status neighborhoods, irrespective of their racial composition, were far more likely to oppose affirmative action than those in high-status settings.

6. For example, in the OLS equations listed in appendix B, the coefficients for percent white in the neighborhood are greater than those for education or age when the scaling of the variables is taken into account.

7. These are listed in online appendix B, table B5. For black respondents in Los Angeles, this was done on views about Asians, Latinos, and whites; for those in Boston, only views about Latinos and whites were measured; and for blacks in Atlanta, only feelings about whites were measured. These differences across cities are due to the small Latino and Asian populations in Atlanta and the small Asian population in Boston, which provide little basis for geographic comparison. The Detroit portion of the MCSUI data was excluded from this analysis because almost the entire black sample lived in all-black neighborhoods and had little difference in the racial composition of their neighborhoods.

8. The full equations are listed in online appendix B, table B4. Because of the small portion of blacks in the population and their high levels of segregation, I employed a quadratic term (the percent black in the neighborhood squared) to estimate nonlinear effects.

9. The full equations for the figures are listed in online appendix B, table B5. Once again, as with white Bostonians' views, black Bostonians' views about Latinos tend to run opposite to all of the other findings. The exact reason for this may

have to do with the particular growth of the Puerto Rican community in Boston and the particular neighborhoods it are encroaches upon. The difference in black Atlantans' views is definitely due to the higher levels of integration in Atlanta and the proportionately larger black population. Unlike in Los Angeles or Boston, a neighborhood that is 50 percent black in the Atlanta metropolitan area is not disproportionately black relative to the city population. It is only neighborhoods in the Atlanta metropolis that are more than 50 percent black that could be considered disproportionately black.

10. For a full description, see chapter 2.

11. These questions were not asked in the Atlanta survey.

12. The results are listed in online appendix B, table B5.

13. Unlike the predictions in the hypotheses, blacks' opposition to interracial marriage with Latinos or Asians in particular was not significantly affected by the percent of either group in the metropolitan area. For example, 8 percent of blacks opposed interracial marriage with Latinos in metropolitan areas that were at least 20 percent Latino, the same number that opposed interracial marriage in metropolitan areas that were under 20 percent Latino. Similarly, 11 percent of blacks in metropolitan areas that were 20 percent Asian opposed interracial marriage with Asians, compared with 9 percent in metropolitan areas that were less than 10 percent Asian. It should be noted, however, that these results are based on relatively small samples from the heavily Asian and Latino metropolitan areas.

14. Interestingly, blacks' attitudes toward affirmative action programs that benefit either Latinos or Asians were largely insensitive to neighborhood or regional racial composition: blacks who live in predominantly black neighborhoods were no more opposed to affirmative action programs that benefit Latinos or Asians than those who live in integrated settings. The one difference was that blacks who live in predominantly black neighborhoods were more in favor of affirmative action programs that benefit blacks. Whereas whites' feelings about affirmative action seem to reflect white racial resentment toward out-groups, for blacks, opinions about affirmative action seem to reflect greater in-group solidarity.

15. The full equation is listed in online appendix B, table B6.

16. When the OLS equation estimating perceptions of discrimination is run without the variable measuring language of interview, there is a large and statistically significant difference predicted in the scores of Latinos: those in predominantly Latino neighborhoods were far more likely to agree that discrimination hurts Latinos' job chances than those in integrated neighborhoods. When the measure of Spanish language interview is included, however, the coefficient for the percent Latino in the neighborhood diminishes by half and loses statistical significance.

17. In the nationwide sample of the SCCBS data, there was no evidence that feelings of ethnic solidarity (measured by the "how much of a sense of community do you get from people in your ethnic group) varies according to the racial composition of the neighborhood. In OLS regressions that estimated the relationship between this ethnic solidarity measure and the racial composition of the metropolitan

area and neighborhood, there were no significant findings. Just as with the MCSUI data from Boston and Los Angeles, there is little evidence that feelings of solidarity with Latinos are influenced by the racial composition of the environment.

18. The five-point opposition to interracial marriage variable was regressed on variables measuring the percent of the target group in the metropolitan area, the percent Latino in the neighborhood or the percent of the target group in the neighborhood, and a set of control variables including neighborhood income and individual-level age, education, homeownership, length of residence, citizenship, and political knowledge. The full results are listed in online appendix B, table B9.

19. To estimate the impact of Asian racial contexts, OLS regressions were run estimating changes in the predicted negative stereotype scores for blacks, Latinos, and whites by the percent of Asians in the Asian respondents' neighborhood with controls for language of interview and immigration and citizenship status and a list of individual-level controls such as education, income, age, homeownership, and length of residence. Full results are listed in online appendix B, table B10.

20. Interestingly, among the Asian sample, the regression equations show a positive relationship between education levels and negative stereotypes. Asian Americans with higher education levels were more likely to hold negative stereotypes of all other groups, a trend that is in opposition to that of all other racial groups in which education generally corresponds with less negative stereotypes. As this result is contrary to so many theories about the positive effects of education on racial attitudes, it certainly deserves more exploration in future research.

21. In fact, these results are not the consequence of simply being an ethnic Korean. Among respondents who were interviewed in English but who spoke Korean at home, there were no significant differences in the average negative stereotype scale. The results are only valid for those respondents interviewed in Korean.

22. Online appendix B, table B11, lists the effects of neighborhood racial environment (measured by the percent of Asians in the neighborhood) for the sample divided by their language of interview from interaction terms from OLS regression analyses. In other words, the figures are derived from the interaction terms between the interview language and the percent Asian in the neighborhood in addition to the standard set of controls.

23. Unincorporated Koreans who live in neighborhoods with a higher percentage of blacks were slightly more negative in their views of blacks than those in neighborhoods with few blacks, although the distribution of the measure was quite limited, and a similar pattern emerged for other Asian groups. Over 75 percent of unincorporated Koreans live in neighborhoods that are under 12 percent black, and 98 percent live in neighborhoods that are under 30 percent black. Nevertheless, despite these smaller numbers, Korean interviewees were the most likely of any Asian group in the MCSUI sample to live in neighborhoods with African Americans. For example, 98 percent of the Chinese interviewees live in neighborhoods that are under 5 percent black, and over 90 percent of the English-speaking Asian respondents live in neighborhoods that are under 12 percent black. While Asian

Americans in Los Angeles are highly segregated from blacks as a group, unincorporated Koreans were comparatively more integrated. It is also possible that these results are picking up neighborhood proximity. In other words, Asians who live in neighborhoods that are proximate to black areas are probably more negative in their views of African Americans. Unfortunately, the available data do not allow this assertion to be tested further.

24. When regression analyses are run measuring the effects of percent white on Asians' attitudes toward whites, the results are basically replicated. English-speaking interviewees who live in predominantly white neighborhoods are less negative in their views of whites, while Chinese interviewees in white neighborhoods tend to be more negative in their views of whites.

25. Admittedly, however, this is a very small number of cities with which to make a comparison.

Chapter 4

1. The MCSUI data also provide other mechanisms for testing neighborhood racial preferences including a measure of neighborhoods the respondent would not move into and a measure for which respondents fill in the racial composition of their ideal neighborhood using a blank card. Similar results are derived with these alternative measures too: whites who prefer whites as neighbors (or resist having minorities as neighbors) are more likely to live in predominantly white neighborhoods.

2. Respondents ordered the neighborhoods from most to least desirable. Respondents who listed their top two neighborhoods as the ones that were mostly or all black were coded 5, those who listed either the all- or mostly black neighborhood as one of their top two choices were coded 4, and so on.

3. Online appendix B, table B15, lists the coefficients from ordinary least squares regression equations in the MCSUI data predicting negative stereotype scores by the percent white in the neighborhood for all three racial groups, before and after controlling for neighborhood racial preference. In each of the equations, the first column lists the coefficients for an equation that estimates just the impact of the percent white in a white's neighborhood along with the three interaction terms between percent white and Atlanta, Boston, and Detroit, as well as the standard set of controls. In other words, these are the coefficients from which the estimates in chapter 3 were derived. The second set are the same equations only adding two terms that control for neighborhood racial preference: the five-point scale for white neighbor preference and another item scored from one to twelve based on a question that asked respondents to pick how many white neighbors they would have if they could choose. These two items serve as controls for the preference for white neighbors among the white MCSUI respondents.

4. The full equations are in online appendix B, table B15.

Chapter 5

1. Despite its consistency with the findings in this book, the Welch et al. study leaves several questions unanswered. First, it did not control for geographic self-selection of the residents. Although the previous chapter indicates that self-selection is generally not a contributing factor in the overall pattern of racial attitudes, it did have some effect on whites' racial attitudes. Since most of Welch et al.'s research focused on how contact influenced whites' racial views, it is unclear whether self-selection underlies their findings. Second, the data for the Welch et al. study only came from Detroit, which, because of its extreme levels of segregation, provides little variation in social contexts. In other words, those few whites who do live in "integrated" neighborhoods in Detroit may themselves to be something of an anomaly. Third, the Welch et al. study did not analyze the impact of multiethnic settings on patterns of social contact. It is unclear whether social contact and segregation operate in the same manner for Latinos and Asian Americans as they do for blacks and whites.

2. Data from the SCCBS show that among whites, there are significant differences in the level of interracial friendships, particularly with Asians and Latinos, by the percentage of these groups in a person's metropolitan area. On average, 75 percent of whites in metropolitan areas with large Asian or Latino populations (over 20 percent) had friendships with people of these races, compared with only 35 percent of whites in metropolitan areas with few Asians or Latinos (under 10 percent). Whites who lived in areas with smaller black populations, under 10 percent, had slightly lower rates of black friendship, although these differences were not as great as with Latinos and Asians. In metropolitan areas that are more than 30 percent black, 70 percent of whites report having a black friend, as opposed to only 60 percent in metropolitan areas that are under 10 percent black. African Americans were also twice as likely to have Asian or Latino friends if they lived in a metropolis with larger numbers of these groups. In fact, the only friendship patterns to be relatively unaffected by the racial composition of a metropolitan area were among minorities and whites—there were few differences in the amounts of friendships that Asians, blacks, or Latinos had with whites between metropolitan areas with large and smaller white populations. This is due largely to the fact that whites make up such a large percentage of most metropolitan areas. Nevertheless, these findings accord with an expectation—the likelihood of whites having contact with minorities and minorities having contact with each other depends somewhat on the size of the available minority population.

3. Respondents in SCCBS were asked whether they participate in any civic organizations (this item will be explained in greater depth in chapter 6). Among those who said they participated in such organizations, a follow-up question was posed on whether the other members of the group were of the same race as the respondent (the respondent could answer all, most, some, few, or none). Those

who said that some, few, or none of their fellow group members were of their race were counted as belonging to an interracial group. This measure did not include church membership.

4. There are also significant differences between Asian American and Latino citizens and noncitizens, with citizens being more likely to participate in integrated civic associations than noncitizens.

5. For a full listing of the results, see online appendix B, table B16.

6. Although some researchers using sophisticated statistical modeling have sorted through these various effects and still found evidence of contact (e.g., Welch et al. 2001), generally speaking it is all but impossible to identify, outside an experimental situation, whether contact with people of other races changes people's racial attitudes.

7. The MCSUI data, which have the largest numbers of cases and good measures of racial attitudes, do not have any good indicators of people's social contacts. The SCCBS data have only limited measures of both social contact (self-reports of friends with particular groups) and only two measures of racial attitudes. The CID data have only a small number of cases, particularly of minorities, and not enough cases to measure sufficient differences across racial contexts

8. The results are depicted in online appendix B, table B17.

Chapter 6

1. The civic participation scale was a simple count of the number of civic activities the respondent said he or she had engaged in during the past year, including voting, signing a petition, attending a political meeting, working on a community project, and participating in a demonstration. The civic participation index was rescaled to 0 to 1 for this table. The informal social interaction scale was a composite measure of five activities: having friends visit one's home, visiting with relatives, socializing with coworkers outside of work, hanging out with friends in public places, and playing cards or board games with friends). At least two of the activities had to be engaged in for the scale to be calculated. The index was calculated as the mean of the standardized responses to the five questions. The index was rescaled to 0 to 1.

2. The predicted probability at each point was calculated using CLARIFY software. The full equations are listed in online appendix B, table B18. Together, these items comprise a good battery of indicators of people's civic activities, and the latter three are the best indicators of their participation in local activities. Each of these measures was regressed on a set of predictive variables including the percent white in the metropolitan area and the percent white in the neighborhood as well as a host of individual-level controls for race, income, education, sex, and homeownership.

3. Civic associations are counted as sports clubs, hobby clubs, trade unions, professional associations, consumer organizations, organizations for human rights,

environmental associations, religious organizations, political parties, organizations for education, social clubs (for the elderly or the retired or fraternal organizations), neighborhood associations, veterans' organizations, self-help groups, welfare organizations, and any other voluntary civic associations. Questions were asked in order: after seeing the list of civic groups, respondents were asked to report whether they actively participate or do any voluntary works in those associations.

4. Of course, race is not the only contextual determinant of American associational life; the level of affluence is also negatively associated with most civic activities. This finding, which is consistent with that of a prior study (Oliver 2001), suggests that people are highly individualized and socially disconnected particularly in rich and small geographic areas.

5. Online appendix B, table B19, lists the results from multivariate linear regressions that estimate the relationship of individual-level and geographic-level variables to scale, measuring how much they informally socialized with neighbors and whether they participated in a neighborhood group. Once again, the equations control for individual-level factors such as age, education, length of residence, and homeownership and for the level of incorporation into American society using variables for citizenship and political knowledge. The remaining variables estimate the effects of the racial composition of the neighborhood (measured by the percent white) with interaction terms for each of the three minority groups. These interaction terms measure the additional impact of the white percentage of the neighborhood for each minority group and should be viewed in conjunction with the variable measuring the participation rate attributed to that specific group as well as the variable measuring the baseline effect of the white percentage of the neighborhood.

6. Interestingly, black informal social ties do not follow a linear pattern with respect to the black percentage in their neighborhood. Rather, much like their racial views, blacks' informal social activity scores are highest in the middle range of black neighborhoods. Blacks in neighborhoods that are 40–60 percent black score significantly higher on the informal social activity scale than those in neighborhoods that are much less black or predominantly black.

7. For the trust question, respondents were asked, "How much can you trust people in your neighborhood? Can you trust them a lot, trust them some, trust them only a little, or trust them not at all?" The answers to this question were coded on a four-point scale from not trusting to most trusting. For the neighborhood belonging, respondents were asked, "Do people in your community give you a sense of belonging" to which they could answer yes or no. To rate the quality of life in their community, respondents were asked, "On the whole, how would you rate your community as a place to live—poor, only fair, good, or excellent." This was coded into a four-point scale from poor to excellent. These items were then regressed on the same set of predictors used to measure civic and social involvement above. The results are listed in online appendix B, table B20.

8. This last figure was derived from probability estimates from logistic regression equations. Logistic regression was not employed, despite the fact of a

dichotomous dependent variable, in order to maintain comparability of coefficients across all equations. There are no substantive differences in the findings between the OLS and logistic regression equations.

9. There are, of course, many individual accounts of Latinos and Asian Americans in American life (e.g., Kim 2000; Portes and Bach 1985), but I could find no systematic research on the civic and social patterns of these groups in relationship to their social surroundings.

Chapter 7

1. The exception here is among Asian Americans who, as a very small portion of the population, tend to be much more integrated and who are very diverse by virtue of nationality.

2. Which contrasts with the voluntary character of the Gautreaux housing program.

3. Although not listed in chapter 5, the SCCBS data show a similar trend among Latinos in feelings of community with the racial composition of their neighborhood. Like African Americans, Latinos who live in predominantly same-group neighborhoods are more likely to feel a sense of community from their neighborhood and were more likely to report a feeling a community from their ethnic group membership.

4. We can also contrast the voluntary immigrant experience with the involuntary immigration of people caught in the slave trade from Africa.

References

Achen, Christopher, and W. Phillips Shiveley. 1993. *Cross-Level Inference*. Chicago: University of Chicago Press.

Alba, Richard, and Victor Nee. 1997. Rethinking Assimilation Theory for a New Era of Immigration. *International Migration Review* 31 (4): 826–74.

Alesina, Albert, and E. La Ferrara. 2000. Participation in Heterogeneous Communities. *Quarterly Journal of Economics* (August): 847–904.

Allport, Gordon. 1954. *The Nature of Prejudice*. Boston: Beacon Press.

Anderson, Elijah. 2001."The Social Situation of the Black Executive: Black and White Identities in the Corporate World. In *Problem of the Century*, edited by Elijah Anderson and Douglas Massey. New York: Russell Sage Foundation.

Auerbach, Susan, ed. 1994. *Encyclopedia of Multiculturalism*. New York: Marshall Cavendish.

Banfield, Edward. 1970. *The Unheavenly City*. Boston: Little, Brown.

Bean, Frank D., and Gillian Stevens. 2003. *America's Newcomers: Immigrant Incorporation and the Dynamics of Diversity*. New York: Russell Sage Foundation.

Bell, Derrick. 1992. *Faces at the Bottom of the Well*. New York: Basic Books.

Berry, Kate, and Martha Henderson. 2002. *Geographical Identities of Ethnic America: Race, Space, and Place*. Reno: University of Nevada Press.

Bettleheim, Bruno, and Morris Janowitz. 1964. *Social Change and Prejudice*. New York: Basic Books.

Blalock, Hubert M., Jr. 1967. *Toward a Theory of Minority-Group Relations*. New York: John Wiley.

Bledsoe, Timothy, Susan Welch, Lee Sigelman, and Michael Combs. 1995. Residential Context and Racial Solidarity among African Americans. *American Journal of Political Science* 39 (2): 434–58.

Bluestone, Barry, and Mary Huff Stevenson. 2000. *The Boston Renaissance: Race, Space, and Economic Change in an American Metropolis*. New York: Russell Sage Foundation.

Blumer, Herbert. 1958. Race Prejudice As a Sense of Group Position. *Pacific Sociological Review* 1(1): 3–7.

Bobo, Lawrence. 1983. Whites' Opposition to Busing: Symbolic Racism or Re-
alistic Group Conflict? *Journal of Personality and Social Psychology* 45 (6):
1196–210.
————. 1999. Prejudice as Group Position: Microfoundations of a Sociological Ap-
proach to Racism and Race Relations. *Journal of Social Issues* 55 (3): 445–72.
Bobo, Lawrence, and Vincent L. Hutchings. 1996. Perceptions of Racial Group
Competition: Extending Blumer's Theory of Group Position to a Multiracial
Social Context. *American Sociological Review* 61 (6): 951–72.
Bobo, Lawrence D., and Devon Johnson. 2000. Racial Attitudes in the Prismatic
Metropolis: Identity, Stereotypes, and Perceived Group Competition in Los
Angeles. In *Prismatic Metropolis: Inequality in Los Angles*, edited by Lawrence
D. Bobo, Melvin L. Oliver, James H. Johnson, Jr., and Abel Valenzuela. New
York: Russell Sage Foundation.
Bobo, Lawrence D., and James R. Kluegel. 1993. Opposition to Race Targeting:
Self-Interest, Stratification Ideology, or Racial Attitudes? *American Sociologi-
cal Review* 58 (4): 443–64.
Bobo, Lawrence D., and Michael P. Massagli. 2001. Stereotypes and Urban Inequal-
ity. In *Urban Inequality: Evidence from Four Cities*, edited by Alice O'Conner,
Chris Tilly, and Lawrence Bobo. New York: Russell Sage Foundation.
Bobo, Lawrence D., Melvin L. Oliver, James H. Johnson, Jr., and Abel Valenzuela.
2000. *Prismatic Metropolis: Inequality in Los Angeles*. New York: Russell Sage
Foundation.
Bobo, Lawrence, and Camille L. Zubrinsky. 1996. Attitudes on Residential In-
tegration: Perceived Status Differences, Mere In-Group Preference, or Racial
Prejudice? *Social Forces* 73 (3): 883–909.
Boger, John Charles, and Judith Welch Wegner. 1986. *Race and Poverty in Ameri-
can Cities*. Chapel Hill: University of North Carolina Press.
Borjas, George. 1999. *Heaven's Door: Immigration Policy and the American Econ-
omy*. Princeton, NJ: Princeton University Press.
Branscombe, Nyla, and Daniel Wann. 1994. Collective Self-Esteem Consequences
of Outgroup Derogation When a Valued Social Identity Is on Trial. *European
Journal of Social Psychology* 24 (3): 641–57.
Brewer, Marilynn B., and Norman Miller. 1988. Contact and Cooperation: When
Do They Work? In *Eliminating Racism*, edited by Phyllis Katz and Dalmas
Taylor. New York: Plenum Press.
Brown, Roger. 1986. Ethnocentrism and Hostility. In *Social Psychology*, by Roger
Brown. 2d ed. New York: Free Press.
Buchanan, Patrick. 2006. *State of Emergency: The Third World Invasion and Con-
quest of America*. New York: Thomas Dunne Books.
Campbell, David. 2006. *Why We Vote: How Schools and Communities Shape Our
Civic Life*. Princeton, NJ: Princeton University Press.
Carsay, Thomas. 1995. The Contextual Effects of Race on White Voter Behavior.
Journal of Politics 57 (1): 221–28.

Cederman, Lars-Erik, and Luc Girardin. 2000. Beyond Fractionalization: Mapping Ethnicity onto Nationalist Insurgencies. *American Political Science Review* 101:173–85.

Charles, Camille Zubrinsky. 2000. Socioeconomic Status and Segregation: African Americans, Hispanics, and Asians in Los Angeles. In *Problem of the Century*, edited by Elijah Anderson and Douglas Massey. New York: Russell Sage Foundation.

————. 2001. Residential Segregation in Los Angeles. In *Prismatic Metropolis: Inequality in Los Angles*, edited by Lawrence D. Bobo, Melvin L. Oliver, James H. Johnson, Jr., and Abel Valenzuela. New York: Russell Sage Foundation.

Clampet-Lundquist, Susan, Kathryn Edin, Jeffrey R. Kling, and Greg J. Duncan. 2006. Moving At-Risk Teenagers out of High Risk Neighborhoods: Why Girls Fare Better than Boys. Princeton IRS Working Paper no. 509.

Clark, William A.V. 1992. Residential Preferences and Residential Choices in a Multi-Ethnic Context. *Demography* 29 (3): 451–66.

Cohen, Cathy, and Michael Dawson. 1993. Neighborhood Poverty and African American Politics. *American Political Science Review* 87:286–302.

Costa, Dora, and Matthew Kahn. 2003. Civic Engagement and Community Heterogeneity: an Economist's Perspective. *Perspectives on Politics* 1:103–11.

Cummings, S., and T. Lambert. 1997. Anti-Hispanic and Anti-Asian Sentiments among African Americans. *Social Science Quarterly* 78:338–53.

Dawson, Michael C. 1994. *Behind the Mule: Race, Class, and African-American Politics*. Princeton: Princeton University Press.

de la Garza, Rodolfo O., Louis DeSipio, F. Chris Garcia, John Garcia, and Angelo Falcon. 1992. *Latino Voices: Mexican, Puerto Rican, and Cuban Perspectives on American Politics*. Boulder, CO: Westview Press.

Denton, Nancy, and Douglas S. Massey. 1989. Racial Identity among Caribbean Hispanics: The Effect of Double Minority Status on Residential Segregation. *American Sociological Review* 54 (4): 790–808.

Deutsch, Morton, and Mary Collins. 1951. *Interracial Housing: A Psychological Evaluation of a Social Experiment*. Minneapolis: University of Minnesota Press.

Dixon, Jeffery. 2006. The Ties That Bind and Those That Don't: Reconciling Group Threat and Contact Theories of Prejudice. *Social Forces* 84:2179.

Dollard, John. 1989 [1957]. *Caste and Class in a Southern Town*. Madison, WI: University of Wisconsin Press, reprint.

D'souza, Dinesh. 1996. *The End of Racism: Principles for a Multiracial Society*. New York: Free Press.

Dyer, James, Arnold Velditz, and Stephen Worchel. 1989. Social Distance among Ethnic Groups in Texas: Some Demographic Correlates. *Social Science Quarterly* 70 (3): 607–16.

Ellison, Christopher G., and Daniel A. Powers. 1994. The Contact Hypothesis and Racial Attitudes among Black Americans. *Social Science Quarterly* 75 (2): 385–400.

188 REFERENCES

Espinosa, Kristen, and Douglas S. Massey. 1997. Determinants of English Proficiency among Mexican Migrants to the United States. *International Migration
Review* 31 (1): 28–50.

Espiritu, Yen Le. 1992. *Asian American Panethnicity: Bridging Institutions and
Identities*. Philadelphia: Temple University Press.

Espiritu, Yen Le, and Michael Omi. 2000. "Who Are You Calling Asian?": Shifting
Identity Claims, Racial Classifications, and the Census." In *The State of Asian
Pacific America: Transforming Race Relations*, edited by Paul Ong. Los Ange-
les: LEAP Asian Pacific American Public Policy Institute and UCLA Asian
American Studies Center.

Estlund, Cynthia. 2003. *Working Together*. New York: Oxford University Press.

Farley, Reynolds, Sheldon Danziger, and Harry Holzer. 2001. *Detroit Divided*. New
York: Russell Sage Foundation.

Farley, Reynolds, Charlotte Steeh, Tara Jackson, Maria Krysan, and Keith Reeves.
1993. Continued Racial Residential Segregation in Detroit: "Chocolate City,
Vanilla Suburbs" Revisited. *Journal of Housing Research* 4 (1): 1–38.

Forbes, H. D. 1997. *Ethnic Conflict: Commerce, Culture, and the Contact Hypothesis*. New Haven: Yale University Press.

Fossett, Mark, and Jill Kiecolt. 1989. The Relative Size of Minority Populations
and White Racial Attitudes. *Social Science Quarterly* 70 (4): 820–35.

Fredrickson, George. 2002. *Racism: A Short History*. Princeton, NJ: Princeton University Press.

Frey, William H. 1994. Minority Suburbanization and Continued "White Flight" in
U.S. Metropolitan Areas: Assessing Findings from the 1990 Census. *Research in
Community Sociology* 4:15–42.

Frey, William, and Reynolds Farley. 1996. Latino, Asian, and Black Segregation
in the U.S. More Metropolitan Areas: Are Multiethnic Metros Different? *Demography* 33 (1): 35–50.

Frey, William H., Bill Abresch, and Jonathan Yeasting. 2001. *America by the Numbers: A Field Guide to the U.S. Population*. New York: New Press.

Gaertner, Sam, and Jack Dovidio. 2000. *Reducing Intergroup Bias: The Common
Ingroup Identity Model*. Philadelphia, PA: Psychology Press.

Galster, George, and Edward Hill. 1992. *The Metropolis in Black and White*. Washington, D.C.: Center for Urban Policy Research.

Gilens, Martin. 1999. *Why Americans Hate Welfare*. Chicago: University of Chicago Press.

Giles, Michael W., and Melanie Buckner. 1993. David Duke and Black Threat: An
Old Hypothesis Revisited. *Journal of Politics* 55 (4): 702–13.

Giles, Michael W., and Arthur S. Evans. 1985. External Threat, Perceived Threat,
and Group Identity. *Social Science Quarterly* 66 (1): 50–66.

Giles, Michael W., and Kaenan Hertz. 1994. Racial Threat and Partisan Identification. *American Political Science Review* 88 (2): 317–26.

Glaser, James. 1994. Back to the Black Belt: Racial Environment and White Racial Attitudes in the South. *Journal of Politics* 56 (1): 21–41.

Glassner, B. 2000. *The Culture of Fear: Why Americans Are Afraid of the Wrong Things*. New York: Basic Books.

Green, Donald, Dara Strolovitch, and Janelle Wong. 1998. Defended Neighborhoods, Integration, and Racially Motivated Crime. *American Journal of Sociology* 104:372–403.

Guterbock, Thomas, and Bruce London. 1983. Race, Political Orientation, and Participation: An Empirical Test of Four Competing Theories. *American Sociological Review* 48:439–53.

Guzman, Betsy. 2001. The Hispanic Population, Census 2000 Brief. U.S. Census Bureau Report, Series C2KBR/01–03, Washington, D.C.

Hamilton, David L., Sandra Carpenter, and George D. Bishop. 1984. Desegregation of Suburban Neighborhoods. In *Groups in Contact: The Psychology of Desegregation*, edited by Norman Miller and Marilynn B. Brewer. Orlando: Academic Press, Inc.

Hogg, Michael, and Dominic Abrams. 1990. Social Identifications: A Social Psychology of Intergroup Relations and Group Processes. New York: Routledge.

Hollinger, David. 2006. *Post-Ethnic America: Beyond Multiculturalism*. New York: Basic Books.

Hood, M. V., and I. Morris 1997. Amigo o Enemigo? Context, Attitudes and Anglo Public Opinion toward Immigration. *Social Science Quarterly* 78:309–23.

Horowitz, Donald. 1998. *Ethnic Groups in Conflict*. Berkeley: University of California Press.

Huckfeldt, Robert, and Carol Weitzel Kohfeld. 1989. *Race and the Decline of Class in American Politics*. Urbana, IL: University of Illinois.

Hum, Tarry, and Michela Zonta. 2000. Residential Patterns of Asian Pacific Americans. In *The State of Asian Pacific America: Transforming Race Relations*, edited by Paul Ong. Los Angeles: LEAP Asian Pacific American Public Policy Institute and UCLA Asian American Studies Center.

Humes, Karen, and Jesse McKinnon. 2000. The Asian and Pacific Islander Population in the United States: March 1999, U.S. Census Bureau, Current Population Reports, Series P20–529, U.S. Government Printing Office, Washington, D.C.

Huntingon, Samuel. 2004. *Who Are We? The Challenges to America's National Identity*. New York: Simon and Schuster.

Ignatiev, Noel. 1996. *How the Irish Became White*. New York: Routledge.

Jackman, Mary R., and Marie Crane. 1986. "Some of My Best Friends Are Black": Interracial Friendship and Whites' Racial Attitudes. *Public Opinion Quarterly* 50 (2): 459–86.

Jackson, Kenneth T. 1985. *Crabgrass Frontier: The Suburbanization of the United States*. New York: Oxford University Press.

Jones-Correa, Michael, and David Leal. 1996. Becoming Hispanic: Secondary Panethnic Identification among Latin American-Origin Populations in the United States. *Hispanic Journal of Behavioral Sciences* 18 (1): 214–54.

Key, V. O. 1949. *Southern Politics in State and Nation*. Knoxville: University of Tennessee Press.

Kim, Claire. 2000. *Bitter Fruit: The Politics of Black-Korean Conflict in New York City*. New Haven: Yale University Press.

Kim, Elaine H. 1997. Korean Americans in U.S. Race Relations: Some Considerations. *Amerasia Journal* 23 (2): 69–78.

Kinder, Donald R., and Lynn M. Sanders. 1996. *Divided by Color: Racial Politics and Democratic Ideals in the American Republic*. Chicago: University of Chicago Press.

Kling, Jeffrey, Jeffrey Liebman, Lawrence Katz, and Lisa Sanbonmatsu. 2006. Moving to Opportunity and Equality. Unpublished paper. Princeton University.

Krysan, Maria, and Reynolds Farley. 2002. The Residential Preferences of Blacks: Do They Explain Persistent Segregation? *Social Forces* 80:937–80.

Lau, Richard R. 1989. Individual and Contextual Influences on Group Identification. *Social Psychology Quarterly* 52 (3): 220–31.

Lee, Jennifer, and Frank D. Bean. "America's Changing Color Lines: Race/Ethnicity, Immigration and Multiracial Identification." *Annual Review of Sociology* 30:221–242.

Lee, Taeku. 2000. Racial Attitudes and the Color Line(s) at the Close of the Twentieth Century." In *The State of Asian Pacific America: Transforming Race Relations*, edited by Paul Ong. Los Angeles: LEAP Asian Pacific American Public Policy Institute and UCLA Asian American Studies Center.

Lee, Robert. 2000. Fu Manchu Lives! Asian Pacific Americans as Permanent Aliens in American Culture. In *The State of Asian Pacific America: Transforming Race Relations*, edited by Paul Ong. Los Angeles: LEAP Asian Pacific American Public Policy Institute and UCLA Asian American Studies Center.

Leighley, Jan, and A. Vedlitz. 1999. Race, Ethnicity and Political Participation: Competing Models and Contrasting Explanations. *Journal of Politics* 61: 1092–114.

Lewis, Oscar. 1965. *La Vida: A Puerto Rican Family in the Culture of Poverty—San Juan and New York*. New York: Random House.

Lien, Pei-te. 1994. Ethnicity and Political Participation: A Comparison Between Asian and Mexican Americans. *Political Behavior* 16 (1): 237–64.

———. 2001. *The Making of Asian Americans through Political Participation*. Philadelphia: Temple University Press.

Lien, Pei-te, Margaret Conway, Taeku Lee, and Janelle Wong. 2001. The Mosaic of Asian American Politics: Preliminary Results from the Five-City Post-Election Survey. Paper Presented at the Annual Meeting of the Midwest Political Science Association, Chicago, Illinois.

Lien, Pei-te, and Taeku Lee. 2001. The Political Significance of Ethnic and Panethnic Group Dynamics among Asians in America. Paper presented at the Annual Meeting of the American Political Science Association, San Francisco, CA.

Logan, John. 2001. Ethnic Diversity Grows, Neighborhood Integration Lags Behind. Report to the Lewis Mumford Center, SUNY Albany.

Marshall, Mellisa, and Dietland Stolle. 2004. Race and the City: Neighborhood Context and the Development of Generalized Trust. *Political Behavior* 26: 573–86.

Massey, Douglas S. 2000. The Residential Segregation of Blacks, Hispanics, and Asians, 1970–1990. In *Immigration and Race: New Challenges for American Democracy*, edited by Gerald D. Jaynes. New Haven: Yale University Press.

———. 2001. Residential Segregation and Neighborhood Conditions in U.S. Metropolitan Areas. In: *America Becoming: Racial Trends and Their Consequences*, edited by Neil Smelser, William Julius Wilson, and Faith Mitchel. Washington, DC: National Academy Press.

Massey, Douglas S., and Nancy A. Denton. 1993. *American Apartheid: Segregation and the Making of the Underclass*. Cambridge: Harvard University Press.

Meyer, Stephen. 2001. *As Long as They Don't Move Next Door: Segregation and Racial Conflict in American Neighborhoods*. New York: Rowman and Littlefield Publishers.

McLaren, Lauren M. 2003. Anti-Immigrant Prejudice in Europe: Contact, Threat Perception, and Preferences for the Exclusion of Immigrants. *Social Forces* 81:909–36.

Morawska, Ewa. 2001. Immigrant-Black Dissensions in American Cities: An Argument for Multiple Explanations. In *Problem of the Century: Racial Stratification in the United States*, edited by Elijah Anderson and Douglas Massey. New York: Russell Sage Foundation.

Oboler, Suzanne. 1995. *Ethnic Labels, Latino Lives*. Minneapolis: University of Minnesota Press.

O'Connor, Alice, Chris Tilly, and Lawrence Bobo. 2000. *Urban Inequality: Evidence from Four Cities*. New York: Russell Sage Foundation.

Oliver, J. Eric. 2001. *Democracy in Suburbia*. Princeton: Princeton University Press.

Oliver, J. Eric, Fredric Gey, Jon Stiles, and Henry Brady. 1995. *Pacific Rim States Asian Demographic Data Book*. University of California, Office of the President, Research Report.

Oliver, J. Eric., and Tali Mendelberg. 2000. Reconsidering the Environmental Determinants of Racial Attitudes. *American Journal of Political Science* 44 (3): 574–89.

Oliver, Melvin, and Thomas Shapiro. 1997. *Black Wealth, White Wealth: New Perspectives on Racial Inequality*. New York: Roultledge.

Olzak, Susan. 1989. Labor Unrest, Immigration, and Ethnic Conflict in Urban America, 1880–1914. *American Journal of Sociology* 94 (4): 1303–33.

———. 1994. *The Dynamics of Ethnic Competition and Conflict*. Palo Alto: Stanford University Press.

Ong, Paul M. 2000. The Asian Pacific American Challenge to Race Relations. In *The State of Asian Pacific America: Transforming Race Relations*, edited by Paul Ong. Los Angeles: LEAP Asian Pacific American Public Policy Institute and UCLA Asian American Studies Center.

Orfield, Gary. 1988. Separate Societies: Have the Kerner Warnings Come True? In *Quiet Riots: Race and Poverty in the United States*, edited by Fred R. Harris and Roger Wilkins. New York: Pantheon Books, 1988.

Patterson, Orlando. 1997. *The Ordeal of Integration: Progress and Resentment in America's Racial Crisis*. Washington, DC: Counterpoint.

Pettigrew, Thomas F. 1959. Regional Differences in Anti-Negro Prejudice. *Journal of Abnormal and Social Psychology* 59 (1): 28–36.

———. 1979. Racial Change and Social Policy. *Annals of the American Academy of Political and Social Science* 441:114–31.

———. 1998. Intergroup Contact Theory. *Annual Review of Psychology* 49: 65–85.

Pettigrew, Thomas F., and Linda R. Tropp. 2000. Does Intergroup Contact Reduce Prejudice? Recent Meta-analytic Findings. In *Reducing Prejudice and Discrimination: The Claremont Symposium*, edited by Stuart Oskamp. Mahwah, NJ: Erlbaum.

Portes, Alejandro. 1984. The Rise of Ethnicity: Determinants of Ethnic Perceptions among Cuban Exiles in Miami. *American Sociological Review* 49 (2): 383–97.

Portes, Alejandro, and Robert L. Bach. 1985. *Latin Journey: Cuban and Mexican Immigrants in the United States*. Berkeley: University of California Press.

Portes, Alejandro, and Ruben G. Rumbaut. 1990. *Immigrant America: A Portrait*. Berkeley, CA: University of California Press.

———. 2001. *Legacies: The Story of the Immigrant Second Generation*. Berkeley, CA: University of California Press.

Portes, Alejandro, and Cynthia Truelove. 1987. Making Sense of Diversity: Recent Research on Hispanic Minorities in the United States. *Annual Review of Sociology* 13:359–85.

Portes, Alejandro, Robert Nash Parker, and Jose A. Cobas. 1980. Assimilation or Consciousness: Perceptions of U.S. Society among Recent Latin American Immigrants to the United States. *Social Forces* 59 (1): 200–24.

Putnam, Robert. 2000. *Bowling Alone: The Collapse and Revival of American Community*. New York: Simon and Schuster.

Quillian, Lincoln. 1995. Prejudice as a Response to Perceived Group Threat: Population Composition and Anti-Immigrant and Racial Prejudice in Europe. *American Sociological Review* 60 (4): 586–611.

———. 1996. Group Threat and Regional Change in Attitudes toward African Americans. *American Journal of Sociology* 3 (4): 816–60.

Rainwater, Lee, and William Yancey. 1967. *The Moynihan Report and the Politics of Controversy*. Cambridge: MIT Press.

Rieder, Jonathan. 1987. *Canarsie: The Jews and Italians of Brooklyn against Liberalism*. Cambridge, MA: Harvard University Press.

Roediger, David. 2005. *Working Toward Whiteness: How America's Immigrant's Became White. The Strange Journey from Ellis Island to the Suburbs*. New York: Basic Books.

Rubinowitz, Leonard, and James Rosenbaum. 2000. *Crossing the Class and Color Lines*. Chicago: University of Chicago Press.

Saito, Leland. 1998. *Race and Politics: Asian Americans, Latinos, and Whites in a Los Angeles Suburb*. Urbana, IL: University of Illinois Press.

Schuman, Howard, and Shirley Hatchett. 1974. *Trends in Racial Attitudes*. Ann Arbor: University of Michigan, Institute for Social Research.

Schuman, Howard, Charlotte Steeh, Lawrence Bobo, and Maria Krysan. 1997. *Racial Attitudes in America*. Cambridge: Harvard University Press.

Sears, David O. 1993. Symbolic Politics: A Sociopsychological Theory. In *Explorations in Political* Psychology, edited by Shante Iyengar and William J. McGuire. Durham: Duke University Press.

Sears, David O., and Donald Kinder. 1985. Whites' Opposition to Busing: On Conceptualizing and Operationalizing Group Conflict. *Journal of Personality and Social Psychology* 48:1141–47.

Sears, David, James Sidanius, and Lawrence Bobo. 2000. *Racialized Politics: The Debate about Racism in America*. Chicago: University of Chicago Press.

Shingles, Richard D. 1981. Black Consciousness and Political Participation: The Missing Link. *American Political Science Review* 75 (1): 76–91.

Sidanius, Jim, and Felicia Pratto. 2001. *Social Dominance: An Intergroup Theory of Social Hierarchy and Oppression*. New York: Cambridge University Press.

Sigelman, Lee, and Susan Welch. 1993. The Contact Hypothesis Revisited: Interracial Contact and Positive Racial Attitudes. *Social Forces* 71 (5): 781–95.

Sjoquist, David. 2002. *The Atlanta Paradox*. New York: Russell Sage Foundation.

Smelser, Neil, William Julius Wilson, and Faith Mitchell, 2001. *America Becoming: Racial Trends and Their Consequences*. Washington, DC: National Academy Press.

Sniderman, Paul, and Tom Piazza. 1993. *The Scar of Race*. Cambridge: Harvard University Press.

Sniderman, Paul, and Phil Tetlock 1986. Symbolic Racism: Problems of Motive Attribution in Political Analysis. *Journal of Social Issues* 42 (1): 129–50.

Sowell, Thomas. 1994. *Race and Culture: A World View*. New York: Basic Books.

Stein, Robert, Stephanie Post, and Allison Rinden. 2000. Reconciling Context and Contact Effects on Racial Attitudes. *Political Research Quarterly* 53:285–303.

Tajfel, Henri, and John C. Turner. 1979. An Integrative Theory of Intergroup Conflict. In *The Social Psychology of Intergroup Relations*, edited by William G. Austin and Stephen Worchel. Monterey, CA: Brooks-Cole.

Taylor, Marylee. 1998. How White Attitudes Vary with the Racial Composition of Local Populations: Numbers Count. *American Sociological Review* 63 (2): 512–35.

Thernstrom, Stephan, and Abigail Thernstrom. 1999. *America in Black and White, One Nation Indivisible*. New York: Touchstone Books.

Therrien, Melissa, and Roberto Rameriz. 2000. The Hispanic Population in the United States: March 2000, Current Population Reports, pp. 20–535. U.S. Census Bureau, Washington D.C.

Varshney, Ashutosh. 2002. *Ethnic Conflict and Civic Life: Hindus and Muslims in India*. New Haven: Yale University Press.

Verba, Sidney, Kay Schlozman, and Henry Brady. 1995. Voice and Equality: Civic Voluntarism in American Politics. Cambridge, MA: Harvard University Press.

Waldinger, Roger. 1996. Ethnicity and Opportunity in the Plural City. In *Ethnic Los Angeles*, edited by Roger Waldinger and Mehdi Bozorgmehr. New York: Russell Sage Foundation.

Waters, Mary. 2000. *Black Identities: West Indian Immigrant Dreams and American Realities*. Cambridge, MA: Harvard University Press.

Wei, William. 1994. *The Asian American Movement: A Social History*. Philadelphia: Temple University Press.

Welch, Susan, and Lee Sigelman. 2000. Getting to Know You? Latino-Anglo Social Contact. *Social Science Quarterly* 81 (1): 67–83.

Welch, Susan, Lee Sigelman, Timothy Bledsoe, and Michael Combs. 2001. *Race and Place: Race Relations in an American City*. New York: Cambridge University Press.

Wilner, Daniel M., Rosabelle P. Walkley, and Stuart W. Cook. 1955. *Human Relations in Interracial Housing: A Study of the Contact Hypothesis*. Minneapolis: University of Minnesota Press.

Wilson, William Julius. 1980. *The Declining Significance of Race*. Chicago: University of Chicago Press.

———. 1985. *The Truly Disadvantaged: The Inner City, the Underclass and Public Policy*. Chicago: University of Chicago Press.

Wilson, William Julius, and Richard Taub. 2006. *There Goes the Neighborhood: Racial, Ethnic, and Class Tensions in Four Chicago Neighborhoods and Their Meaning for America*. New York: Alfred A. Knopf, 2006.

Wong, Cara. 1998. Group Closeness. A Pilot Study Report to the 1997 NES Pilot Study Committee and the American National Election Study Board of Overseers.

Wong, Janelle. 2006. *Democracy's Promise: Immigrants and America's Civic Institutions*. Ann Arbor, MI: University of Michigan Press.

Wright, Gerald. 1977. Contextual Model of Electoral Behavior: The Southern Wallace Vote. *American Political Science Review* 71:497–508.

Yancey, George. 2003. Who Is White? Asians, Latinos, and the New Black/Non-Black Divide. Boulder, CO: Lynne Reinner Publishers.

Zajonc, Robert B. 1968. Attitudinal Effects of Mere Exposure. *Journal of Personality and Social Psychology* 9: 1–27.

Index

affirmative action, whites' opinions about, 175n5, 178n14

African Americans: Asians' negative attitudes toward, 91–94, 92f; Latinos' negative attitudes toward, 86–88, 87f; and racial environment, 76–85; viewed more negatively than other groups, 164; whites' negative stereotypes of, 68–72, 69f, 71f; whites opposed to marriage with, 73–75, 74f

African Americans' racial attitudes: environmental influences on, 25–32; toward other racial groups, 77–80

Allport, Gordon W., 18. *See also* contact hypothesis

Asian Americans, 32–33, 89–95; blacks' feelings of zero-sum competition with, 80–81, 80f; blacks' negative attitudes toward, 78f, 79; blacks opposed to marriage with, 82–84, 82f; diversity, 39, 50–65; Latinos' negative attitudes toward, 86–88, 87f; panethnic identity, 161; whites' negative stereotypes of, 70–72, 71f. *See also specific topics*

Asian Americans' racial attitudes: environmental influences on, 32–35; by nationality, 57, 58f

assimilation: segmented, 51. *See also* incorporation

blacks. *See* African Americans
Blumer, Herbert, 27
Bobo, Lawrence, 27

"Cablinasian," 37
Chicago, 1–2

Chinese Americans, 92–93, 92f, 93f. *See also* Asian Americans

Citizen, Information, and Democracy (CID) Survey, 170

citizenship and civic participation, 138–40, 139f

civic associations, 20–21

civic participation, 182nn1–3; motivations for, 137; neighborhood racial segregation and, 141–47; race, citizenship, and, 138–40, 139f

civic ties, interracial: and whites' racial attitudes, 18–21

civil life, racial environments and, 136–40

Clark, William, 101–2

closeness, racial: comparative perspectives on, 45–47, 46t; incorporation levels, interracial friendship patterns, and, 124, 125t, 126, 127f

community, feelings of: racial environment and, 136–40

competition, racial (zero-sum): and African Americans' racial attitudes, 27–28, 81; and Asians' racial attitudes, 94; comparative perspectives on, 17, 46t, 47; interracial friendship patterns, 125t; and Latinos' racial attitudes, 88–89; and whites' racial attitudes, 44, 72–73

conflict hypothesis, 24, 85. *See also* power-threat hypothesis; "real conflict" hypothesis; threat hypothesis

contact, interracial: among various racial groups, 117–18, 117f; and differences in attitudes across racial environments, 128–29; measuring, 114–17; in multiethnic America, 114–22; and racial